W. T. Rowe

SHAKESPEARE AT WORK

1592-1603

SHAKESPEARE AT WORK

1592-1603

BY

G. B. HARRISON

With a New Preface by the Author

ANN ARBOR PAPERBACKS

THE UNIVERSITY OF MICHIGAN PRESS

First edition as an Ann Arbor Paperback 1958

To
HARLEY GRANVILLE-BARKER

Manufactured in the United States of America

PREFACE TO THE ANN ARBOR PAPERBACKS EDITION

THE present reprint of *Shakespeare at Work 1592-1603* has been made photographically, and therefore without alteration, from the original edition of 1933. The book was written in 1931, before the burgeoning of the new criticism and the innumerable studies of Shakespeare's images and patterns which have appeared during the last twenty-five years. Some of the opinions in this book I would now modify or expand; but in general I believe that this account of the Elizabethan world in which Shakespeare lived and worked is still valid. Whatever the wider cosmic, psychological, theological, or ethical significances which modern critics may distill from Shakespeare's plays, it is still an elementary fact that he wrote plays (and not metaphysical poetical dramas) to interest and entertain his contemporaries; and a playwright is successful as he reflects the immediate interests of his audience. To some extent *Shakespeare at Work* covers much the same ground as *Elizabethan Plays and Players* (also reprinted in the Ann Arbor Paperbacks), but the intention of that book was different.

G. B. HARRISON

University of Michigan
31st July 1957

PREFACE TO THE FIRST EDITION

THIS book is a sequel to the three volumes of my *Elizabethan Journal*, wherein were recorded those events, books, ideas and emotions which were uppermost in the minds of Englishmen in the last twelve years of the reign of Queen Elizabeth. In *Shakespeare at Work* I have tried, so far as is now possible, to show Shakespeare against the background of his times, which included his own world of the theatre. It is a personal interpretation, a conjectural reconstruction built up from such fragments as remain. Much of the book is, and must be, sheer guesswork; but, since the documentary evidences for the life of Shakespeare and the history of the stage are easily available in well-known works of reference, I have chosen the form of plain narrative, unqualified by "doubtless," "probably," "we may be sure that" and other phrases expressing scholarly diffidence. All who are familiar with Shakespeare's work and times create their own Imaginary Portrait of the Author: this is mine.

G. B. H.

CONTENTS

I

THE UPSTART CROW

THERE were three playhouses in London in the winter of the year 1591; the Theatre and the Curtain to the north of the City in Shoreditch; and south of the Thames, not far from London Bridge, stood the Rose. The Rose Theatre was the property of one Philip Henslowe. It had been built some four and a half years and now needed renovation. Accordingly, in January 1592, Henslowe called in the workmen; and being a good man of business, he was exact in his accounts. He determined to keep a separate account for his theatre property, and having by him an old vellum-bound manuscript book that had belonged to his brother he turned it about, and opening at a clean page, he wrote at its head the word "Jesus." He added the date, "1592."

Then he set down in detail the charges laid out upon his playhouse; they amounted to over a hundred pounds. There were wages, lime, sand, boards, nails innumerable; a new mast, which cost 12s.; two dozen turned balusters at 2¼d. each, and a further two dozen, but he paid only 2d. apiece for those. With a new thatch, fresh plaster in the

Lord's room and the room over the tiring house, the stage repainted, the house was now ready.

A few days later Henslowe turned over three pages in his ledger book and began a new account with the words "In the name of God"; for although a pawnbroker and a landlord of brothels, Henslowe was a pious man, and the coming of the Lord Strange's players to play at his theatre was an event fraught with possibility. The company of players that looked to the Lord Strange as their protector were greatly distinguishing themselves this winter. Whilst other companies had appeared at Court once only, they played four times in the Christmas holidays; and now again this Shrovetide they were summoned twice. They were an experienced and competent company, but their present success was due to their leader, Edward Alleyn.

Alleyn was twenty-five and he had been an actor for nine years. He was moreover a great man of business who knew a good part when he saw it, and realised that if he was to get the fullest effects from his own fine presence and great voice he needed a good poet, someone more talented than himself or his fellow actors. He was not above asking the help of these young men from the Universities on reasonable terms. There was no rarer sight than to see him as Tamburlane the Great, bending his brows and fetching his stations up and down the stage with furious gestures, or whipping his team of pampered jades of Asia, or wooing his Zenocrate with high astounding terms or raging against Death himself. And Marlowe had provided him with some magnificent lines.

Alleyn was a very great man; not even Roscius or Æsop, those actors of antiquity whose fame still survived from before Christ's birth, could perform more than Ned Alleyn, who could turn his poorest play into a rare work of art. Unfortunately *Tamburlane* was the property of the Admiral's men, and though Alleyn still served the Lord Admiral he could not play the Scythian tyrant so long as he was with Strange's men; but they had other good plays.

On Saturday afternoon the 19th February the Rose Theatre was reopened with a performance of *Friar Bacon.* The play was Robert Greene's work, and provided the Lord Strange's men with something that could rival the attraction of the Admiral's new play, Marlowe's *Tragical History of Doctor Faustus.*

Everyone in London knew Robin Greene and talked of his dissolute and licentious living; his vain flaunting of his Master of Arts degree of both Universities; his horrible oaths and profanation of sacred texts. He was a handsome man, and well proportioned, and he dressed like a scholar but for a trick of wearing his red beard overlong, uncut and hanging down in a long point. His manners were scandalous. He was forever shifting his lodgings; at his first coming he would surfeit and riot with roisterly acquaintances, but he would slip away like a beggar leaving the score unpaid. He was well known on the Bankside, and in Shoreditch, but no one dared arrest him, for he employed a ruffian called Cutting Ball to guard him with his men. Once in a tavern he made an apparitor eat up his own citation, wax and all, very handsomely served between two dishes. He kept Ball's sister as his mistress, a sorry ragged quean, who was the mother of his bastard son Fortunatus.

Yet he had his good qualities. When pressed for money he settled to work and in a day and a night he could yark up a book, and any printer would gladly pay him dear for the very dregs of his wits. He was not proud. He made no account of winning credit by his works; his only care was to have a spell in his purse to conjure up a good cup of wine at all times.

A few years ago Greene wrote only for gentlemen readers, priding himself on his style, and scorning those scholars who wrote for the stage. When they taunted him for holding aloof from play writing, he answered that he disdained to make his verses "jet upon the stage in tragical buskins, every word filling the mouth like the faburden of Bow Bell, daring God out of Heaven with that atheist Tamburlane." As for those that set the end of scholarism in an English blank verse, either it was the humour of a novice that tickled them with self-love, or too much frequenting the hot house that had sweat out the greatest part of their wits.

Nevertheless at last he too prostituted his Muse to writing stage plays, being greatly importuned thereto by the players themselves, and in *Alphonsus of Arragon* and *Orlando Furioso* he created heroes who outranted even Tamburlane in his rages.

This last winter Greene suddenly developed a conscience and a new style of writing. Instead of a tale full of eloquent phrases and fine figurative conveyance, he wrote a pamphlet called *A Notable Discovery of Cosenage*, for he was filled with remorse at the wantonness of his younger years. "I have seen the world," he said, "and rounded it, though not with travel yet with experience, and I cry out with Solomon, *Omnia sub sole vanitas*."

Greene indeed was sickening of chronic excess, and when in bodily distress or maudlin drunk, he would cast up his debit account with his Maker and turn over a new leaf whereon to record his repentance as a credit. He was very conscious of the wickedness around him and knew from inside how mercilessly simple folk were fleeced of their goods. In the *Notable Discovery* he exposed card sharpers and crossbiters that preyed on men wantonly given who were enticed into brothels. Greene was now exploiting a new public and this new book was dedicated, contrary to his previous custom, to merchants, apprentices, farmers and plain countrymen. They bought the pamphlet eagerly and other things too that Greene wrote, so that his virtue brought him immediate profit; and seeing that there was an appetite for tales of the wicked, Greene set about a *Second Part of Connycatching*. Both books were selling well in these early weeks of 1592.

The season at the Rose opened quietly. At *Friar Bacon* on 19th February the house was half empty. In the following week the company played *Muly Mulocco*, Greene's *Orlando Furioso*, *The Spanish Comedy of Don Horatio*, *Sir John Mandeville* and *Harry of Cornwall*. Their first successful afternoon was on Saturday the 26th when Marlowe's *Jew of Malta* drew a good house. It was a far better play than *Tamburlane*, and though there was nothing to equal the high poetry, there was a greater dramatic power in the situations and speeches. Tamburlane's ambition to be a King and ride in triumph through Persepolis was lofty and picturesque, but the Jew's more sordid lust for power through money was nearer to common reality as understood in the city of London. Barabas too was the embodiment of the most terrifying of Elizabethan bogeys; he was the incarnate spirit of Machiavel, and a Jew. The Jew of Malta was one of Alleyn's more notable parts, highly regarded by his fellow actors and followers, amongst whom was a young man from Stratford who had not yet attracted much notice.

Marlowe brought on the spirit of Machiavel to act as admiring prologue to his play. Then he opened the scene with Barabas in his counting house, brooding over his wealth:

So that of thus much that return was made:
And of the third part of the Persian ships,
There was the venture summed and satisfied.
As for those Samnites, and the men of Uz,
That bought my Spanish oils and wines of Greece
Here have I purs'd their paltry silverlings.
Fie; what a trouble 'tis to count this trash!

For this Jew is no mere usurer to weary his fingers with reckoning coins; he deals rather in seldseen costly stones of such a price that one of them might serve to ransom great Kings from captivity:

This is the ware wherein consists my wealth;
And thus methinks should men of judgment frame
Their means of traffic from the vulgar trade,
And as their wealth increaseth, so inclose
Infinite riches in a little room.

The Jew had two passions besides his wealth—a daughter and a hate for Christians. When the Christians of Malta convert his house to a nunnery and turn him out, he persuades his daughter to pretend Christianity and so be admitted to the house. In the night he waits under the balcony for her to come out and when the bags are thrown down to him, he hugs them passionately as he cries out:

O my girl,
My gold, my fortune, my felicity!
Strength to my soul, death to mine enemy!

Welcome the first beginner of my bliss!
O Abigail, Abigail, that I had thee here too!
Then my desires were fully satisfied:
But I will practise thy enlargement thence:
O girl! O gold! O beauty! O my bliss!

Thus armed again with the means of power, he proceeds to rebuild his fortunes, with the added zest of an intensified hatred for all Christians and a passion for vengeance:

I am not of the tribe of Levi, I,
That can so soon forget an injury.
We Jews can fawn like spaniels when we please:
And when we grin we bite; yet are our looks
As innocent and harmless as a lamb's.
I learned in Florence how to kiss my hand,
Heave up my shoulders when they call me dog,
And duck as low as any barefoot friar;
Hoping to see them starve upon a stall,
Or else be gather'd for in our synagogue,
That, when the offering-basin comes to me,
Even for charity I may spit into't.

And the audience of London citizens shuddered with satisfaction at the thought that Englishmen were not tainted either with Judaism or Machiavellianism, except for a few Italianate politicians.

On the Friday following, 3rd March, the first new play of the season was put on. It was called *Harry the Sixth* and dealt with that patch of the history of England and France between the death of Harry the Fifth and the wedding of the boy king with Margaret of Anjou.

A play concerned with Anglo-French history was opportune for at this time affairs in France were occupying general attention. For the last three and a half years since the great Armada was shattered in the August of '88, the war with Spain dragged on without any decisive result. In 1589, the theatre of war had shifted from the seas to France where Henri of Navarre was fighting for the throne of France against the Catholic League who were opposing him. The Queen aided him royally with £22,000 in gold and a force of 5,000, but though he won a victory at Arques he was unable to take Paris. The English army was withdrawn and the Spaniards entered France as allies to the League. In the next year Henri was forced back to the north and the Spaniards pressed nearer to the English Channel. There was indeed no great zest at first to help the French, for who could trust a Frenchman? They murdered their late King who was a Catholic, and they rebelled against his successor who was a Protestant; and they so often deceived the English in money matters that when they beguiled simple-minded creditors of their own they would derisively mock them as "Englishmen!" On the other hand the Spaniards had now reached Brittany, and with a base on the English Channel they could assemble a fleet and invade England at their own good time. A second expedition was despatched to France, and in April 1591 Sir Roger Williams with 600 men entered Dieppe in Normandy, and to allay any doubts as to the legality of the war, a proclamation was issued declaring that Henri of Navarre was justly entitled Henri the Fourth of France, and that any Englishman who succoured his enemies was a traitor to his Queen. Another force under Sir John Norris entered Brittany.

The English soldiers won glory in both provinces. Norris took Guincamp, and the English claimed the honours of the day. Early in May, Williams with 300 English and 400 French after a long night march fell upon the Leaguers' garrison at Cinqsens at noon. After two hours' fight the barricades were forced and every man within slain. They paused but to thank God on their knees and to sing a psalm, and then were away back to Dieppe before the enemy could come after them. This Welshman was a great soldier, and the author of a text book on war too.

At Midsummer the Queen agreed to augment the Normandy force to 4,000, and the Earl of Essex (who was now aged 26) was sent over to take command. As autumn came on, the King's army, supported by the English, drew round Rouen and settled down to a siege. The Earl was accompanied by a volunteer company of gentlemen, as well as the gentlemen who served in his special regiment of cavalry. Once more the French wars were in every Londoner's mind; Englishmen again were fighting over the ground familiar to their ancestors in the great days of the third Edward, and Harry the Fifth.

Moreover national feeling was growing, as well as bitterness against the enemy. Of late years the Pope was sending over more and more Jesuits and seminaries, who went about in disguise, some as gentlemen or gallants, some as soldiers, mariners or merchants, or even as ruffians whom no one would suspect of any holy calling. The Council were perturbed and in November 1591 a new and stern proclamation had been set forth, warning the people of the preparations that were being made against the realm by the King of Spain, the Pope, and the English fugitives beyond seas. Commissions were everywhere set up to collect the names of those suspected of recusancy and to warn them.

At Rouen the siege dragged on indeterminately. The Earl of Essex issued romantic challenges to the Governor within; raids and sorties were made by either party; but by the end of the year two thirds of the army had melted away by death, sickness or desertion.

In the spring of 1592 the fortunes of the French King were ebbing. The Duke of Parma was at the head of a well-trained, efficient Spanish army, advancing to relieve Rouen. Henri asked for more English soldiers, and the Queen after some change of mind agreed to send a further 1,600. Essex by this time had returned to England, and the command was resumed by Sir Roger Williams.

The play of *Harry the Sixth* began with the funerals of King Harry the Fifth. The nobles immediately reveal their self-seeking ambitions; and the coffin has not been carried off the stage before the news comes of the revolt of France, the coronation of the Dauphin in Rheims, and the capture of Sir John Talbot. The scene then shifts to France to show the coming of Joan La Pucelle to the French Court. In London the hatred between the Duke of Gloucester, Lord Protector, and Beaufort, Bishop of Winchester, breaks out into open riot. In France Joan and the French prevail and the valiant old Salisbury is slain; but Talbot reasserts his old valour and puts to flight the Dauphin and Joan. The quarrels between the English nobles increase, and the beginning of the ambition of the young Earl of Somerset is shown in an episode in the Temple Garden where he quarrels with Richard Plantagenet. Plantagenet plucks a white rose, and is supported by Warwick; Somerset plucks a red and is supported by Suffolk. Winchester and Gloucester quarrel in presence of the King. Plantagenet urges his rights; general outward reconciliation follows and Plantagenet is created Duke of York. The wars in France go on with varying fortune, until Joan persuades the Duke of Burgundy to desert the English. Young Henry is crowned King of France, but the controversy of the Temple Garden is renewed and again quieted by the young King, who puts on a red rose and so appears to favour Somerset's party.

The war continues, the odds now being heavily against Talbot, especially when Somerset and York, who suspect each other, fail to give him support; so that both Talbot and his son are overcome in battle and die valiantly. Gloucester now works for peace. The Pucelle's power wanes; she conjures up her fiends but they can only give silent forewarning that infernal powers have forsaken her; and the English take her. Suffolk captures Margaret, daughter of Reignier (King of Naples and Duke of Anjou), falls in love with her but woos her for the King. Joan is led off cursing, to be burnt as a witch and a strumpet. The play ended with King Henry's promise to marry Margaret; after which, to whet the appetite for further instalments, Suffolk came forward alone to declare:

> Thus Suffolk hath prevail'd; and thus he goes,
> As did the youthful Paris once to Greece;
> With hope to find the like event in love,
> But prosper better than the Trojan did.
> Margaret shall now be queen, and rule the king;
> But I will rule both her, the king, and realm.

The Rose playhouse was crowded and the audience enthusiastic, and particularly at the heroic speeches of brave Talbot, whose single-minded patriotism was so notably in contrast to the crooked greed of the other noblemen, and especially at the end when he saw that escape was impossible:

> How are we park'd and bounded in a pale,
> A little herd of England's timorous deer,

Maz'd with a yelping kennel of French curs!
If we be English deer, be then in blood;
Not rascal-like, to fall down with a pinch,
But rather moody-mad and desperate stage,
Turn on the bloody hounds with heads of steel,
And make the cowards stand aloof at bay:
Sell every man his life as dear as mine,
And they shall find dear deer of us, my friends.
God and Saint George, Talbot and England's right,
Prosper our colours in this dangerous fight!

The takings at the new play were the best of the season, and the Lord Strange's men realised that they had found a new playwright who could write speeches that would draw an audience as well as Marlowe and better than Greene. His name was Shakespeare.

William Shakespeare was now in his twenty-eighth year. He had been born and bred at Stratford upon Avon where his father at the time was a man of some substance, a person of importance in the town; he was, however, a recusant, and though well liked by his neighbours he had dropped out of public life. No one, apparently, knew much about the new playwright. He was not one of the young men from the Universities who had recently monopolised play writing. There were some conflicting tales of his youth. He had got with child a woman of the neighbourhood before he was nineteen, and then married her. Some said that he had been a schoolmaster; others that his youth was lively and spoke of trouble over some deer stealing connected with Sir Thomas Lucy, a great man of those parts. He was now an actor of no great distinction.

It was a liberal education for Shakespeare to serve under Alleyn, and to watch him at closest quarters. After Tamburlane, Alleyn's greatest success was as Hieronimo in Kyd's play *The Spanish Tragedy*, the most popular of all tragedies. *The Spanish Tragedy*, although four years old or more, was the best drama that had yet been seen on English stages. Its motive was revenge. It began with the appearance of the Ghost of Don Andrea accompanied by Revenge to demand his rights upon his slayers. The play which followed was full of exciting episodes of courts and policy, of secret love, midnight murder, hangings and stabbings and passionate excesses. Alleyn took the part of old Hieronimo, marshal of Spain, and the story told how Horatio, his son, was cruelly murdered, and how the father found out the murderers, and at last of the ghastly vengeance which he inflicted on them. There were some fine speeches too, of which Elizabethan audiences seemed never to tire, particularly in the scene where Hieronimo roused from sleep by shrieks in his arbour comes out to find the corpse of his son:

> What outcries pluck me from my naked bed,
> And chill my throbbing heart with trembling fear,
> Which never danger yet could daunt before?
> Who calls Hieronimo? Speak, here I am. . . .

Equally effective was Hieronimo's next outburst when as the distraught father, maddened with grief but as yet ignorant of the murderers, he broke out:

> O eyes! no eyes, but fountains fraught with tears;
> O life! no life, but lively form of death;
> O world! no world but mass of public wrongs,
> Confus'd and fill'd with murder and misdeeds!

Step by step the old man was led on to the discovery of the murderers and his own plan for revenge, a revenge

> not as the vulgar wits of men,
> With open but inevitable ills
> As by a secret, yet a certain mean,
> Which under kindship will be cloaked best.
> Wise men will take their opportunity,
> Closely and safely fitting things to time.
> But in extremes advantage hath no time;
> And therefore all times fit not for revenge.
> This therefore will I rest me in unrest,
> Dissembling quiet in unquietness,
> Not seeming that I know their villainies,
> That my simplicity may make them think
> That ignorantly I will let all slip:
> For ignorance, I wot, and well they know
> *Remedium malorum iners est.*
> Nor ought avails it me to menace them
> Who, as a wintry storm upon a plain,
> Will bear me down with their nobility.
> No, no, Hieronimo thou must enjoin
> Thine eyes to observation, and thy tongue
> To milder speeches than thy spirit affords,
> Thy heart to patience, and thy hands to rest,

> Thy cap to courtesy, and thy knee to bow,
> Till to revenge thou know, when, where and how.

And this speech was the whole essence of that type of revenge tragedy which Kyd made popular in the English theatre.

Kyd ended his play with a quick succession of murders and suicides; all debts of blood were fully paid and the ghost of Don Andrea, satisfied at last, goes off with Revenge who promises:

> This hand shall hale them down to deepest hell,
> Where none but furies, bugs and tortures dwell.

Kyd packed *The Spanish Tragedy* with incidental horrors, a public hanging, a play within a play, and some mad scenes; but he had hit upon such fundamental principles of tragic drama as irony, suspense, pathos, surprise and climax. He had too some sense of character.

In such a school of drama and acting Shakespeare first learned his art. One of his earliest tasks was in an effort to outdo the horrors of *The Spanish Tragedy* in a drama called *Titus Andronicus*. Its motive also was revenge, with the added attractions of rape and mutilation, severed heads and hands, brothers falsely executed for fratricide, murdered sons served up in a pasty for their unwitting mother to feed upon, and nauseating villainies beyond even Kyd's sportive imagination. Of its own bloody kind, it was a good stage play, and in some of the speeches there was music and a vigour new to the English stage, particularly in the utterances of old Titus and the Moor Aaron; as in Titus' lament:

> For now I stand as one upon a rock
> Environ'd with a wilderness of sea,
> Who marks the waxing tide grow wave by wave,
> Expecting ever when some envious surge
> Will in his brinish bowels swallow him.

Or:

> If there were reason for these miseries,
> Then into limits could I bind my woes.
> When heaven doth weep, doth not the earth o'erflow?
> If the winds rage, doth not the sea wax mad,
> Threatening the welkin with his big-swoln face?
> And wilt thou have a reason for this coil?
> I am the sea; hark! how her sighs do blow;
> She is the weeping welkin, I the earth;
> Then must my sea be moved with her sighs;
> Then must my earth with her continual tears
> Become a deluge, overflow'd and drown'd;
> For why my bowels cannot hide her woes,
> But like a drunkard must I vomit them.
> Then give me leave, for losers will have leave
> To ease their stomachs with their bitter tongues.

Or Aaron's spirited defence of his black bastard:

> Stay, murderous villains! will you kill your brother?
> Now, by the burning tapers of the sky,
> That shone so brightly when this boy was got,
> He dies upon my scimitar's sharp point
> That touches this my first-born son and heir.
> I tell you, younglings, not Enceladus,
> With all his threatening band of Typhon's brood,

Nor great Alcides, nor the god of war,
Shall seize this prey out of his father's hands.
What, what, ye sanguine, shallow-hearted boys!
Ye white-lim'd walls! ye alehouse painted signs!
Coal-black is better than another hue,
In that it scorns to bear another hue;
For all the water in the ocean
Can never turn the swan's black legs to white,
Although she lave them hourly in the flood.
Tell the empress from me, I am of age
To keep mine own, excuse it how she can. . . .
Why, there's the privilege your beauty bears.
Fie, treacherous hue! that will betray with blushing
The close enacts and counsels of the heart:
Here's a young lad fram'd of another leer:
Look how the black slave smiles upon the father,
As who should say, 'Old lad, I am thine own,'
He is your brother, lords, sensibly fed
Of that self blood that first gave life to you;
And from that womb where you imprisoned were
He is enfranchised and come to light:
Nay, he is your brother by the surer side,
Although my seal be stamped in his face.

Strange's men enjoyed an unbroken and successful run of plays throughout the spring and early summer, but on 11th June they were unwittingly implicated in a fierce riot in Southwark. It arose because the Knight Marshal's men, in a very high-handed and objectionable manner, arrested the servant of a feltmaker and thrust him into the Marshalsea. That afternoon there was a new play at the Rose called *A Knack to know a Knave*, which concluded with a jig by Kemp. The playhouse was crowded with apprentices, and when the play was over they marched in a body on the Marshalsea and demanded the prisoner. The Marshal's men emerged, armed with daggers and cudgels, belaboured all and sundry, and then drew their swords. They were only rescued from the angry mob by the arrival of the Lord Mayor and his men. For the next few days there was an uneasy feeling in the City, for the apprentices threatened trouble on Midsummer Eve, a traditional night of disorder, insomuch that the Council gave special orders that an extra watch should be set for three nights composed of householders and masters of families, whilst masters were made responsible for their servants. It was also ordered that no plays should be shown from henceforth until Michaelmas.

The activities of the Lord Strange's men were thus brought to an abrupt end. Since their opening in February, they had acted on 105 days out of 125. *Harry the Sixth* continued to be a most popular play and it was estimated that at least ten thousand spectators had thrilled to the eloquence of brave Talbot. Greene's plays, however, failed to draw full houses. As there was no further profit to be made in London, the players moved off for the country. Early in August the Court went on progress. The summer was hot and rainless, and plague broke out. The City was deserted.

Throughout this year Greene had been doing well. The vogue for connycatching pamphlets was passing off and Greene, as ever, sensed the changing feelings of his readers. He tried his hand at a new kind of social commentary, which was in fact a revival of a mediæval mode, the allegorical satire on different types in the Commonwealth. He called it *A Quip for an Upstart Courtier* or *A dialogue between Cloth Breeches and Velvet Breeches*—the old theme that ancient yeomanry is better than newfangled gentility. The book gave him a chance of passing in review a number of different kinds of persons, and as he was at the moment at odds with Dr. Gabriel Harvey, the Cambridge scholar, the opportunity was too good to lose. Harvey's father made ropes at Saffron Walden; so Greene slipped in a paragraph about the Harvey family.

When the book appeared in print the passage was uncomfortably prominent. Harvey was a vindictive man and might have influence with powerful persons. Greene was pressed to withdraw it; and after a few copies had been sold the offending sheet was altered. It was a worrying business. Then there was a debauch with Nashe and a surfeit of pickled herrings and Rhenish wine—ill fare in a hot August for an invalid with diseased kidneys. The dropsy increased daily but Greene at first was not unduly alarmed. Writing grew more difficult. He had promised to publish a Black Book of the rogues about London; it was still unfinished, but he had in hand a short treatise of two connycatchers. The first part only was complete, a brief, hurried performance.

He sent it along to the printer as it was, for he needed money.

Greene now grew very lonely. All who could had left London to avoid the plague. Nashe had gone. The players who might have given him something on account, or even for charity, were in the country. Everyone seemed to have deserted him, and as his illness increased he began to feel bitter. He started a novel about himself in the old euphuistic strain, but he laid it aside. He penned some pages of autobiography. Then as despair settled in upon him, he wrote a few precepts warning young men against harlots, taverners and usurers. Above all he was obsessed with the ingratitude of the professional players; they battened on the works of his brain and pestered him for plays; and now that they were bloated and prosperous they left him to die destitute. Not only that, but there was this new upstart who was learning his trade by copying his betters, and drawing crowds to his plays. And so as a legacy to his old friends that had served the stage along with him—Marlowe, Nashe and Lodge—he wrote a letter of pitiful warning against the ingratitude of players: "Yes, trust them not: for there is an upstart crow, beautified with our feathers, that with his 'Tiger's heart wrapt in a player's hide' supposes he is as well able to bombast out a blank verse as the best of you; and being an absolute *Johannes factotum*, is in his own conceit the only Shake-scene in a country. O that I might intreat your rare wits

ofitable courses: and let
ast excellence, and never
your admired inventions."
ght of the 2nd September.
road and the vultures de-
Iarvey was in town on his
ring upon ways of making
nsult of *Cloth Breeches*. As
his enemy was gone, he hur-
lodging to gather details, and
to interview Greene's mistress,
hostess, and Mistress Appleby,
ls.

as tearful and voluble. She told
n his last days he begged for a
msey, and how lousy he was, and
the poor soul, to borrow her hus-
st his own was a washing; and how
hose and sword were sold for three
esides, the cost of his winding sheet,
ur shillings; and the charges of his
new churchyard near Bedlam, which
ngs and fourpence; and how deeply he
l to her poor husband. She showed Dr.
ene's bond for ten pounds and besought
the writing beneath, which was a letter
doned wife, charging her by their former
ay the debt, "for if he and his wife had
ured me, I had died in the streets." And
when he was dead, Mistress Isam crowned

him with a garland of bays for a tende

Whereupon Dr. Harvey hurried back t ings, and wrote a long letter to a friend Walden, adding an extempore epitaph:

Here lies the man, whom Mistress Isam crowned
She, she that joyed to hear her nightingale's swee

Others too came to pick over the scr Greene's papers would be well worth the p Cuthbert Burby laid hands on the autobio the farewell letter to his wife, and some od Wright, another of the scavenging printers, off the letter to the dramatists and the unf novel, which he turned over to Chettle to p gether as quickly as possible into some sort of This Chettle was a hack of several trades, p playwright, pamphleteer, a fat, puffing Wright's publication was first; his editio Greene's *Groatsworth of Wit* was ready for on 20th September. Burby entered *The Repent of Robert Greene, Master of Arts*, on the 6th tober.

Meanwhile Nashe's new book called *Piers P niless* had been issued by Richard Jones. It was s ilar in vein to *Cloth Breeches*, a new version of old allegory of the *Seven Deadly Sins* brought up date, attacking a number of recognisable worthi but including a fine praise of poets and playwright and justifying plays against their detractors. It w bought avidly and the first edition was soon exhausted.

In October Alleyn completed another good piece of business. On the 22nd he married Joan Woodward, Henslowe's step-daughter, and so united himself with the family and capital of the owner of the Rose Theatre.

The *Groatsworth* raised a storm and all kinds of rumours were set going. Some said that Nashe had written it, but this he indignantly denied in the preface to the new edition of *Piers Penniless*, calling it a "scald, trivial, lying pamphlet." "God never have care of my soul," he added, "but utterly renounce me if the least word or syllable in it proceeded from my pen, or if I were any way privy to the writing or penning of it."

Both Shakespeare and Marlowe protested; for Marlowe the accusation of atheism so publicly made was embarrassing and dangerous. Chettle thought it necessary to offer an apology. Early in December Wright published his *Kindhart's Dream*, and Chettle in the *Epistle to the Gentlemen Readers* took the opportunity of explaining the situation. The *Groatsworth of Wit* was all Greene's, so he declared; but as Greene's writing was none of the best he copied it, striking out certain passages which it would have been intolerable to print. With neither of those that take offence was he acquainted, "and with one of them I care not if I never be"—for it was dangerous to be too friendly with that atheist

Marlowe. As for the other, he had now met Shakespeare and was impressed by the charm of his manners and his easy good nature. He was sorry, he wrote, that he did not use his discretion more freely, "because myself have seen his demeanour no less civil than he excellent in the quality he professes; besides, divers of worship have reported his uprightness of dealing which argues his honesty, and his facetious grace in writing that approves his art."

About three weeks later the Lord Strange's men came back to the Rose from their country tour and opened with *Muly Mulocco* on the afternoon of the 30th December. The season began well, and in a month they played twenty-nine times, giving the old favourites *The Spanish Tragedy*, *The Jew of Malta*, *Titus*, *Friar Bacon*, *Henry the Sixth*, and two new plays, Marlowe's *Massacre at Paris* and *The Jealous Comedy*. But the plague was still about, so that the theatres were obliged to close on the 2nd February. The company stayed on in London hoping for an improvement, but the weekly returns of mortality still showed over thirty plague deaths a week. In May they abandoned hope for the year, and a small travelling company was formed by Alleyn, Kemp, Pope, Heminges, Phillips and Brian who secured a special licence from the Privy Council authorising them to play in any city, town or corporation outside an area of seven miles from London or the Court, that they might be in the better readiness hereafter for her Majesty's service whensoever they should be thereunto called, and calling upon all concerned to permit them to use their exercise at their most convenient times and places, the accustomed times of divine prayers excepted.

Shakespeare did not go with them; he had found encouragement elsewhere.

II

EDUCATION OF A DRAMATIST

AFTER the first success of the Talbot scenes, Shakespeare had enlarged his experience in a number of plays. Two further instalments of *Henry the Sixth* appeared, and the series was completed by *Richard the Third*. He was still learning, and admiring the greater playwrights of his time, and writing with Alleyn's voice and person constantly in his mind.

In *The Second Part* of *Henry the Sixth* he began the story with the marriage of young Henry to Margaret of Anjou. It was a much firmer performance than *The First Part:* the characters had real life, especially the young king, ruthful, and pious, and ineffective amidst his quarrelling nobility, and Margaret his Queen whose impatience was gradually growing to fury, and Richard Plantagenet, Duke of York, who was scheming for the crown for himself. The history gave Shakespeare no opportunity for passages of great depth or passion, but the play was balanced and the scenes dramatic, and without undue bombast except for the incident of Suffolk's murder by pirates. There were some good episodes, particularly the quarrel between Queen Margaret and the Duchess of Gloucester; the Duchess's sorcery, and penance, Cardinal Beaufort's delirium on his death-bed, and the rebellion of Jack Cade and the men of Kent. In *The Second Part* he brought the history down to the first battles of the Wars of the Roses.

In *The Third Part* Shakespeare traced the story through the complex issues and treacheries of the Wars of the Roses to the murder of King Henry in the Tower and the firm establishment of Edward the Fourth upon the throne. There was some change in his dramatic method. As the story drew towards its conclusion, he treated certain of the characters more fully, and in some of the speeches he was more elaborately poetical. Richard, afterwards Duke of Gloucester, was of the kind of person created by Marlowe, with the ambition of Tamburlane, the unscrupulousness of Barabas and the language of both. When his father, Richard of York, hesitates to break oath with King Henry, he argues him round:

> An oath is of no moment, being not took
> Before a true and lawful magistrate
> That hath authority over him that swears:
> Henry had none, but did usurp the place;
> Then, seeing 'twas he that made you to depose,
> Your oath, my lord, is vain and frivolous.
> Therefore, to arms! And, father, do but think
> How sweet a thing it is to wear a crown,
> Within whose circuit is Elysium,
> And all that poets feign of bliss and joy.

But the black depth of his nature is not truly revealed till later in the play when Shakespeare elaborated the character in a soliloquy of over seventy lines wherein he was made to brood admiringly upon the deformities of his body and soul, and the ruthless ambition which will hew him a way to the throne:

Why, I can smile, and murder while I smile,
And cry, 'Content,' to that which grieves my heart,
And wet my cheeks with artificial tears,
And frame my face to all occasions.
I'll drown more sailors than the mermaid shall;
I'll slay more gazers than the basilisk;
I'll play the orator as well as Nestor,
Deceive more slily than Ulysses could,
And, like a Sinon, take another Troy.
I can add colours to the chameleon,
Change shapes with Proteus for advantages,
And set the murderous Machiavel to school.
Can I do this, and cannot get a crown?
Tut! were it farther off, I'll pluck it down.

King Henry murdered, Shakespeare again made Richard delight in his own unparalleled villainy, and detail the steps by which he will remove his brother from the way of his ambition:

I have no brother, I am like no brother;
And this word 'love,' which greybeards call divine,
Be resident in men like one another
And not in me: I am myself alone.

Parallel to Richard of Gloucester he set Margaret, the Queen, whose strength of character is acerbated into cruelty by her own woes and the actions of her enemies. She is shown at her worst in the scene when she has Richard of York at her mercy and torments him, giving him the napkin stained with his boy's blood to wipe away his tears and mocking him with a paper crown. There is, however, some excuse for Margaret.

The third character which Shakespeare selected for special emphasis was King Henry, a saintly incompetent, from whose weakness most of these troubles had origin. He drew the King with sympathy and stressed the pathos of the man with a gentle speech on the simple country contentments which Fate had denied him:

> O God! methinks it were a happy life,
> To be no better than a homely swain;
> To sit upon a hill, as I do now,
> To carve out dials, quaintly, point by point,
> Thereby to see the minutes how they run,
> How many make the hour full complete;
> How many hours bring about the day;
> How many days will finish up the year;
> How many years a mortal man may live.
> When this is known, then to divide the times:
> So many hours must I tend my flock;
> So many hours must I take my rest;
> So many hours must I contemplate;
> So many hours must I sport myself;
> So many days my ewes have been with young;
> So many weeks ere the poor fools will ean;
> So many years ere I shall shear the fleece;
> So minutes, hours, days, months and years,

Pass'd over to the end they were created,
Would bring white hairs unto a quiet grave.
Ah! what a life were this! how sweet! how lovely!

By the time this trilogy of plays was finished Shakespeare had a very considerable experience of the practical problems of stagecraft, and of transmuting narrative into drama. It was journeyman work for the most part, for in none of these plays were there any serious attempt to elevate the story into a theme or a problem. Nor in a drama of the Houses of York and Lancaster was it necessary. Queen Elizabeth herself was but the second generation from Henry of Richmond. Several of the great houses of those times still flourished; there were still Percies of Northumberland and Stanleys of Derby. In truth the memory of the Wars of the Roses was deeply ingrained in Shakespeare's audience, and at the back of their minds lurked perpetually the fear that at any time the crown of England would again be in bloody dispute; for the Queen had no heir and the signs for the future were dark and uncertain, threatening turmoil and civil wars on her death.

Shakespeare's last play in the series was *Richard the Third*. It was, in a way, a commentary on the whole story, underlining its significances. Villainy is punished, perfidy rewarded, and the many curses that have been uttered so largely flutter home to roost. As a result the history became less dramatic and more symbolical. There were fewer scenes of rapid and noisy event. Instead Shakespeare concentrated his attention on certain long passages wherein he sacrificed the drama of clamorous incident to a dialogue of verbal cleverness, as in Richard's amazing wooing of the Lady Anne at the funeral of Henry the Sixth, the Lady Anne being the widow of Edward, the late King's son; and Richard had murdered both father and son. The device was repeated in a second wooing, when, after Anne has been murdered, Richard persuaded the widow of Edward the Fourth to match her daughter to himself.

Another set of episodes which Shakespeare introduced rather for their verbal possibilities than for any dramatic purpose was the appearance of old Queen Margaret, who in defiance of historic fact or even possibility haunts her ancient enemies like a Fury to curse them. Shakespeare even brought her face to face with Richard to indulge in a cursing match. Later, when the women both of the White Rose and the Red have equal cause to hate Richard, she reappears to gloat over the misfortunes of her old enemies, to claim her seniority in sorrow, and to teach them how to curse. Again at the end, the night before Bosworth Field, Shakespeare symbolised the moral issues of the drama. The tents of King Richard and of Henry of Richmond were pitched on either side of the stage, and in the recess between appeared in succession the ghosts of those whom Richard had murdered to curse their slayer and to bless his enemy.

Shakespeare was indeed finding his power over words and experimenting with the possibilities of dialogue, repartee, conceits, and that form of irony which consists in so repeating a phrase that with the alteration of a single word it comes back upon the head of the first speaker. As a contrast to this kind of writing he composed an elaborate piece of epic description in the recital of Clarence's dream:

> Methought that I had broken from the Tower,
> And was embark'd to cross to Burgundy;
> And in my company my brother Gloucester,
> Who from my cabin tempted me to walk
> Upon the hatches: thence we look'd toward England,
> And cited up a thousand heavy times,
> During the wars of York and Lancaster,
> That had befall'n us. As we pac'd along
> Upon the giddy footing of the hatches,
> Methought that Gloucester stumbled; and, in falling,
> Struck me, that thought to stay him, overboard,
> Into the tumbling billows of the main.
> Lord, Lord! methought what pain it was to drown:
> What dreadful noise of water in mine ears!
> What sights of ugly death within mine eyes!
> Methought I saw a thousand fearful wracks;
> A thousand men that fishes gnaw'd upon;
> Wedges of gold, great anchors, heaps of pearl,
> Inestimable stones, unvalu'd jewels,
> All scatter'd in the bottom of the sea.
> Some lay in dead men's skulls; and in those holes
> Where eyes did once inhabit, there were crept,
> As 'twere in scorn of eyes, reflecting gems,

That woo'd the slimy bottom of the deep,
And mock'd the dead bones that lay scatter'd by.

The play ended with the death of Richard the Third, and the long struggle was brought to an end. But Shakespeare reminded his audience how that they had their part in this history in a prayer that the past might not be repeated:

Abate the edge of traitors, gracious Lord,
That would reduce these bloody days again,
And make poor England weep in streams of blood!
Let them not live to taste this land's increase,
That would with treason wound this fair land's peace!
Now civil wounds are stopp'd, peace lives again:
That she may long live here, God say amen!

Shakespeare was thus forming a new conception of historical drama, using his story rather as an excuse for fine writing. Richard himself was like one of Marlowe's characters, and Shakespeare opened the play as Marlowe had opened *The Jew*, bringing forward his villain-hero to soliloquise upon himself, and to descant on his own deformity; and to proclaim that since he is cheated of feature by dissembling nature, and sent into the world scarce half made up, he is determined to prove a villain, and is even now about it. The story of Richard was thus no longer merely a record, in dramatic form, of events, but a play on a theme, the portrait of a man whom nature had formed with a misshapen body and a warped soul, but who was for this very reason filled with a demoniac power because, like Barabas, he was entirely free from the moral scruples which clogged the actions of lesser villains. Shakespeare owed much to Marlowe.

To the respectable and middle-aged, Christopher Marlowe was a monster of depravity, and there were many choice tales of his atheistical opinions and blasphemous conceits. Greene in the notorious letter had pointedly urged him to amend his ways and repent: "Wonder not," he wrote, "thou famous gracer of tragedians, that Greene, who hath said with thee (like the fool in his heart), 'there is no God,' should now give glory unto His greatness: for penetrating is His power; His hand lies heavy upon me; He hath spoken unto me with a voice of thunder, and I have felt He is a God that can punish enemies. Why should thy excellent wit, His Gift, be so blinded that thou should'st give no glory to the Giver? Is it pestilent Machiavellian policy that thou hast studied? O peevish folly! What are his rules but mere confused mockeries, able to extirpate in small time the generation of mankind?"

Machiavellianism, he went on, brought no advantage in this world to its author, and in the next he was inheriting the portion of Judas. "And wilt thou, my friend," Greene continued, "be his disciple? Look but to me, by him persuaded to that liberty, and thou shalt find it an infernal bondage. I know the least of my demerits merit this miserable death, but wilful striving against known truth exceedeth all the terrors of my soul. Defer not, with me, till this last point of extremity: *for little knowest thou how in the end thou shalt be visited.*"

Marlowe was not greatly moved by this appeal from the grave; poor Greene was always a weakling at heart, and sick men's fancies turn readily to the consolations of repentance. Others shivered a little at the prophecy; sometimes strange truths are revealed to dying men.

Marlowe was no company for those with conventional minds: but men who refused to worship the Deity by law established in the Realm of England liked his company, and were fascinated by the daring of his talk. He had some illustrious friends and patrons, Sir Walter Ralegh, the Earl of Northumberland, notorious for his interest in suspected sciences, and Harriot, the mathematician and geographer, George Chapman, the poet and others. They formed a little clique, much suspected of being in league with the Prince of Darkness. Their discussions were even noted in print. Ralegh, it was said, kept a School of Atheism, with a conjuring astrologer as schoolmaster, where no small company of noble young men were taught to jibe at the Old Law of Moses and the New Law of Christ; where divinity, the immortality of the soul, and the hope of a future life were ridiculed, and the scholars taught among other things to spell God backwards.

To these ribaldries Marlowe made his own blasphemous contribution, for his hatred of the professionally religious was so bitter that he took all occasions to mock their holiest beliefs. Marlowe indeed, with a few others of his generation, allowed his reason full license, and it led him to hate religion as mere political cozenage to keep men in awe. He made no secret of his opinions. At all times in table talk he would jest at the Scriptures, jibe at prayers, and strive in argument to frustrate and confute the writings of the prophets and fathers. When miracles were urged, he answered that things supposed to be done by divine power might have as well been done by observation of men. As for Moses, he was a juggler; it was an easy matter for one brought up in all the arts of the Egyptians to abuse the Jews, who were a rude and gross people; besides Harriot, Sir Walter Ralegh's man, could do better. In his more serious moments he would earnestly persuade men to atheism, willing them not to be afeared of bugbears and hobgoblins.

To men of orthodox views in Church and State matters no word could be too bad for such a reprobate. Those who knew him intimately were fond of the man, admiring his poetry, his fervour, and his wit.

Narrative poems retelling some of the amorous Greek myths were coming into fashion. Lodge had written *Scilla's Metamorphosis* four years earlier; two years ago Clapham told the story of Narcissus in Latin verse. Marlowe himself whose admiration for male loveliness was at times excessive had expressed it in *Edward the Second*. Now he began on a version of the story of *Hero and Leander*. As he visualised the legend, it was a story of the sudden, spontaneous love of a youth for a maid. He wrote two sestiads, carrying the narrative down to the point where Leander won his desire. The poem was passed around and Shakespeare with others read it.

The plague was so severe that there would be no market for plays for some time. Shakespeare already admired Marlowe to the point of close imitation; now he ventured on rivalry. He too would write a poem in the same style, claim a place amongst the poets, and perhaps win the poet's reward in the patronage of some great Lord. He found his theme in the embroidery of Hero's garments:

> Her wide sleeves green, and bordered with a grove
> Where Venus in her naked glory strove
> To please the careless and disdainful eyes
> Of proud Adonis that before her lies.

The story was not uncommon in his reading. He met it in Ovid's *Metamorphoses*, together with a similar adventure of Venus with Salmacis. Spenser retold it in the third book of the *Faery Queen*. He had seen it pictured, with Adonis painted by a running brook and Venus spying on him from the sedges.

Marlowe, as was his manner, made the tale gorgeous with all manner of verbal decoration, setting the first meeting of Leander and Hero in the temple of Venus:

So fair a church as this had Venus none;
The walls were of discoloured jasper stone
Wherein was Proteus carved, and o'erhead
A lively vine of green sea agate spread;
Where, by one hand, light headed Bacchus hung,
And with the other, wine from grapes out wrung.
Of crystal shining fair the pavement was;
The town of Sestos call'd it 'Venus' glass.'
There might you see the gods in sundry shapes,
Committing heady riots, incests, rapes. . . .

But Shakespeare knew better than to try to rival Marlowe in such descriptions. He set his story in the open air. His Venus wooed Adonis in the woods and he chose to decorate his poem not with jewels, needlework or statuary, culled from books or a teeming imagination, but with little observations made with his own eyes, such as the

dive-dapper peering through a wave
Who, being looked on, ducks as quickly in. . . .

Or, as the snail, whose tender horns being hit,
Shrinks backward in his shelly cave with pain,
And there all smother'd up, in shade doth sit,
Long after fearing to creep forth again . . .

or the long description of the hunted hare. Nor did he attempt Marlowe's rhymed decasyllabic couplets, but preferred the more elaborate six line stanza used by Lodge.

Marlowe's lovers, though the details of their union at the end were human enough, were somewhat idealised, creatures of art, at the beginning.

There was little of the myth about Shakespeare's poem. Venus was a woman in her prime of beauty and desire, Adonis was a youth whose passion was for hunting and manly sports, for he was as yet in the virgin dawn of adolescence when love is still ideal, and bodily love repugnant and disgusting. Venus accosts him and pulls him from his horse, as a whore in the Bankside suburbs might claw a shy and modest youth of decent breeding, blushing, indignant and protesting.

Shakespeare carried the story through to the fatal end of the hunting, and then he grew less interested; so that the description of Venus' lamentation was artificial and far-fetched after Venus' lust. Shakespeare as yet had no experience of deep sorrow.

When the poem was finished, it was printed by Richard Field. He was himself a Stratford man, two and a half years older than Shakespeare, and there was some friendship between the two families. In the previous year when his father died, John Shakespeare was one of those appointed to make an inventory of his goods. Field had been apprenticed first with George Bishop, and then with Thomas Vautrollier, a French printer and a master of the craft. Vautrollier died in 1587, and Field, after the manner of good apprentices, married the widow and succeeded to the business. He specialised in fine printing, and in 1591 had brought out the memorable edition of Harington's translation of *Orlando Furioso.*

Shakespeare now sought a patron for his work. For this poem one was conspicuously suitable. The young Earl of Southampton was himself an Adonis and his acceptance of Clapham's *Narcissus* showed that he enjoyed such a theme.

Henry Wriothesly, Earl of Southampton, was now aged nineteen. His father, the second Earl, had died in 1581. He was a Catholic peer who had spent some time in the Tower for his sympathies with the Duke of Norfolk. The young Earl, succeeding to the title at the age of eight, thus became according to custom a royal ward, and passed under the care of Sir William Cecil, Lord Burleigh, Lord High Treasurer, who supervised his education. At the age of twelve he was sent up to St. John's College, Cambridge, where he remained till the summer of 1589 when he took his Master of Arts degree *per gratiam.* Thence he was entered at Gray's Inn, after the manner of young gentlemen of means and birth, to complete his education in manners and the law. He was then sixteen, and of marriageable age, and it was the profitable duty and privilege of his guardian to provide him with a suitable wife. Lord Burleigh therefore proposed his own granddaughter, the Lady Elizabeth Vere, and negotiations were opened with the Countess of Southampton, but when she broached the matter to her son his answer was that he had no disposition to be tied yet and pleaded a respite of one year. His mother and his grandfather, Lord Montacute of Beaulieu, continued to press upon him the great advantage of such a match but he evaded a decision, to Lord Burleigh's surprise and irritation.

Southampton's ambitions were elsewhere. He had fallen under the glamour of the Earl of Essex and was hoping to go with him to France in the following spring. Essex, however, did not sail until the autumn of 1591 and Southampton did not accompany him. In the summer the Queen in her progress visited his house at Tichfield. A few weeks later he was one of the noblemen in the Court when the Queen made her brilliant state visit to Oxford in September 1592, and was conspicuous amongst the courtiers for his beauty and learning. He was still a bachelor when Shakespeare first came before him.

To Southampton accordingly *Venus and Adonis* was presented with the customary epistle:

To THE RIGHT HONOURABLE HENRY WRIOTHESLY,
Earl of Southampton, and Baron of Tichfield,
Right Honourable,

I know not how I shall offend in dedicating my unpolished lines to your lordship, nor how the world will censure me for choosing so strong a prop to support so weak a burden: only, if your honour seem but pleased, I account myself highly praised, and vow to take advantage of all idle hours, till I have honoured you with some grave labour. But if the first heir of my invention prove deformed, I shall be sorry it had so noble a godfather, and never after ear so barren a land, for fear it yield me still so bad a harvest. I leave it to your honourable survey, and your honour to your heart's content; which I wish may always answer your own wish and the world's hopeful expectation.

Your honour's in all duty,
WILLIAM SHAKESPEARE.

The poem was now ready for general publication and Field entered it on 18th April. It was sensationally well received, quoted, noted, and soon imitated.

A piece of literary art was one of the recognised means of bringing a young man of promise to the notice of great men, and by this poem Shakespeare was transported into a new world. Southampton showed personal favour which was something more than patronage, and promised advancement into the greater world. It produced also in Shakespeare for a time that wild exhilaration which a clever young man feels when suddenly transplanted from school into the brave new world of an ancient University, where he is treated as an equal by his superiors and encouraged to display his talents. With Shakespeare there was added that he was an older man, mixing with younger, of better birth than himself, accepted on his own merits by a society that was witty, cultured, intellectual and worldly wise after the manner of young gentlemen of wealth. The large household of an Elizabethan nobleman was in itself a little court, and there were some notable persons about Southampton, amongst them John Florio, the Italian who acted as his secretary.

In his first ecstasy Shakespeare fell in with the new fashion of poets and turned sonneteer. During the '80's poets from time to time ventured to experiment with sonnets. Gascoigne in 1575 had briefly described the form, saying, "Then have you sonnets; some think that all poems, being short, may be called sonnets, as indeed it is a diminutive word derived of *sonare;* but I can best allow to call those sonnets which are of fourteen lines, every line containing ten syllables. The first twelve do rhyme in staves of four lines by cross metre, and the last two rhyming together do conclude the whole. There are dizains and sixains which are of ten lines and of six lines, commonly used by the French, which some English writers do also term by the name of sonnetter." In 1582 Thomas Watson published a sequence called *Hecatompathia or Passionate Century of Love.* More illustrious persons included occasional sonnets in their writings.

The sudden vogue, however, of the sonnet in the early 1590's was due to the unwarranted publication of Sir Philip Sidney's famous sequence called *Astrophel and Stella,* with an impudent preface by Nashe. Anything that bore Sidney's name was sure of an honoured welcome, and these poems were obviously so much finer than any of their kind. The explanation of their success was to be found in the first sonnet. Sidney, as all the rest, read, translated and borrowed, but he had something to say for himself in addition:

Loving in truth, and fain my love in verse to show,
That she, dear She, might take some pleasure of my pain,—
Pleasure might cause her read, reading might make her know,
Knowledge might pity win, and pity grace obtain,—
I sought fit works to paint the blackest face of woe;
Studying inventions fine, her wits to entertain,
Oft turning others' leaves to see if thence would flow
Some fresh and fruitful showers upon my sun-burn'd brain.
But words came halting forth, wanting Invention's stay;
Invention, Nature's child, fled step-dame Study's blows;
And other's feet still seem'd but strangers in my way.
Thus, great with child to speak, and helpless in my throes,
Biting my truant pen, beating myself for spite;
'Fool,' said my Muse to me, 'look in thy heart, and write.'

And as his first readers read on they realised that these sonnets were indeed written from the heart, for Sir Philip was not writing on abstract themes of Love, Reason and Desire, but was setting forth in incomparable verse the story of his own disastrous love for Stella. He himself was Astrophel, and his star had been my Lord of Essex's sister, the Lady Penelope, so unhappily mated with Lord Rich. To make living poetry the poet needed a real mistress and not a feigned muse, and though the adornings of his verse might be borrowed, its passion must first be felt.

Within a few months of the publication of *Astrophel and Stella*, other poets were sending off their sonnets to the press. Some of Daniel's had been included in the first printing of *Astrophel*. At the beginning of 1592 he published his own copy, giving it the title of *Delia, containing certain sonnets.* He added also a narrative poem called *The Complaint of Rosamund.* The next year was published Watson's volume called *The tears of Fancy*, Barnabe Barnes' *Parthenophil and Parthenope*, Lodge's *Phillis* and Giles Fletcher's *Licia or poems of love.* Others too were at work for the press, Constable was writing *Diana*, William Percy was puling sonnets to his fairest Cœlia, and Drayton was immortalising his Idea. Love was the commonest theme, and there was much ransacking of Petrarch and Ronsard for fine conceits. Nevertheless English poets were learning through their sonnets to look inwards and to explore their own sensations.

The interest in sonnet writing was keen, but narrow. The sonneteers were gentlemen or retainers in great men's houses, and their readers were to be found in the Court and gentle society. Shakespeare followed in the movement but, unlike most of the rest, he expressed his affection not for a mistress but for the beautiful young noblemen whose affection he had won; and the young male, of pedigree stock, is one of the loveliest of God's creatures. The first group of seventeen were all on one theme, a topic much discussed in the Southampton household, the young man's refusal to fulfil the obligation of his rank and marry. His reluctance was genuine and notable; he was not yet interested in the love of woman; and Shakespeare in setting into verse the plea that he should marry, urged him not to love but to preserve his beauty in posterity:

When forty winters shall besiege thy brow,
And dig deep trenches in thy beauty's field,
Thy youth's proud livery, so gaz'd on now,
Will be a tatter'd weed, of small worth held:
Then being ask'd where all thy beauty lies,
Where all the treasure of thy lusty days,
To say, within thine own deep-sunken eyes,
Were an all-eating shame and thriftless praise.
How much more praise deserv'd thy beauty's use,
If thou couldst answer, 'This fair child of mine
Shall sum my count, and make my old excuse,'
Proving his beauty by succession thine!
  This were to be new made when thou art old,
  And see thy blood warm when thou feel'st it cold.

A few weeks after the presentation of *Venus and Adonis*, Marlowe died tragically and dramatically. Parliament had been assembled in February, its main business being to provide for the growing expenses of the Spanish war; but there were other anxieties nearer home. In the general persecution of recusants Puritans suffered as well as Catholics. Now there were many signs, very disturbing to the Council, that some sort of conspiracy was being hatched. Early in March a secret gathering of Barrowists was surprised at Islington. On the 22nd Barrow and Greenwood, the two most prominent of the Puritan leaders, were arraigned and condemned to death as traitors. The condemnation was bitterly criticised in many places and for eleven days they were kept in suspense. On the 31st May they were led out to Tyburn but at the last moment respited and taken back to prison. Four days later a Bill against the Brownists was brought forward in Parliament at the promptings of Archbishop Whitgift; it was severely attacked in the Lower House and rejected. Early next morning, Barrow and Greenwood were hanged, victims—so malicious gossip said—of the Archbishop's chagrin.

Parliament dissolved on the 10th but it was clear that the Council had not yet discovered the root of the trouble. Lewd and mysterious libels were being circulated warning the Flemings in London to take themselves out of the country, for all the apprentices would rise and then "down with all Flemings and strangers." Special commissioners were appointed to search out the offenders, and some arrests were made; but the principal author was evidently still at large for the libels continued to be put abroad.

In the night of 15th May a threatening poem was set up on the walls of the Dutch churchyard. The Commissioners were therefore urged to make even greater efforts, and given authority to apprehend any suspected persons, to make search anywhere for papers or writings that might give light for the discovery of the offenders, and if the suspected were reluctant to give evidence they could be put to the torture as often as the Commissioners deemed necessary.

It seemed likely that the offender would be found amongst the needy hack writers. Accordingly next day Thomas Kyd was arrested and carried off to Bridewell whilst his papers were examined; and among them was found, not a libel against the Flemings, but some portions of a disputation denying the divinity of Jesus Christ. Kyd was asked to explain the existence of so damnable a document. He answered that it was left in his study by Marlowe two years before, when they were working together.

Marlowe was now summoned to appear before the Council. He presented himself on the 20th May and was ordered to attend daily. Meanwhile the Lord Keeper set about procuring further evidence of Marlowe's activities and opinions; it was soon available.

Marlowe's case, however, was removed to a Higher Court. In the morning of Wednesday, 30th May, Marlowe went to a house at Deptford Strand in company with three men, whose names were Ingram Frizer, Skeres, and Nicholas Poley, all persons with a disreputable record. After dinner they strolled in the garden, and then about six in the evening they returned to the room. Skeres and Poley were sitting at the table with Frizer between them, Marlowe was lying on a bed, when a quarrel began. Marlowe in rage sprang up, snatched Frizer's dagger from the sheath at his back and struck him on the head. Frizer seized Marlowe by the wrist. In the struggle Marlowe suddenly wrested the dagger away, but the point being upwards, it was jabbed into his eye, and after a few moments of screaming agony he was dead.

There was the usual inquest. The only direct testimony came from the three surviving companions who naturally protested their own innocence, and the jury concluded that Frizer had acted "in the defence and saving of his own life." Greene's warning was too soon fulfilled: "little knowest thou how in the end thou shalt be visited."

Marlowe's friends said little, but the godly were exultant and retailed the story with elevating comment. See, they exclaimed, what a hook the Lord put in the nostrils of this barking dog! Herein did the justice of God most notably appear in that He compelled his own hand that had written those blasphemies to be the instrument to punish him, and that in his brain which had devised them!

Southampton's patronage of Shakespeare quickly developed into an intimacy which Shakespeare continued to express with zest in occasional sonnets, and Southampton by the practical favours which he was in a position to bestow on his admirer. A new prospect now lay before Shakespeare, an entrance into the larger social life, for he always yearned after those outward distinctions which take away a man's sense of inferiority amongst his fellows:

> Let those who are in favour with their stars
> Of public honour and proud titles boast,

Whilst I, whom fortune of such triumph bars,
Unlook'd for joy in that I honour most.
Great princes' favourites their fair leaves spread
But as the marigold at the sun's eye,
And in themselves their pride lies buried,
For at a frown they in their glory die.
The painful warrior famoused for fight,
After a thousand victories once foil'd,
Is from the book of honour razed quite,
And all the rest forgot for which he toil'd:
  Then happy I, that love and am belov'd,
  Where I may not remove nor be remov'd.

Shakespeare burgeoned during these months in the nobleman's household, and the zest still lives in the plays which he wrote whilst the memory was fresh and untainted. Berowne, Longaville and Dumain in *Love's Labour's Lost*, Valentine and Proteus, Gratiano and Bassanio, Mercutio, Tybalt and Benvolio all bear traces of the young men of fashion that Shakespeare knew at this time.

Not only had his life become suddenly full of colour, his wit and intelligence were sharpened by contact. He learnt much of drama and literary art, realising at first-hand that the tastes of gentlemen and the appetities of groundlings were very diverse. At the Rose the contrasts of drama were rough and noisy: shoutings, groans, the clashing of swords, bladders of calf's blood, were the chief trappings of a tragedy; and for comedy, a knave, a fool, a cuckold and a cudgel. Working dramatists were hired to purvey bombast for Alleyn, and bawdry for

Kemp. Gentlemen despised such crudity and preferred the lighter wit of the comedies which Lyly provided for them.

Lyly wrote his plays in the '80's for the children of the Chapel Royal and Paul's to perform before the Queen and private audiences, but most of them had remained unprinted until the end of 1591 when the widow Broom rather timidly published *Endymion* in the hope that it might appeal to the gentleman reader. When *Galatea* and *Midas* and further editions of *Campaspe* followed in 1592, anyone could judge for himself the difference in standard between court drama and playhouse stuff.

Accordingly late in this year 1593 Shakespeare set about a light comedy of his own to amuse Southampton and his friends. Certain conditions must be observed. It must be witty, fashionable and topical, full of those subtleties which would tickle the fancy of those for whom it was written and yet be caviare to the general.

A play needed a plot, and a comedy must deal of love. But Southampton and his intimates affected to scorn love, much to the amusement of the older man who had already trod that same path some years ahead. However, it gave him the germ of a play of Dan Cupid's revenge. He called it *Love's Labour's Lost*.

So Shakespeare began with a theme much canvassed by some of his audience. A king and three of his courtiers determined to shut out women from their lives and to bend themselves to study for three years. He set the story in France, and these French wars furnished him with good names. Navarre, for instance, for the king; it was a neat touch for the real Navarre was a notorious ladies' man. Two of his commanders were the Marshal Biron and the Duc de Longueville—good stage names; and for a fourth Du Mayne, Navarre's chief enemy among the Leaguers. The idea of these four cloistering themselves in amity and celibacy would itself raise a laugh at the very outset.

This playwright and his audience had certain jests, and ideas, and arguments in common. The theme of love was one, and learning another. Some of the more learned poets had of late come out as heavy champions of wit against barbarism. Spenser began it in *The Tears of the Muses;* Daniel followed in *Delia and Rosamund;* Chapman, most solemnly of all, in *The Shadow of Night* pompously claimed that skill would only show her secrets with invocation, fasting, watching, and the very sweat of the soul. The upstart crow thought otherwise, that many who passed for learned knew nothing, and through the mouth of Berowne he championed both love and book ignorance:

> Why, all delights are vain; but that most vain
> Which, with pain purchas'd doth inherit pain:
> As, painfully to pore upon a book,
> To seek the light of truth; while truth the while

Doth falsely blind the eyesight of his look:
  Light seeking light doth light of light beguile:
So, ere you find where light in darkness lies,
Your light grows dark by losing of your eyes.
Study me how to please the eye indeed,
  By fixing it upon a fairer eye,
Who dazzling so, that eye shall be his heed,
  And give him light that it was blinded by.
Study is like the heaven's glorious sun,
  That will not be deep-search'd with saucy looks;
Small have continual plodders ever won,
  Save base authority from others' books.
These earthly godfathers of heaven's lights
  That give a name to every fixed star,
Have no more profit of their shining nights
  Than those that walk and wot not what they are.
Too much to know is to know nought but fame;
And every godfather can give a name.

For the rest he filled up his play with characters who were three parts fancy and one part caricature. Southampton was not over fond of Sir Walter Ralegh, and Ralegh these last two years had made himself notorious. In the summer of '92 he was recalled from the fleet which he was commanding and sent to the Tower, for the Queen had learnt that the Captain of her personal Bodyguard had been intriguing with one of her own Maids of Honour. Moreover Marlowe's sensational death, and Ralegh's own championship of the Brownists in the last Parliament had again drawn attention to the School of Atheism, and Harriot the figure caster. There were little touches in some of the characters which reminded the audience of Ralegh and his circle; Armado, for instance, with his melancholy, his extravagant letters, his intrigues with the serving wench, and his lofty humour, his discourse peremptory, his tongue filed, his eye ambitious, his gait majestical, and his general behaviour vain, ridiculous and thrasonical. Holofernes had certain affinities with Harriot, a foolish extravagant spirit, full of forms, figures, shapes, objects, ideas, apprehensions, notions, revolutions; one who taught boys the horn book, but was nonplussed by Moth's request to spell a. b. backwards.

There were many more butterfly quips born to die a few hours after their hatching. Shakespeare profited not a little from the experiment; he learnt how to draw from life and not from copies.

Meanwhile Shakespeare was writing another long poem. The theme of *Venus and Adonis* was lust disdained; the new poem was the old story of *Lucrece*, or chastity forced. It was published in May 1594, and was even more popular than the former. Again Shakespeare dedicated his poem to the Earl of Southampton, with an acknowledgment of his favours of the past year:

To the Right Honourable Henry Wriothesly,
Earl of Southampton, and Baron of Tichfield,

The love I dedicate to your lordship is without end; whereof this pamphlet, without beginning, is but a superfluous moiety. The warrant I have of your honourable disposition, not the worth of my untutored lines, makes it assured of acceptance. What I have done is yours; what I have to do is yours; being part of all I have, devoted yours. Were my worth greater, my duty would show greater; meantime, as it is, it is bound to your lordship, to whom I wish long life, still lengthened with happiness.

Your lordship's in all duty,

WILLIAM SHAKESPEARE.

III

EXPERIMENTS

ALL the hot summer of 1593 the plague continued, and throughout July and August it increased week by week. In September there were still over a thousand deaths a week; but in the late autumn it began to decline and by December the danger was apparently over. On 26th December Sussex's men ventured to open at the Rose. They played for five weeks and were doing well, but the Council grew apprehensive that the infection would break out again and on 3rd February, 1594, the playhouses were closed. Early in April, however, playing was again sanctioned and the Rose was occupied for a few days by a combined company formed of the Queen's and Sussex's men.

In the spring of this year 1594 there was a sensational alarm at Court. At the end of January it was learnt that Dr. Roderigo Lopez, one of the physicians at Court, was accused by the Earl of Essex of having convenanted with the Spaniards to poison the Queen. Dr. Lopez was a Portuguese Jew who had come to England many years before and now had a considerable practice amongst courtiers. He had also a knowledge of state secrets. Some years before Mr. Secretary Walsingham, knowing of Lopez's good connections in Portugal, employed him in receiving and forwarding information to his spies. When Walsingham died in 1590, Essex, who was beginning to regard himself as a statesman, proposed that Lopez should in future act as his agent and supply him with news. Lopez agreed, but privately made a similar arrangement with the Queen herself. From time to time he received information which he imparted to the Queen, and then went on to Essex. Essex hastened to Court to tell the Queen, who laughed at him for bringing stale news. As a result Essex became deeply incensed against Lopez. At the end of 1593 a mysterious stranger named Tinoco told an English merchant at Calais that he had strange revelations to make concerning the King of Spain's secretary. He was sent over to Court and closely examined when he declared that he, with another man called Ferrara, had been dispatched to England to win Lopez over to the Spanish King's service. Further he said that Lopez had already accepted a jewel of great value from the King. Lopez was arrested and lodged at Essex House whilst his papers were examined. Nothing incriminating was found and when Essex came to report to the Queen, she rebuked him severely, saying that she knew Lopez was innocent and that the whole business was due to Essex's malice and nothing else. Essex was so angry that he flung back to his chamber and sulked there for two days.

Rumours began to fly round. It was said that on

further examination Lopez was found to be deeply implicated and discovered to have been the King of Spain's pensioner for seven years. At Court all access to the Queen was forbidden except to the Council and ladies on immediate attendance. Essex meanwhile worked day and night in the attempt to vindicate himself, and within the next month a very dark case was made out against the Doctor.

Lopez was arraigned at the Guildhall on 28th February, and ample evidence was produced by Sir Edward Coke, the Attorney General, to satisfy the jury that he was indeed guilty, and he was condemned to death. A fortnight later Tinoco and Ferrara were also condemned. The Queen, however, for a long time was unwilling to agree to Lopez's death, and there was considerable anxiety lest he should die before the sentence could be carried out. At last on the 7th June, the three men were brought up before the King's Bench in Westminster Hall, where their sentence was pronounced. They were then taken back to the city and dragged thence on hurdles to Tyburn, where they were hanged and quartered. Lopez protested his innocence at the passing of the sentence, and at the gallows he declared that he loved the Queen as well as he loved Jesus Christ—which, coming from a Jew, moved the crowd to great laughter. The whole affair confirmed the general prejudice against Machiavellians and Jews.

The players were now beginning to drift back to London, but after nearly two years of forced absence their affairs were in a poor way. General reorganisation followed. Alleyn re-formed the Admiral's company, and on 14th May they played at the Rose, but for three days only. The players hitherto known as the Lord Strange's men had changed their title twice during the plague months. Ferdinando Stanley, Lord Strange, had succeeded as Earl of Derby in the previous September but in April 1594 he died in great agony of a mysterious illness, and there were many suspicious signs that his end had been brought about by witchcraft. His actors found a new master in Henry Carey, Lord Hunsdon, Lord Chamberlain. The Lord Chamberlain's men also returned to London, and on 3rd June they united with the Admiral's for a few days to play to poor houses at the little theatre in Newington Butts. They acted ten times, their plays being *Hester and Ahasuerus*, *The Jew of Malta*, *Titus Andronicus*—twice each, *Bellendon*—a new play of the Admiral's, *Cutlack*, *Hamlet* and *The Taming of the Shrew*.

The alliance was soon dissolved. On 15th June Alleyn took the Admiral's men back to the Rose. The best of the Chamberlain's men did not follow him. There was room only for one Tamburlane in Alleyn's company; individuals with ambitions of their own had small chance against the financial strength of the Alleyn-Henslowe combine. For a time the Chamberlain's men had no London theatre and were obliged to go on tour, but they were back in London in October and found a home in the Theatre in Shoreditch.

During these months Shakespeare's friendship with Southampton began to change, for Adonis did not shun Venus for ever. The position of the player in the nobleman's company was peculiar and caused some comment which was plainly reflected in a curious poem that appeared in October 1594. It was called *Willobie His Avisa or The True picture of a modest maid and of a chaste and constant wife*, and purported to tell the story of an English country girl of great beauty who was the wife of an innkeeper. She was pestered by all kinds of gallants but rebuffed them sternly and remained constant to her husband. Names and places were disguised but in such a way that they were obvious to those who knew the real story. In the 43rd Canto the writer left verse and continued in prose:

Henrico Willobego. Italo-Hispalensis

H. W. being suddenly infected with the contagion of a fantastical fit, at the first sight of A, pineth a while in secret grief, at length not able any longer to endure the burning heat of so fervent a humour, bewrayeth the secrecy of his disease unto his familiar friend W. S. who not long before had tried the courtesy of the like passion, and was now newly recovered of the like infection; yet finding his friend let blood in the same vein, he took pleasure for a time to see him bleed, and instead of stopping the issue, he enlargeth the wound, with the sharp razor of a willing conceit, persuading him that he thought it a matter easy to be compassed, and no doubt with pain, diligence and some cost in time to be obtained. Thus this miserable comforter comforting his friend with an impossibility, either for that he would now secretly laugh at his friend's folly, that had given occasion not long before unto others to laugh at his own, or because he would see whether another could play his part better than himself, and in viewing afar off the course of this loving Comedy, he determined to see whether it would sort to a happier end for this new actor than it did for the old player. But at length this Comedy was like to have grown to a Tragedy by the weak and feeble estate that H. W. was brought unto, by a desperate view of an impossibility of obtaining his purpose, till Time and Necessity, being his best physicians, brought him to a plaster, if not to heal, yet in part to ease his malady. In all which discourse is lively represented the unruly rage of unbridled fancy, having the reins to rove at liberty, with the divers and sundry changes of affections and temptations, which Will set loose from Reason can devise.

After this preface a series of twenty-one cantos followed in which W. S. urged H. W. to greater efforts, and Avisa very decidedly repulsed his offers.

Of course H. W. might not be Henry Wriothesly, Earl of Southampton, nor W. S. be William Shakespeare, but there was enough fact in the relationship of nobleman and player for the coincidence to be most embarrassing.

Whatever hopes and promises Shakespeare may have received during the last eighteen months, Southampton for the present was not in a position to do very much for him; he had more than enough troubles of his own. He was obliged at last to decide whether he would or would not marry the Lady

Elizabeth Vere, and he refused. The penalty for disdaining Lord Burleigh's wishes was a payment of £5,000.

As yet there was no break in his friendship, and Shakespeare continued to express his hopes and disappointments in intimate sonnets.

When in disgrace with fortune and men's eyes
I all alone beweep my outcast state,
And trouble deaf heaven with my bootless cries,
And look upon myself, and curse my fate,
Wishing me like to one more rich in hope,
Featur'd like him, like him with friends possess'd,
Desiring this man's art, and that man's scope,
With what I most enjoy contented least;
Yet in these thoughts myself almost despising,
Haply I think on thee,—and then my state,
Like to the lark at break of day arising
From sullen earth, sings hymns at heaven's gate;
For thy sweet love remember'd such wealth brings
That then I scorn to change my state with kings.

Friendship was severely strained over the affair of the Black Woman. She was a courtesan, notorious to fashionable young gentlemen of the Inns of Court who took their pleasures in Clerkenwell; and for a time Shakespeare became her lover. The adventure stirred him profoundly. By ordinary standards the woman was not beautiful, yet irresistibly fascinating; his will led him to her; his reason was revolted, as he expressed it in a sonnet:

The expense of spirit in a waste of shame
Is lust in action, and till action, lust

Is perjur'd, murderous, bloody, full of blame,
Savage, extreme, rude, cruel, not to trust,
Enjoy'd no sooner but despised straight,
Past reason hunted, and no sooner had
Past reason hated as a swallow'd bait,
On purpose laid to make the taker mad.
Mad in pursuit and in possession so,
Had, having, and in quest to have extreme,
A bliss in proof and proud and very woe,
Before a joy propos'd behind a dream,
All this the world well knows yet none knows well,
To shun the heaven that leads men to this hell.

Nor was he blindly in love, for he could stand aside from himself and criticise both himself and her:

My mistress' eyes are nothing like the sun,
Coral is far more red, than her lips' red.
If snow be white, why then her breasts are dun:
If hairs be wires, black wires grow on her head:
I have seen roses damask'd, red and white,
But no such roses see I in her cheeks,
And in some perfumes is there more delight,
Than in the breath that from my mistress reeks.
I love to hear her speak, yet well I know,
That music hath a far more pleasing sound:
I grant I never saw a goddess go,
My mistress when she walks treads on the ground.
And yet by heaven I think my love as rare,
As any she belied with false compare.

The woman however was after the highest game and when Southampton came her way she readily deserted Shakespeare. It was a galling situation. He wanted his mistress again, but not at the expense of friendship, and all that friendship might still bring; so he made the best of it, and tried to cover his disappointments with a half-hearted gesture of renunciation. To each of them he protested in a run of sonnets. To Southampton he wrote:

That thou hast her, it is not all my grief,
And yet it may be said I lov'd her dearly;
That she hath thee, is of my wailing chief,
A loss in love that touches me more nearly.
Loving offenders, thus I will excuse ye:
Thou dost love her, because thou know'st I love her;
And for my sake even so doth she abuse me,
Suffering my friend for my sake to approve her.
If I lose thee, my loss is my love's gain,
And losing her, my friend hath found that loss;
Both find each other, and I lose both twain,
And both for my sake lay on me this cross:
  But here's the joy; my friend and I are one;
  Sweet flattery! then she loves but me alone.

To the woman:

Two loves I have of comfort and despair,
Which like two spirits do suggest me still:
The better angel is a man right fair,
The worser spirit a woman, colour'd ill,
To win me soon to hell, my female evil
Tempteth my better angel from my side,
And would corrupt my saint to be a devil,
Wooing his purity with her foul pride.
And whether that my angel be turn'd fiend
Suspect I may, but not directly tell;
But being both from me, both to each friend,
I guess one angel in another's hell:

Yet this shall I ne'er know, but live in doubt,
Till my bad angel fire my good one out.

In the autumn of 1594, however, destiny laid hold upon Shakespeare. In the reorganisation of the Lord Chamberlain's company he was able to acquire a player's share and henceforward took his place on equal terms with the rest. Apart from Alleyn the Chamberlain's men were as good a company as could be found, and they possessed certain advantages over their rivals in that no individual was yet in a position to monopolise the good parts. Their chief tragedian was Richard Burbage, now about twenty-five years old, who had been playing, mostly in minor parts, for some ten years. Burbage learnt in the school of Alleyn and first made a name for himself in the part of Richard the Third, so that the last scene with Richard calling "A horse, a horse, my kingdom for a horse" was almost as famous as "Who calls Hieronimo from his naked bed?"

For clown they had the illustrious Will Kemp, who had succeeded Tarlton as the most popular of comedians. He was a certain draw but not always an entirely satisfactory partner for serious drama as he was apt to take his part a little light-heartedly when any opportunity offered for extemporal merriment. He was especially famous for the jigs which he used to dance after the play was over, a form of pantomime more vigorous than chaste. In his own way Kemp was as famous as Alleyn, and not less popular.

The Theatre in Shoreditch where they now began to play was the property of James Burbage, father to Richard. He had begun life as a joiner and later turned player with such success that he became leader of the great Earl of Leicester's company nearly thirty years ago. In the early 1570's there had been trouble between the players and the Lord Mayor of London which resulted in galling restrictions on plays and ultimately in their banishment from the City. Burbage, who was always a stubborn fighter, was not so easily put down. The power of the Lord Mayor was limited to the boundaries of the City, and beyond, in the suburbs, playing could go on undisturbed. So in 1576 Burbage acquired a piece of waste ground in Shoreditch on a twenty-one years' lease from a gentleman called Giles Alleyn and thereon erected a playhouse which he named the Theatre.

Burbage liked everything about him to be handsome and he spent generously on his playhouse, but as he had little capital of his own he brought in his brother-in-law, whose name was John Brayne, a wealthy grocer. The partnership led to endless trouble, especially after Brayne's death, for Burbage acted arbitrarily, if not dishonestly, with the widow. But the building of the Theatre was a work of genius. It gave the actors a permanent home, and as much as any one he had been ultimately responsible for the financial success of playing.

The Chamberlain's men were at first at some disadvantage compared with their rivals on the Bankside for their repertory contained fewer popular plays, but they had Shakespeare with them as a partner. Moreover both Greene and Marlowe were dead, and Kyd died before the end of the year, and there was no one else at the moment with any reputation as a playwright.

Shakespeare had been experimenting with various types of drama. In *Love's Labour's Lost* he tried a society play in the Lyly manner. He attempted three other kinds of comedy; in the *Comedy of Errors* he deliberately imitated Plautus in a Latinised play of coincidences; in *Two Gentlemen of Verona* he played with a romantic theme of friendship, and with the *Taming of the Shrew* he wrote a farce.

The Comedy of Errors was an adaptation of the story which Plautus contrived in the *Menæchmi.* There were twin brothers each named Menæchmus, exactly alike but long parted. One lived at Epidamnum, the other at Syracuse. Menæchmus of Epidamnum married a shrewish wife but loved elsewhere. Menæchmus of Syracuse having undertaken to seek out his brother came at last to Epidamnum. The play told of the complications which followed when servants, wife and acquaintances confused the two Menæchmi. Shakespeare altered the names, calling his brothers Antipholus, and for Epidamnum he substituted Ephesus. He also added another pair of twins, each Antipholus being provided with a servant called Dromio, and thereby vastly increased the possibility for farce and misunderstanding. The exits and entrances were very adroitly managed, but the language was wooden and over witty. Moreover, Shakespeare had not yet learnt how to contrive his opening scene. The twins according to his story were separated in infancy by shipwreck. He decided to effect the final recognition by producing the parents. Their mother had become an abbess in Ephesus. The father, Ægeon of Syracuse, comes to look for his long lost family. Since Syracuse is at war with Ephesus, Ægeon is arrested, brought before the Duke, and condemned to death. It took Shakespeare twenty-seven lines to explain this fact, and then the Duke observed:

> Well, Syracusian; say in brief the cause
> Why thou departedst from thy native home,
> And for what cause thou cam'st to Ephesus.

Thus encouraged, Ægeon was given a speech, almost continuous, of over a hundred lines wherein to relate his autobiography and family history as prelude to the story.

Farce of this kind depended for its success on rapidity; the broadest of contrasts in characterisation only were necessary; and indeed if once the characters were to become too human the spirit of farce would be abashed. Shakespeare, however, presented a close portrait of a jealous wife in Adriana who seemed to be drawn from the life; and since the husbands of such seldom have a chance at home of fully stating their own side of the argument he put into the mouth of the abbess a severe homily on the disquiets wrought by jealousy:

> The venom clamours of a jealous woman
> Poison more deadly than a mad dog's tooth.
> It seems, his sleeps were hinder'd by thy railing,
> And thereof comes it that his head is light.
> Thou say'st his meat was sauc'd with thy upbraidings:
> Unquiet meals make ill digestions;
> Thereof the raging fire of fever bred:
> And what's a fever but a fit of madness?
> Thou say'st his sports were hinder'd by thy brawls:
> Sweet recreation barr'd, what doth ensue
> But moody moping, and dull melancholy,
> Kinsman to grim and comfortless despair,
> And at her heels a huge infectious troop
> Of pale distemperatures and foes to life?
> In food, in sport, and life-preserving rest
> To be disturb'd, would mad or man or beast:
> The consequence is then, thy jealous fits
> Have scar'd thy husband from the use of wits.

The Two Gentlemen of Verona was an essay on the theme worn shiny of love and friendship. There were two friends Valentine and Proteus. Proteus was in love with Julia, Valentine was fancy free. Valentine knowing that home-keeping youth hath ever homely wits goes travelling to Milan; Proteus stays behind. In Milan Valentine falls in love with Silvia, the Duke's daughter. Proteus' father sends him away to Milan and the two friends meet in Silvia's company. Proteus is attracted by Silvia and when he learns that Valentine is about to climb up to Silvia's chamber by night he tells the Duke. The Duke encounters Valentine wearing a long cloak which he snatches aside and the ladder of cords is revealed. Valentine is banished and makes his way disconsolately to the woods where the outlaws take him, and finding him to be a presentable young gentleman make him their king. Proteus is admitted to the company of Silvia but she despises his infidelity. Meanwhile Julia, unable to endure the absence of her Proteus, disguises herself as a page and follows. She comes upon Proteus as he is serenading Silvia. She takes service as Proteus' page and is sent for Silvia's picture. Silvia persuades a gentleman named Sir Eglamour to help her to escape from Thurio whom her father would force upon her. She also is taken by the outlaws in the wood. Proteus with the disguised Julia follows to the wood where he finds Silvia and rescues her from her guard. He again makes love but when she repulses him he is about to force her. At this moment, Valentine slips out of the thicket; Proteus confesses his guilt and is sorry. Valentine forgives him and relinquishes all claim to Silvia, whereat Julia swoons and all is explained. Proteus discovers that Julia is fairer after all than Silvia and they are reconciled. The outlaws enter with the Duke and Thurio whom they have captured. Thurio forgoes his claim on Silvia, at which the Duke is so disgusted that he gives her to Valentine; everyone is pardoned; and the lovers are happily paired.

It was a very familiar plot which in one form or another had been told many times, and dramatised. Shakespeare set forth his story plainly, but he made the dialogue sparkle with abundant showers of puns, lover's complaints and sonneteer's conceits. He added, after Lyly's manner, a pair of comic servants, Proteus' Launce and Valentine's Speed, who follow on a lower level their masters' travails. Launce has a dog, a very mongrel cur, and his devotion to his beast is in laudable contrast to Proteus' inconstancy. The play, however, was not a success, and Shakespeare laid it aside; parts of it could be used again.

Shakespeare then wrote a tragedy on the love story of Romeo and Juliet. It was one of the many tales of star-crossed lovers which were familiar to readers of novels, and it had been retold in ambling fourteeners by Arthur Brooke in 1562. To this poem Shakespeare turned. Moreover this family feud, with murder countered by murder, was a close parallel to a tragedy of a few weeks past in which Southampton and his household were still closely involved.

Two of Southampton's especial intimates were the brothers Danvers, Sir Charles and Sir Henry, sons of old Sir John Danvers. Between their family and the Longs, Southampton's neighbours near Titchfield, there existed a bitter feud. It came to a head when Sir John Danvers, as magistrate, committed one of Sir Walter Long's servants for a robbery. Sir Walter by undue proceeding rescued his servant, and Sir John caused him to be severely rebuked by the Judge at the next Assizes. The matter was carried to the Council and Sir Walter committed to the Fleet prison. Sir John also committed another of Sir Walter's servants for a murder.

In retaliation Sir Walter and his brother Henry Long began to egg on their followers to behave insolently and to provoke quarrels with Sir John's household. Feeling grew bitterer, and a servant of Sir John was killed and another dangerously wounded. Brawls followed. Henry Long, guarded by many of his servants, broke into the house of one of Sir John's tenants, and when Sir John's principal officer protested, a glass of beer was thrown into his face, and Master Long cried out in derision that now they dubbed him knight. Still the Longs were unsatisfied, for they wished to provoke the Danvers to open violence. Master Henry wrote bitter letters to Sir Charles Danvers giving him the lie direct, and sending him word that wheresoever he met him, he would untie his points and whip his etc. with a rod, adding that he was an ass, a puppy, a fool, and a boy.

Hereupon Sir Charles was at last moved to great fury, and taking with him his brother and some seventeen of his men, he went after Long. Long was dining with Sir Walter Long, some justices of the peace and other gentlemen in an ordinary at Cosham. Sir Charles entered, went up to Henry Long and struck him twice with a cudgel. He then made off, but the door was now barred, and Long turned on him with his sword. Sir Charles was getting the worst, being wounded in seven places and beginning to faint for loss of blood. At this moment Sir Henry Danvers and the others broke in, and seeing his brother's danger discharged his pistol upon Long who fell mortally wounded.

This was one account. Another said that Sir Henry had thrust himself between Long and his brother as Long had raised his arm to kill, and striking upwards with his dagger accidentally gave Long a fatal wound.

The Danvers party fled and took refuge with the Earl of Southampton, and though warrants were soon out for their arrest he shielded them for some days, until he had arranged for their escape to France. In the mêlée which followed, Signior Florio played his part.

Thus it came about that when Shakespeare began to write *Romeo and Juliet*, he used Brooke's names and situations, but again he borrowed from life, peopling his tragedy with those whom he knew, and especially with the young men, catching their phrases, tones and little mannerisms.

The love story of Romeo and Juliet was a perfect sonnet sequence, passing from love in despair to love at first sight; thence to the ecstasy of troth plight; and as prelude to love's consummation Shakespeare wrote an epithalamium, which Juliet pronounced as a soliloquy:

Gallop apace, you fiery-footed steeds,
Towards Phœbus' lodging; such a waggoner
As Phaëthon would whip you to the west,
And bring in cloudy night immediately.
Spread thy close curtain, love-performing night!
That runaway's eyes may wink, and Romeo
Leap to these arms, untalk'd of and unseen!
Lovers can see to do their amorous rites
By their own beauties; or, if love be blind,
It best agrees with night. Come, civil night,
Thou sober-suited matron, all in black,
And learn me how to lose a winning match,
Play'd for a pair of stainless maidenhoods:
Hood my unmann'd blood, bating in my cheeks,
With thy black mantle; till strange love, grown bold,
Think true love acted simple modesty.
Come, night! come, Romeo! come, thou day in night!
For thou wilt lie upon the wings of night,
Whiter than new snow on a raven's back.
Come, gentle night; come, loving, black-brow'd night,
Give me my Romeo: and, when he shall die,
Take him and cut him out in little stars,
And he will make the face of heaven so fine
That all the world will be in love with night,
And pay no worship to the garish sun.
O! I have bought the mansion of a love,
But not possess'd it, and, though I am sold,
Not yet enjoy'd. So tedious is this day
As is the night before some festival
To an impatient child that hath new robes
And may not wear them.

Brooke was a most useful foundation, for he had himself seen the same argument set forth on the stage, and his narrative grouped itself into scenes with very little rearrangement. Shakespeare however compressed the action and made the plot move more rapidly. In Brooke's story Romeo and Juliet enjoyed each other's love for a month or twain; the play was a gamut of five days, upon Marlowe's theme—

> Whoever lov'd that lov'd not at first sight.

Shakespeare took suggestions also from Brooke for some of the speeches. When Juliet about to drink the potion was filled with horrible imaginings, Brooke essayed to poetise them:

And whilst she in these thoughts doth dwell somewhat too long,
The force of her imagining anon did wax so strong,
That she surmised she saw, out of the hollow vault,
(A grizzly thing to look upon) the carcase of Tybalt;
Right in the selfsame sort that she few days before
Had seen him in his blood embru'd, to death eke wounded sore.
And then when she again within herself had weigh'd
That quick she should be buried there, and by his side be laid,
All comfortless, for she should living fere have none,
But many a rotten carcase and full many a naked bone;
Her dainty tender parts gan shiver all for dread,
Her golden hairs did stand upright, upon her childish head.
Then pressed with the fear that she there lived in,
A sweat as cold as mountain ice pierced through her tender skin,

That with the moisture hath wet every part of hers:
And more besides, she vainly thinks whilst vainly thus she fears,
A thousand bodies dead have compassed her about,
And lest they will dismember her she greatly stands in doubt.
But when she felt her strength began to wear away,
By little and little, and in her heart her fear increased aye,
Dreading that weakness might, or foolish cowardise,
Hinder the execution of the purpos'd enterprise,
As she had frantic been, in haste the glass she cought,
And up she drank the mixture quite, withouten further thought.
Then on her breast she cross'd her armës long and small
And so, her senses failing her, into a trance did fall.

Shakespeare transmuted this jingle into a soliloquy:

I have a faint cold fear thrills through my veins,
That almost freezes up the heat of life:
I'll call them back again to comfort me:
Nurse! What should she do here?
My dismal scene I needs must act alone.
Come, vial.
What if this mixture do not work at all?
Shall I be married then to-morrow morning?
No, no; this shall forbid it: lie thou there.
What if it be a poison, which the friar
Subtly hath minister'd to have me dead,
Lest in this marriage he should be dishonour'd
Because he married me before to Romeo?
I fear it is: and yet, methinks, it should not,
For he hath still been tried a holy man.
I will not entertain so bad a thought.
How if, when I am laid into the tomb,
I wake before the time that Romeo comes?

Or, if I live, is it not very like,
The horrible conceit of death and night,
Together with the terror of the place,
As in a vault, an ancient receptacle,
Where, for these many hundred years, the bones
Of all my buried ancestors are pack'd;
Where bloody Tybalt, yet but green in earth,
Lies festering in his shroud; where, as they say,
At some hours in the night spirits resort:
Alack, alack! is it not like that I,
So early waking, what with loathsome smells,
And shrieks like mandrakes' torn out of the earth,
That living mortals, hearing them, run mad:
O! if I wake, shall I not be distraught,
Environed with all these hideous fears,
And madly play with my forefathers' joints,
And pluck the mangled Tybalt from his shroud?
And, in this rage, with some great kinsman's bone,
As with a club, dash out my desperate brains?
O, look! methinks I see my cousin's ghost
Seeking out Romeo, that did spit his body
Upon a rapier's point. Stay, Tybalt, stay!
Romeo, I come! this do I drink to thee.

Romeo and Juliet was his most successful play hitherto, and with the two poems, firmly established Shakespeare's reputation with the young gentlemen of the Inns of Court. It was attuned to the present fashion for love poetry; and they saw themselves, their own society, their tastes and wit, reflected in the conversation of Romeo and his friends.

In the winter of 1594 the junior members of Gray's Inn set about some revels on a lavish and elaborate scale. They constituted themselves a kingdom, elected a Prince of Purpool and for some weeks kept up a solemn parody of the affairs and ceremonial of the English Court, to which they invited their neighbours of the Inner Temple to send an ambassador. The Revels began on 20th December when the Prince was solemnly installed. On the 28th, elaborate inventions had been prepared but the crowd of guests was great, and of uninvited spectators far greater, so that the Hall was too crowded for the actors to enter. The Ambassador for Templaria took offence and departed, after which some sort of order was restored. The evening ended with a performance by the professional players of *The Comedy of Errors;* but the entertainment as a whole was a lamentable failure, and to bring in common players was considered the crowning disgrace, insomuch as the fiasco was known henceforth as the "Night of Errors."

Six days later—on 3rd January, 1595—the Revels were continued and special officers appointed to keep order. The company was very distinguished; most of the Privy Council were present, including Lord Burleigh, the Earl of Essex, the Lord Keeper, and Sir Robert Cecil, and of the nobility the Earls of Shrewsbury, Cumberland, Northumberland and Southampton. The revels began with a symbolical piece of the restoration of amity between Graius and Templarius. Then the Prince of Purpool held a chapter of his order of knighthood, the Order of the Helmet, and the Articles of Order were designed not only as a skit on graver and nobler bodies but of the foibles of young gentlemen about town, and amongst other commands it was enjoined that they should frequent the Theatre and such like places of experience. Gentlemen were already regarding the Theatre as the playhouse of distinction.

IV

THE PASSING OF AN ECLIPSE

AT the beginning of the year 1595 the Chamberlain's company was commanded to present a new play for the wedding of the young Earl of Derby to the Lady Elizabeth Vere, whose thwarted affections had been so costly to Southampton. The marriage was most royally kept at the Court at Greenwich on 26th January.

Shakespeare therefore began a play suitable for the occasion and audience. Entertainments specially intended for the Queen and her Court were usually of a set pattern. The story was mythological or classical, set out with compliments to the Queen, preferably on the theme of virginity, and a few discreet topicalities to amuse the courtiers; the whole being something light and pleasing which would put everyone in good humour.

These command performances were liable to short notice. The time being limited Shakespeare had little opportunity for new experiment, and, as most writers, when pressed for delivery he took stock of such incidents in his recent plays as could be reworked quickly. The Queen Mab speech in *Romeo and Juliet* suggested the theme of a dream of fairies, and the complications which might arise if Robin

Goodfellow went out looking for mischief. Moreover the company was to be augmented by children for the singing and dancing; children most obviously and suitably could present fairies. *Love's Labour's Lost*, a year ago, pleased a similar audience, and one of its most successful incidents was the pageant of the Nine Worthies. Courtly audiences were always amused by parody of the amateur county actors who insisted on parading their musty fopperies whenever the Court went on progress. Such a play, acted by rude tradesmen, its rehearsal and performance, would be, as it were, a bergomask to the main plot. And as the main plot needed to be light, and concerned with love, what could be better than to rework the theme so successful in *The Comedy of Errors* of a pair of lovers who were continually mistaken by their mistresses. The confusions caused by the similarity of twins could hardly be used again so soon, especially since many of those who would be at Court had been present at the Gray's Inn Revels, but any improbability was laudably natural when there the fairies were about; and the mistakes resulting from the pook's pranks were easier to manipulate than exact likeness of twins.

These threads needed to be united and preferably within some well-known tale of antiquity. So Shakespeare began to turn over his Chaucer and lighting upon the first of the *Canterbury Tales* he read:

> Whilom, as olde stories tellen us,
> Ther was a duc that highte Theseus;

> Of Atthenes he was lord and governour,
> And in his tyme swich a conquerour,
> That gretter was ther noon under the sonne.
> Ful many a riche contree hadde he wonne;
> That with his wysdom and his chivalrie
> He conquered al the regne of Femenye,
> That whilom was y-cleped Scithia;
> And weddede the Queene Ypolita,
> And broghte hire hoom with hym in his contree
> With muchel glorie and greet solempnytee. . . .

And upon the wedding of the Duke Theseus with the conquered Amazon the other stories could appropriately converge: it was a good pretext for the mechanics to present a play; and fairies and the pook were naturally connected, for good or ill, with weddings, as Spenser had remembered in his *Epithalamium* which was just come from the press.

For the love story then there were two pairs of lovers, and a harsh old father. The father commanded his daughter to marry the bridegroom whom he had chosen but she was in love with another. To let true love have its way the official suitor needed his mate; and she as yet doted on him in vain. It was much the same as in *The Two Gentlemen of Verona.* As in that play, all find their way to the woods where after some necessary entanglements, enough to fill up three acts, each pair was happily coupled. Shakespeare was using old work rather lavishly; but there were excuses.

Having elaborated the details, he began to work. The scenes between the lovers were rather heavy, but the fairy lyrics came pleasingly; lyric poetry suited his mood better than blank verse. The episode of the play he divided into three scenes, the casting, the rehearsal, and the performance.

These processes were very familiar, and especially since Shakespeare caused his mechanics to ape the methods of the professional actors, so that their chief player, a weaver, a burly fellow, Nick Bottom by name, took on something of the nature of the great Ned Alleyn, as Shakespeare had observed him at the Rose listening to the synopsis of a new play as it was outlined by one of his poets. Alleyn was always for the chief part, whatever it might be, but his chief humour was for a tyrant, something lofty, in Ercles' vein; and in writing *The most lamentable comedy and most cruel death of Pyramus and Thisby* for Quince's company, Shakespeare irreverently mimicked some of the phrases which rolled so sonorously over Alleyn's tongue, such as:

> O eyes, no eyes, but fountains filled with tears,

Or,

> Alas, it is Horatio my sweet son,
> O no, but he that whilom *was* my son;

or that pathetic last speech of Tom Stukeley before he yielded up his groaning ghost on the sands of Barbary.

In Quince's play Alleyn's reverberating "O's" and "eyes" were echoed by Bottom in:

O grim-look'd night! O night with hue so black!
O night which ever art when day is not!
O night! O night! alack, alack, alack!
    Fear my Thisby's promise is forgot.

And,

    But stay, O spite!
    But mark, poor knight,
What dreadful dole is here!
    Eyes do you see?
    How can it be?
O dainty duck! O dear! . . .

Or,

O wherefore, Nature, didst thou lions frame?
    Since lion vile hath here deflower'd my dear?
Which is—no, no,—which *was* the fairest dame
    That liv'd, that lov'd, that lik'd, that look'd with cheer.

As he wrote Shakespeare was mindful of topical touches, and wove them into the dialogue. The vile weather of the season was still a matter of talk. A bolder joke lay in a remark of Bottom—"Masters, you ought to consider with yourselves; to bring in—God shield us!—a lion among ladies, is a most dreadful thing; for there is not a more fearful wild-fowl than your lion living, and we ought to look to it." Those who had attended the Earl of Sussex when he represented the Queen at the baptism of the Prince Henry of Scotland in the late summer brought back amusing tales of the festivities at the Scottish Court. The ambitious pageant master had devised a triumphant chariot to be drawn in by a real lion, but at the last moment there was some apprehension lest the lion, being unused to courtly entertainments, might forget himself or fright the ladies. Moreover in the running at the ring and glove the King himself competed, choosing as the *impresa* or device on his shield a lion's head with open eyes to signify fortitude and vigilance; whenas indeed his Majesty might have been better fitted with a hare.

Shakespeare called his play *A Midsummer Night's Dream*, and after all the entanglements were loosened and the lovers had gone bedward he let the children have the last word so that the play ended in an atmosphere of dream and unreality, with a fairy blessing of the bride bed.

After this comedy Shakespeare returned to history in the story of Richard the Second. It was notably parallel to the story of the second Edward which Marlowe had dramatised three years before.

Marlowe's *Edward the Second* was a development in the writing of History Plays, for he saw the story not as a series of scenes from history but as a tragic theme of fault and event. Edward so doted on Gaveston, his Ganimede, that he excluded the Queen from his love, insulted the nobles and ruined his kingdom. They rose and destroyed Gaveston; and the King then chose Spenser to be his minion. His Queen, having now taken Mortimer as her lover, with the revolting nobles deposes him from the throne and he is brutally murdered. Edward the third his son succeeds, immediately causes Mortimer to be beheaded, and the play ends with the young king standing by the bier, holding up Mortimer's head as a sacrifice to his father's murdered ghost.

In writing the play Marlowe had held his poetic fancies in check. Except for Gaveston's luscious description of the wanton pleasures that he would prepare for the King there were few lyrical speeches until near the end, when Edward defeated and deposed was given a long passage of woeful lamentation which stressed both his pathos and his weakness as he is reluctant to part with the crown:

> But stay awhile, let me be king till night,
> That I may gaze upon this glittering crown,
> So shall my eyes receive their last content,
> My head the latest honour due to it,
> And jointly both yield up their wished right.
> Continue ever thou celestial sun,
> Let never silent night possess this clime,
> Stand still, you watches of the element,
> All times and seasons rest you at a stay,
> That Edward may be still fair England's king:
> But day's bright beam doth vanish fast away,
> And needs must I resign my wished crown. . . .
> Here receive my crown.
> Receive it? No, these innocent hands of mine
> Shall not be guilty of so foul a crime,
> He of you all that most desires my blood
> And will be called the murderer of a king,
> Take it: what, are you mov'd, pity you me?

There were a few Machiavellian speeches, as Spencer's advice to the traitor Baldock to "cast the scholar off, and learn to court it like a gentleman"; or Mortimer's boast:

> The prince I rule, the Queen I do command,
> And with a lowly congé to the ground,
> The proudest lords salute me as I pass;
> I seal, I cancel, I do what I will.

But there was little room for pause in the rush of events as incident was hustled after incident in the race to present within two hours the history of twenty years.

Marlowe's *Edward the Second*—which was originally a play of Pembroke's men—was entered for printing shortly after his death, in June 1593, so that Shakespeare had the advantage of a pattern in print for his version of the story of *Richard the Second*. The incidents he took from Holinshed who gave him not only an outline but some graphic details which could be worked up into effective scenes, the quarrel between Norfolk and Bolingbroke, the lists at Coventry, Richard's return from Ireland, the quarrels in Parliament, the revolts against King Henry, the murder of Richard and his solemn obsequies. The pageantry of the deposition was compiled from a number of scattered incidents and Shakespeare added from his own imagination a scene of parting between John of Gaunt and his banished son, and another scene of Gaunt on his death bed rebuking the thriftless king.

Shakespeare received many hints from *Edward the Second*. The theme was similar and he treated it in the same way; and he ended his play with the bringing in of the bier of the murdered king and a curse upon the murderer. None of the characters in this story came near his own experience, and he reverted to the earlier poetising method, indulging himself in fine writing and an enjoyment of phrase making; so that Richard was a sonneteer's king, a creature of exquisite sentimentality. He had too something of Marlowe himself, combining a cynical disregard for ordinary morality with an intense beauty of fancy. Shakespeare revelled in the mere poetry of the speeches; but at the same time he did not forget that fine writing by itself would never make a play. The opening scene of the quarrel between the two peers and the pathetic deposition scene were full of quick and vivid emotional change.

Lovers of poetry noted many things in this play, especially Gaunt's swelling praise of England:

> This royal throne of kings, this scepter'd isle,
> This earth of majesty, this seat of Mars,
> This other Eden, demi-paradise,
> This fortress built by Nature for herself
> Against infection and the hand of war,
> This happy breed of men, this little world,
> This precious stone set in the silver sea,
> Which serves it in the office of a wall,
> Or as a moat defensive to a house,
> Against the envy of less happier lands,
> This blessed plot, this earth, this realm, this England,

This nurse, this teeming womb of royal kings,
Fear'd by their breed and famous by their birth,
Renowned for their deeds as far from home,—
For Christian service and true chivalry,—
As is the sepulchre in stubborn Jewry
Or the world's ransom, blessed Mary's Son:

And:

Not all the water in the rough rude sea
Can wash the balm from an anointed king;
The breath of worldly men cannot depose
The deputy elected by the Lord.

And:

O! but they say the tongues of dying men
Enforce attention like deep harmony:
Where words are scarce, they are seldom spent in vain,
For they breathe truth that breathe their words in pain.
He that no more must say is listen'd more
  Than they whom youth and ease have taught to glose;
More are men's ends mark'd than their lives before:
  The setting sun, and music at the close,
As the last taste of sweets, is sweetest last,
Writ in remembrance more than things long past.

Whilst Shakespeare was at work on the play, there was published in April Sir Philip Sidney's *Defence of Poesy*, which had been written fifteen years or so before; it was the first serious attempt in English to enunciate any critical principles of drama. Sidney wrote before Marlowe, Kyd, Greene or Shakespeare had penned a play, and doubtless he might have modified his views if he had seen something better than *Gorboduc*. Yet the main heads of his criticism were as relevant as in 1580: drama was still "very defectious in the circumstances, faulty both in time and place"; many plays were still "neither right tragedies nor right comedies mingling Kings and Clowns, not because the matter so carrieth it, but thrust in clowns by head and shoulders to play a part in majestical matters with neither decency nor discretion." Comedy too erred very grievously, because it lacked "that delightful teaching which is the end of Poesy." There was no obvious and immediate change in the practices of playwrights, but the book was nevertheless discussed.

In June and July normal life in the City was gravely upset by a series of fierce riots. In the bad summer of '94 the crops failed and food was now dear. There was a riot on 5th June in the City and on the 13th the prentices forced the butter women, who were demanding 5d. a lb., to sell at the standard rate of 3d. There was rioting two days later, and again on the 23rd in Billingsgate and on the 29th on Tower Hill. The Council now took drastic action. Martial law was proclaimed on the 4th July and three weeks later five of the prentices who had been arrested on Tower Hill were condemned to death and quartered on the scene of their offence. By this time the price of butter had risen to 7d. a lb. and eggs to 1d. apiece. The players, as usual, suffered, and the playhouses were shut down on 26th June for two months.

As the year went on the general feeling of anxiety increased, and the omens were all lowering. By August it was realised that a new and greater Spanish Armada was preparing. Drake and Hawkins sailed on their last voyage at the end of the month; but their departure at such a time was felt to be a dangerous mistake in policy. Moreover, many, and especially scholarly persons, who had observed or read how God was wont to deal in times and seasons, were alarmed because on September 6th, the Queen entered upon her ninth, or grand climacteric—that is her sixty-third year, when the mystic numbers nine and seven were united. Her eighth climacteric—the fateful year '88 when the Armada came—was a time of threatened disaster, and the prophets were busy that year; but the ninth was astrologically far more alarming.

This uneasiness was expressed in a book put forth at this time at Cambridge by William Covell, Fellow of Queens' College. It was called *Polimanteia; or the means, lawful and unlawful, to judge of the fall of a Commonwealth, against the frivolous and foolish conjectures of this age.* It discussed oracles, divinations, and such subjects, endeavouring to limit the range and reliability of supernatural methods of foreknowledge. Among other opinions which Covell confuted was a dangerous tenet of Bodin, "who saith, that if we mark the great and notable changes of states and kingdoms, we shall find the most part to have been in September, in which month God gave the beginning to all the world." In the book the essay on divination was followed by exhortations in the person of England to her three daughters, Cambridge, Oxford and the Inns of Court, and to all her inhabitants, beseeching them to remain loyal at this most anxious time. In one place England lamented that she was torn in pieces by her own inhabitants; Covell commented in the margin, "England cannot perish but by Englishmen."

Nor were relations between England and France at all happy as Henri IV. became more dissatisfied with the lack of direct help which the Queen would afford him. In October M. de Lomenie was sent over to lay his needs before the Queen and the Council; and he presented the King's letters with such stout speeches that the Queen, who disliked plain speaking, was alarmed and angry.

Early in November the perpetual bogey of the succession suddenly reappeared. A copy of Doleman's book, *A Conference about the next Succession to the Crown of England*, with its embarrassing dedication to the Earl of Essex, came into the Queen's hands. She demanded an explanation, and for a short while Essex was under a cloud. A few days later emergency measures were put in hand to deal with the threat of invasion; and from London and Southampton and fifteen Home and South Coast counties a force of over sixty thousand men was prepared.

By the end of the year the situation in France

was worse. M. de Lomenie brought back no satisfactory answer from London, and the general opinion was that the alliance was rapidly dissolving. Early in January Sir Henry Unton was sent over to the French King to mend matters, if possible; but at his first public audience he was received coldly and scornfully and told that, as nothing would prevail with the Queen, the King must provide for his own safety as best he could.

At Christmas time the Chamberlain's men performed four times at Court. Meanwhile the general alarm at home increased. In January one C. G., another Cambridge man, published a book called *A Watchword for War* to confute various fearful alarms that were being circulated—that the enemy was great; that maybe he will have the aid of the Indians, or the Pope; and perhaps of some that had greater cause to gratify us than be against us. C. G. had no fear of the papists, for, said he, when they should see the Spaniard they would join against them. Nor need they fear civil troubles so long as the common saying remained true—"If we be true within ourselves, we need not care or fear the enemy." To the like effect Thomas Nun, in *A Comfort against the Spaniard*, wrote:

> Is it true that the Spaniards will come this spring? And is it not true that we are ready to receive them? Hath this land at any time had either better provision or more soldiers? braver captains to lead them, or sounder divines to encourage them?

By the end of January 1596, it was believed that Henry was about to desert his allies and make a separate peace with the enemy; the gossip in his camp was that the Cardinal Archduke of Austria, who was then at Namur, had received instructions from the King of Spain to negotiate.

On 12th February, the Admiral's men brought out a new play at the Rose called *The Blind Beggar of Alexandria.* It was the work of Chapman and in its own fantastic way quite a novelty of a kind to appeal to Alleyn and his admirers, for it gave the great tragedian a part wherein he had to play Cleanthes, a Duke, and Irus, a blind beggar, and Count Hermes, a swashbuckler, and Leon, a usurer, all in one person. The plot of this gallimaufry was a trifle far-fetched, even for the Rose, but it was carefully explained to the audience by the beggar:

I am Cleanthes and blind Irus too,
And more than these, as you shall soon perceive,
Yet but a shepherd's son at Memphis born;
And I will tell you how I got that name:
My father was a fortune-teller and from him I learnt his art,
And, knowing to grow great was to grow rich,
Such money as I got by palmistry
I put to use, and by that means became
To take the shape of Leon, by which name
I am well known a wealthy usurer;
And more than this I am two noblemen:
Count Hermes is another of my names,
And Duke Cleanthes whom the Queen so loves;
For, till the time that I may claim the crown,

I mean to spend my time in sports of love,
Which in the sequel you shall plainly see,
And joy, I hope, in this my policy.

This versatile shepherd so enters into the quadruplicity of his personalities that in three of his shapes he woos and enjoys the love of a different lady; and not content with that, he proceeds to diversify the "sports of love" by cuckolding himself, producing a confusion of relationships which grammar is inadequate to express.

At the end of the play, the shepherd survives as Cleanthes, now King of Egypt, Count Hermes has been swallowed quick in the earth and Leon has cast himself into the sea, whilst the blind beggar is forgotten in the final excitements.

Alleyn thus gave a display of his talents as a quick change artist in very diverse parts. Count Hermes was the best of them, his particular and grotesque humour being to wear a patch over his eye, to shroud his person in a large velvet cloak "in rain or snow or in the hottest weather," and to brandish a large pistol, wherewith he would shoot his enemies, as 'twere to emphasise his humour.

The play was popular and especially the Count's thundering oath "by this pistol, which is God's angel." The success of the character was duly noted by the Chamberlain's men.

Shakespeare was now at work on another history, the story of King John, which also was concerned with England and France. No sensitive man could live through the anxious months which followed unaffected by the general mood; and as he wrote the play his own apprehensions were clearly reflected in many of the speeches.

Unton's efforts with the French King were unavailing, and in March he died having accomplished nothing. Meanwhile at home a great fleet (as great as in '88) was being mobilised and fitted out.

At the beginning of April news came that the Cardinal had suddenly invested Calais, which could only hold out for a few days. On the 5th, Mr. John Norden, the topographer, entered *A Christian familiar comfort and encouragement unto all English subjects*, urging his readers not to be alarmed at the Spanish threats. He warned especially the inferior magistrates to beware of sudden and undiscreet hurly-burlies, for it was a policy of the enemy to draw on tumults by sudden reports, dangerous bruits, and open hubbubs. The Queen hesitated to send relief to Calais; but after some ignoble bargaining, orders were given on the afternoon of Good Friday (April 9th) that 6,000 men should march at once for Dover, where Essex and Lord Charles Howard, the Lord Admiral, were waiting to lead over a relief force; and such expedition was used by the Lord Mayor that most of them were ready by 8 o'clock at night.

On that day the Bishop of St. David's preaching before the Queen and Court, most unhappily chose as his text, "O teach us to number our days that we may incline our hearts unto wisdom," whereto he attached a sermon on mystical numbers, and the grand climacteric, devising some suitable prayers for the Queen, as one who had now reached that age when "the senses begin to fail, the strength to diminish, yea, all the powers of the body daily to decay." The prayer included these words:

"O Lord, I am now entered a good way into the climacterical year of mine age, which mine enemies wish and hope to be fatal unto me. But Thou Lord, which by Thy prophet Jeremy didst command the House of Israel not to learn the way of the heathen nor be afraid of the signs of heaven, and who by Thy Almighty hand and outstretched arm, madest the year of greatest expectation, even '88, marvellous by the overthrow of Thine and mine enemies, now, for Thy Gospel's sake, which hath long had sanctuary in this land, make likewise '96 as prosperous unto me and my loyal subjects."

The Queen was not grateful and told him bluntly that he should have kept his arithmetic to himself. Next day it was reported that Calais could hold out no longer and the levies were therefore dismissed. But at 10 o'clock on Easter Sunday they were again demanded. The people at this moment were making their Easter Communion; the constables were therefore sent round to the parish churches to close the doors till the necessary men had again been pressed. The levies were marched off to Dover. Two days later the sound of the cannon could be heard all day in London: on the 16th, when the men had been embarked and were ready to sail, news came that Calais had fallen. Some very ugly stories of French treachery were soon in circulation. One was that 400 old soldiers, sent by the States, succeeded in breaking through the Spaniards and reaching the citadel. But the garrison refused to admit them and they were all slain, the French declaring that they would rather have the Spaniards in Calais than the English or their other friends, for "if the Spaniards win it, yet there is good hope by mediation of the Church to regain it; but if the English repossess it they will never restore it."

Southampton was eager to go over to Calais with Essex, and went down to Dover, but the Queen refused her leave, and he with several other young noblemen was ordered back to Court. Shakespeare's friendship with Southampton had gradually cooled during the last year. On the one side there was jealousy of other poets who sought the Earl's favour, and slights, real or imagined, but tormenting to a sensitive mind; on the other, the increasing responsibility of a nobleman busied with affairs at Court. Moreover, Southampton was at last in love, and his familiarity with Mistress Vernon, one of the Queen's ladies in waiting, had been a matter of gossip since the autumn. It was now three years since Shakespeare had first come into his presence with *Venus and Adonis*, and at this time he wrote a sonnet celebrating their friendship:

THE PASSING OF AN ECLIPSE

To me, fair friend, you never can be old,
For as you were when first your eye I ey'd,
Such seems your beauty still. Three winters' cold
Have from the forests shook three summers' pride,
Three beauteous springs to yellow autumn turn'd
In process of the seasons have I seen,
Three April perfumes in three hot Junes burn'd,
Since first I saw you fresh, which yet are green.
Ah! yet doth beauty, like a dial-hand,
Steal from his figure, and no pace perceiv'd;
So your sweet hue, which methinks still doth stand,
Hath motion, and mine eye may be deceiv'd:
For fear of which, hear this, thou age unbred:
Ere you were born was beauty's summer dead.

There was little response, and he made no further advances for the time.

After the disgrace of Calais, the original plan was continued. The great fleet and army continued to assemble at Plymouth, and after one false start, it sailed away on 3rd June. The old Lord Admiral and Essex were in command, and Ralegh, Sir Francis Vere and other distinguished soldiers served with them.

This summer of 1596 was a wretched time for Shakespeare. He was no longer welcomed into Southampton's house but told with unpleasant bluntness that common players were not suited to the society of gentlemen, so that he became more acutely conscious than ever of the barrier of his profession. He was quarrelling with a certain William Gardiner, a well-known and well-hated

Justice of the Peace of Southwark, and a lawsuit was threatening. Besides, his private and intimate affairs were dragged out of the darkness where they properly belonged, paraded and mocked.

In this state of mind he finished his version of King John. It was founded directly on an old play called *The Troublesome Reign of King John*, which once belonged to the Queen's men and had been published five years ago. For the time he had lost his touch; he was writing rebelliously, with a feeling of disgust with himself that in his brilliant work of the last two years he had been cheapening for sale all that was intimate and dear to him. The plays of '94 and '95 were alive because he had drawn from life, taking this man's features and that man's wit. In this play he avoided all portraits. It opened smoothly; the first two acts had some life in them but thereafter he lost all interest and went on mechanically. It was the worst thing he had written; the characters were flat, the speeches tedious; little Arthur was hysterical. Even the Bastard had no meat in his belly after the second act; yet he intended the Bastard to be a specimen of the bluff, hearty, dishonest captains who were so well known to theatre goers; but though he began well he degenerated into a mere trumpet for heroic sentiments.

This story of King John in some ways bore closely on the present times and Shakespeare stressed its significances, as in Austria's remark:

> I will no more return
> Till Angiers, and the right thou hast in France
> Together with that pale, that white-fac'd shore,
> Whose foot spurns back the ocean's roaring tides
> And coops from other lands her islanders,
> Even till that England, hedg'd in with the main,
> That water-walled bulwark, still secure
> And confident from foreign purposes,
> Even till that utmost corner of the west
> Salute thee for her king.

There was a passing reference to the swarms of young gallants who had just sailed for Cadiz in:

> And all the unsettled humours of the land,
> Rash, inconsiderate, fiery voluntaries,
> With ladies' faces and fierce dragons' spleens,
> Have sold their fortunes at their native homes,
> Bearing their birthrights proudly on their backs,
> To make a hazard of new fortunes here.
> In brief, a braver choice of dauntless spirits
> Than now the English bottoms have waft o'er
> Did never float upon the swelling tide,
> To do offence and scathe in Christendom.

Nor was the Bastard's speech on "commodity" without its special meaning for Englishmen who felt that their ally was deserting them:

> This same bias, this Commodity,
> This bawd, this broker, this all-changing word,
> Clapp'd on the outward eye of fickle France,
> Hath drawn him from his own determin'd aid,
> From a resolv'd and honourable war,
> To a most base and vile-concluded peace

And why rail I on this Commodity?
But for because he hath not woo'd me yet.
Not that I have the power to clutch my hand
When his fair angels would salute my palm;
But for my hand, as unattempted yet,
Like a poor beggar, raileth on the rich.
Well, whiles I am a beggar, I will rail,
And say there is no sin but to be rich;
And being rich, my virtue then shall be
To say there is no vice but beggary.
Since kings break faith upon Commodity,
Gain, be my lord, for I will worship thee!

In the play another Cardinal would separate France from England; and John defied him as a true-blue Protestant should:

What earthly name to interrogatories
Can task the free breath of a sacred king?
Thou canst not, cardinal, devise a name
So slight, unworthy and ridiculous,
To charge me to an answer, as the pope,
Tell him this tale; and from the mouth of England
Add thus much more: that no Italian priest
Shall tithe or toll in our dominions;
But as we under heaven are supreme head,
So under him that great supremacy,
Where we do reign, we will alone uphold,
Without the assistance of a mortal hand:
So tell the pope; all reverence set apart
To him, and his usurp'd authority.

The passage which followed was but a slight transposition of the situation of Henri IV. of France.

The hubbubs and hurly-burlies which troubled

John's London, Shakespeare sketched from his own immediate observations:

> Old men and beldams in the streets
> Do prophesy upon it dangerously:
> Young Arthur's death is common in their mouths;
> And when they talk of him, they shake their heads
> And whisper one another in the ear;
> And he that speaks doth gripe the hearer's wrist
> Whilst he that hears makes fearful action,
> With wrinkled brows, with nods, with rolling eyes.
> I saw a smith stand with his hammer, thus,
> The whilst his iron did on the anvil cool,
> With open mouth swallowing a tailor's news;
> Who with his shears and measure in his hand,
> Standing on slippers,—which his nimble haste
> Had falsely thrust upon contrary feet,—
> Told of a many thousand warlike French,
> That were embattailed and rank'd in Kent.
> Another lean unwash'd artificer
> Cuts off his tale and talks of Arthur's death.

Uneasily stirring in everyone's mind was the terrible dread of what would surely happen when anarchy was let loose at the Queen's death. The author of the *Conference about the next Succession* declared that the issue would not be decided without a war; it was the common opinion, for there was no clear candidate for the throne, so that in the Bastard's words over dead Arthur, Shakespeare indulged in grim and likely prophecy:

> How easy dost thou take all England up!
> From forth this morsel of dead royalty,

The life, the right and truth of all this realm
Is fled to heaven; and England now is left
To tug and scramble and to part by the teeth
The unow'd interest of proud swelling state.
Now for the bare-pick'd bone of majesty
Doth dogged war bristle his angry crest,
And snarleth in the gentle eyes of peace:
Now powers from home and discontents at home
Meet in one line; and vast confusion waits,—
As doth a raven on a sick-fallen beast,—
The imminent decay of wrested pomp.

And yet, however gloomy the future seemed, Shakespeare ended his play with a quiet confidence which reflected the mood of ordinary, level-headed Englishmen:

This England never did, nor never shall,
Lie at the proud foot of a conqueror,
But when it first did help to wound itself.
Now these her princes are come home again,
Come the three corners of the world in arms,
And we shall shock them. Nought shall make us rue,
If England to itself do rest but true.

To fill up the tale of his own troubles, at the be-beginning of August, Shakespeare's only boy Hamnet died.

And then the sky suddenly cleared.

The gallants came back from the expedition full of excitement and enthusiasm, and many of them affecting great beards in imitation of the fashion set by the Earl of Essex. It had been most spectacular and triumphant, and on Sunday 8th August a great service of Thanksgiving was celebrated in London. Less than three weeks after sailing from Plymouth the expedition appeared before Cadiz. On the 21st June the fleet forced a way past the Spanish ships and forts and by nightfall the soldiers had disembarked and cleared a way into the city, and all but the Castle and one fort had surrendered. These too were yielded in the morning. The Spanish fleet was burnt, except for two great galleons which were now brought home; a great ransom was exacted; infinite damage was inflicted on the enemy; and above all King Philip had shown that he was powerless against Englishmen, even in his own country. To add to the general feeling of elation the alliance with the French was solemnly renewed on 29th August. A few days later the Queen passed out of her grand climacteric; the prophets of disaster were again confounded and put off for another seven years.

Shakespeare's friendship with Southampton was renewed at this time. He was once more admitted into his presence and treated with kindliness and favour. Southampton too had his troubles. He was ambitious of following Essex's lead, but the Queen perpetually thwarted him, keeping him at Court by her side when all the others had been proving their manhood at Cadiz. Shakespeare celebrated the reunion with a batch of twenty sonnets. In the first of them, he rejoiced at the silencing of those who would have kept him away from his friend:

Not mine own fears, nor the prophetic soul
Of the wide world dreaming on things to come,
Can yet the lease of my true love control,
Suppos'd as forfeit to a confin'd doom.
The mortal moon hath her eclipse endur'd,
And the sad augurs mock their own presage;
Incertainties now crown themselves assur'd,
And peace proclaims olives of endless age.
Now with the drops of this most balmy time
My love looks fresh, and Death to me subscribes,
Since, spite of him, I'll live in this poor rime,
While he insults o'er dull and speechless tribes:
And thou in this shalt find thy monument,
When tyrants' crests and tombs of brass are spent.

But in the fourth and fifth, he unburdened himself of the bitterness of the past six months:

Alas! 'tis true I have gone here and there,
And made myself a motley to the view,
Gor'd mine own thoughts, sold cheap what is most dear,
Made old offences of affections new;
Most true it is that I have look'd on truth
Askance and strangely; but, by all above
These blenches gave my heart another youth,
And worse essays prov'd thee my best of love.
Now all is done, save what shall have no end:
Mine appetite I never more will grind
On newer proof, to try an older friend,
A god in love, to whom I am confin'd.
Then give me welcome, next my heaven the best,
Even to thy pure and most most loving breast.

O! for my sake do you with Fortune chide
The guilty goddess of my harmful deeds,

That did not better for my life provide
Than public means which public manners breeds.
Thence comes it that my name receives a brand,
And almost thence my nature is subdu'd
To what it works in, like the dyer's hand:
Pity me, then, and wish I were renew'd;
Whilst, like a willing patient, I will drink
Potions of eisel 'gainst my strong infection;
No bitterness that I will bitter think,
Nor double penance, to correct correction.
  Pity me, then, dear friend, and I assure ye
  Even that your pity is enough to cure me.

One effective answer at least could be made to those who curled the lip at the player. Shakespeare's family was not ignoble. His father could claim gentility on the strength of his own record. On 29th October Garter King of Arms with language of due pomp granted a coat of arms to the family of John Shakespeare:

Gold, on a Bend sables, a spear of the first steeled argent. And for his crest or cognizance a falcon his wings displayed Argent standing on a wreath of his colours; supporting a spear gold steeled as aforesaid set upon a helmet with mantels and tassels as hath been accustomed and doth more plainly appear depicted on this margent: Signifying hereby and by the authority of my office aforesaid ratifying that it shall be lawful for the said John Shakespeare, gentleman, and for his children, issue and posterity (at all times and places convenient) to bear and make demonstration of the same blazon or achievement upon their shields, targets, escutcheons, coats of arms, pennons, guidons, seals, rings, edifices, buildings, utensils, liveries, tombs or monuments or otherwise for all warlike facts or civil use or exercises, according to the Law of Arms, and customs that to gentlemen belongeth without let or interruption of any other person or persons for use or bearing the same.

The motto chosen was significant, and self-conscious, *Non Sanz droict:* Not Without Right.

V

MATURITY

THE favourable turns of Fortune were reflected in Shakespeare's next play, which was a return to comedy. He tried the theme of a malevolent Jewish usurer in *The Merchant of Venice*, and in creating Shylock the Jew he borrowed some features from Marlowe's *Jew of Malta.* Shylock also had an only daughter and his love was balanced equally between her and his ducats. He had too a very reasonable hate for Christians, as Italian Jews might well have, but he was a more human figure than Barabas, with neither the powers nor the will to achieve such orgies of vengeance.

Shakespeare had a certain advantage over Marlowe for the theme of the Christian-hating Jew had gained a new intensity through the case of Dr. Lopez; and he put into Gratiano's mouth a speech which associated his Shylock with Lopez:

O, be thou damn'd, inexecrable dog!
And for thy life let justice be accus'd.
Thou almost mak'st me waver in my faith
To hold opinion with Pythagoras,
That souls of animals infuse themselves
Into the trunks of men: thy currish spirit
Govern'd a wolf, who, hang'd for human slaughter,
Even from the gallows did his fell soul fleet,

And whilst thou lay'st in thy unhallow'd dam,
Infus'd itself in thee; for thy desires
Are wolfish, bloody, starv'd and ravenous.

There was a maturity about the play which showed that Shakespeare had not only regained his touch but was reaching new heights in his development as a dramatic artist. The disappointments, restraints and uncertainties which cramped him in writing *King John* were gone. He was surer of himself and finding satisfaction in his art, for the profession of playing and the dignity of play writing were visibly waxing. His first efforts in the *Henry the Sixth* series were exercises in dramatic themes copied from his masters. Then followed a period when he drew rather closely from life. In *The Merchant of Venice* he achieved that state of dramatic craftsmanship when an artist no longer draws from copies but blends his own experiences of men, customs and matters into a pattern of his own free choosing. The smallest thread that ever spider twisted came from her own womb, and great plays were only to be written from the heart. Henceforward he would pawn all experience to his art.

There was a great leap forward in the competence and the variety of his dramatic expression. Without any unnecessary preliminaries the play opened with Antonio the Merchant, the sketch of his character, and his wealth, and the suggestion of a mood. Shakespeare saw the play as a musical harmony of contrasting characters and tones. From Antonio's melancholy he passed to Portia the heiress and Nerissa her maid, idly chatting over the strange conditions of marriage which her dead father has imposed upon her, and the odd suitors who have come to venture for the prize—a passage which Shakespeare took over from his own neglected *Two Gentlemen of Verona.*

Thence back to Venice and a complete change of tone. Bassanio enters in talk with Shylock. Shakespeare was developing this method of beginning a scene in the middle of a conversation; it was a great economy of dialogue, conveying so much and so naturally in the briefest words:

"Three thousand ducats; well?"
"Ay, sir, for three months."
"For three months; well?"
"For the which, as I told you, Antonio shall be bound."
"Antonio shall become bound; well?"
"May you stead me? Will you pleasure me? Shall I know your answer?"
"Three thousand ducats, for three months, and Antonio bound."
"Your answer to that."
"Antonio is a good man. . . ."

Antonio joins them, treating Shylock with contempt and goading him into a display of temper unusual in one who was accustomed to assume an unctuous servility in dealing with Gentiles, which was Shakespeare's version of Barabas's outburst of hate against all Christians:

Signior Antonio, many a time and oft
In the Rialto you have rated me
About my moneys and my usances:
Still have I borne it with a patient shrug,
For sufferance is the badge of all our tribe.
You call me misbeliever, cut-throat dog,
And spet upon my Jewish gaberdine,
And all for use of that which is mine own.
Well then, it now appears you need my help:
Go to then; you come to me, and you say,
'Shylock, we would have moneys': you say so;
You, that did void your rheum upon my beard,
And foot me as you spurn a stranger cur
Over your threshold: moneys is your suit.
What should I say to you? Should I not say,
'Hath a dog money? Is it possible
A cur can lend three thousand ducats?' or
Shall I bend low, and in a bondman's key,
With bated breath, and whispering humbleness,
Say this:
'Fair sir, you spet on me on Wednesday last;
You spurn'd me such a day; another time
You call'd me dog; and for these courtesies
I'll lend you thus much moneys?'

And then again to Belmont, and the stiff formality of Portia's reception of the Prince of Morocco which was succeeded by the sudden inruption of Launcelot Gobbo (own younger brother to Launce of the mongrel) to debate with himself whether the fiend or his conscience shall have the upper hand, and to cockneyfy into real life the mental debates of the stiff heroes and heroines of

Euphues with their interminable contrasts of "ay, but—"

At this point Shakespeare held up the story of Bassanio to allow the intrigue between Lorenzo and Jessica to move forward. Thence to Belmont to watch the Prince of Morocco foiled by his own vanity; and back again to Venice for a report of Shylock's rage at the flight of Jessica and of Antonio's parting with Bassanio, which showed clearly how Shakespeare was combining poetry with drama. Shylock's rage was not shown but reported:

> My daughter! O my ducats! O my daughter!
> Fled with a Christian! O my Christian ducats!
> Justice! the law! my ducats, and my daughter!
> A sealed bag, two sealed bags of ducats,
> Of double ducats, stol'n from me by my daughter!
> And jewels! two stones, two rich and precious stones,
> Stol'n by my daughter! Justice! find the girl!
> She hath the stones upon her, and the ducats;

and again Shakespeare brought Barabas' similar outburst down to the level of common humanity.

The successful wooing of Portia had yet to come, but Shakespeare wished also to show that destruction was blowing up towards Antonio. He therefore kept Bassanio out of sight, and suggested the passing of time by a second unsuccessful wooing of Portia, and another scene between Salanio and Salarino, wherein they talk of Antonio's misfortunes and encounter Shylock who again loses his self-control at the torment of Antonio's insolencies:

He hath disgraced me, and hindered me half a million, laughed at my losses, mocked at my gains, scorned my nation, thwarted my bargains, cooled my friends, heated mine enemies; and what's this reason? I am a Jew. Hath not a Jew eyes? Hath not a Jew hands, organs, dimensions, senses, affections, passions? fed with the same food, hurt with the same weapons, subject to the same diseases, healed by the same means, warmed and cooled by the same winter and summer, as a Christian is? If you prick us, do we not bleed? if you tickle us, do we not laugh? if you poison us, do we not die? and if you wrong us, shall we not revenge? If we are like you in the rest, we will resemble you in that. If a Jew wrong a Christian, what is his humility? Revenge. If a Christian wrong a Jew, what should his sufferance be by Christian example? Why, revenge. The villainy you teach me I will execute, and it shall go hard but I will better the instruction.

To point the increasing bitterness in Shylock's heart, Shakespeare wrote this speech in unrestrained prose; in the former outburst there was the restraint of verse speech.

From this atmosphere of impending thunder, he shifted his scene to Belmont. Bassanio has been for some time a member of Portia's household and she fears to lose him. The crackle of temper in the preceding scene is succeeded by a scene of pure lyric as Bassanio makes his choice of the caskets to music. And having chosen aright Portia surrenders herself to him:

You see me, Lord Bassanio, where I stand,
Such as I am: though for myself alone
I would not be ambitious in my wish,

To wish myself much better; yet, for you
I would be trebled twenty times myself;
A thousand times more fair, ten thousand times
More rich;
That only to stand high in your account,
I might in virtues, beauties, livings, friends,
Exceed account: but the full sum of me
Is sum of nothing; which, to term in gross,
Is an unlesson'd girl, unschool'd, unpractis'd;
Happy in this, she is not yet so old
But she may learn; happier than this,
She is not bred so dull but she can learn;
Happiest of all is that her gentle spirit
Commits itself to yours to be directed,
As from her lord, her governor, her king.

The pause of four beats in the seventh line was a masterly use of silence to express unutterable emotion.

The lyric mood was suddenly changed to tragic; news comes that Antonio is ruined and the Jew demands his forfeit. For the scene of the trial of the case of Shylock versus Antonio, Shakespeare assembled his full cast, proceeding with dignity and formality towards the tragic conclusion which seemed inevitable. One by one the hopes of a happy issue are put out, when suddenly relief comes and a reversal of situation so entire that Shylock's punishment is dramatically just.

The play, however, could not end here, for the love of Bassanio and Portia needed its proper fulfilment. Shakespeare therefore returned to Belmont and finished his play daringly in moonlight and music. *The Merchant of Venice* was the last piece of his apprenticeship. Henceforward he was master dramatist.

This same autumn of 1596 there were troubles in the Theatre. Old James Burbage had originally leased the ground whereon the playhouse stood for a period of twenty-one years. In less than a year the lease would fall in and his landlord was showing great reluctance to renew the contract. After a lengthy negotiation Burbage realised that he would be obliged to go elsewhere.

James Burbage was as shrewd a man of business as ever. As twenty years before he had realised the possibilities of a permanent theatre so now he saw that theatrical conditions were changing rapidly. The future of the playhouse lay not with the prentices and groundlings but the gentlemen spectators. In the '80's Lyly had managed a very successful little private theatre in the Blackfriars where the children of Paul's and the Chapel Royal had played exclusively to gentlemen. When Lyly's efforts were brought to an end by an unsympathetic landlord, part of the building, which included the old great hall of the monastery, was let to Rocco Bonetti, an Italian fencing master, who established a famous and expensive school for noblemen and gentlemen. After Bonetti's time, the building was turned into apartments. Burbage acquired this hall and at great expense converted it into an indoor theatre.

In November the building was almost ready to be opened when the aristocratic residents signed a petition to the Privy Council praying them to forbid the playhouse. Burbage's scheme therefore came to nothing for the time. In the following February James Burbage died, leaving the Theatre to his son Cuthbert, and the Blackfriars to Richard.

At the beginning of 1597 public life was becoming noticeably bitter. For the last two years and more the ambitions of the Earl of Essex had caused some apprehension and the triumph of Cadiz had bred violent quarrels. Essex wished to keep the ransoms of his prisoners and when the Queen demanded them there had been a regrettable scene at Court. Now Essex and the Cecils—old Lord Burleigh and his son Sir Robert—were openly at variance and the Queen was supporting the Cecils. Early in February the deaf and choleric Earl of Northumberland quarrelled with the Earl of Southampton and sent him a challenge; but the affair was patched up by the Council. The spirit of faction spread outwards and thoughtful men began to grow more disgusted with the times; but as yet no one had quite devised a suitable medium of expressing this general mood.

Early in April, however, there appeared a book called *Virgidemiarum* which pointed the way; it contained three books of toothless satires, written in rhymed couplets, a very pertinent metre for epigrammatic criticism of men and matters. This book started a new vogue and those young gallants, especially of the Inns of Court, who felt the urgent need to express their feelings about their neighbours and betters, turned to satire and epigram with some relish.

A month later the Admiral's men put on a new play at the Rose which showed how public taste was moving. It was the work of Chapman and was called *A humorous day's mirth*. Chapman had been writing regularly for the Admiral's men at the Rose for some months, but this new comedy was somewhat different. It was a complicated play but in the main a study of the humours. There was the jealous doting old Count Labervele and his young Puritan wife Florilla, the old Countess Moren jealous of her young husband, Lemot the courtier and wit, Dowsecer the pensive, melancholic man. They had their origins in common stage types, but yet in many ways they had their living counterparts in London society. Shakespeare and Lyly before him had sketched this kind of society, but without malice. Chapman had succeeded in infusing a general air of cynicism in his play. He had at least realised the true rule of Comedy, that folly should be made ridiculous.

Shakespeare followed up the grant of arms by taking further steps to establish himself as a gentleman of good family and substance, and in May he completed the purchase of New Place, a large house in the centre of Stratford-on-Avon. So the Shakespeares of Stratford were now visibly and legally to be regarded as people of worth and standing.

In the summer of 1597 another expedition was prepared for a secret destination and the Earl of Essex was given the command. Southampton sailed in his company. This year the Earl was continuously unlucky. The men sent up by the press masters were of poor quality and the victuals were bad. They set sail in the middle of July but a few days later were driven back to Plymouth by tempests. Meanwhile there was trouble in the City and unpleasantness between the Lord Mayor and the Council. The Council had ordered 700 men to be pressed for Picardy out of the ex-soldiers and vagrants. The Lord Mayor disliked the order and let it be known publicly that he was about to make a round up, with the expected result that the vagrants shifted themselves into the counties. The Council were angry.

At this tactless moment the Earl of Pembroke's players chose to produce a satire on the times called *The Isle of Dogs* at the Swan Theatre. The first two acts of the play had been written by Nashe, who then abandoned it, being a little apprehensive that there was too much mustard in it. It was finished by a new writer called Jonson who was also an actor with Pembroke's men.

Ben Jonson was now twenty-five years old—eight years younger than Shakespeare—and his career had been varied and exciting. His grandfather, so he claimed, was a gentleman of Carlisle; his father lost all his estate under Queen Mary, and at last turned minister, and died a month before his son was born. His mother was then married again to a bricklayer in London, and young Ben was brought up poorly in a private school in St. Martin's Church; but by the kindness of a friend he was sent to Westminster School where he had Camden for his master. Thence he was withdrawn and put to his step-father's trade of bricklaying, which he could not endure. So he went off as a soldier to the Low Countries, where—so he said—in face of both the camps he had killed an enemy and despoiled him. His service was brief. When he returned he became an actor in one of the inferior strolling companies, which were never known in the London theatres, and with them he played Hieronimo in the inevitable *Spanish Tragedy*.

The Isle of Dogs was very popular but not with the authorities. On the 28th July the Lord Mayor petitioned the Council for the immediate prohibition and final suppression of stage plays at the Theatre, Curtain, Bankside and all other places. He alleged four reasons in particular, the first being that plays were a special cause of corrupting youth, containing nothing but unchaste matters, lascivious devices, shifts of cosenage, and other lewd and ungodly practices, being so as that they impress the very quality and corruption of manners which they represent, contrary to the rules and art prescribed for the making of comedies even among the heathen, who used them seldom and at certain set times, and not all the year long as our manner is; whereby such as frequent them, being of the base and refuse sort of people or such young gentlemen as have small regard of credit or conscience, draw the same into imitation and not to the avoiding of the like vices which they represent. From which it was seen that someone in the City had been taking an interest in dramatic criticism.

The Council took immediate action, not on account of the Lord Mayor's æsthetic objection to plays, but because this play of the *Isle of Dogs* contained very seditious and slanderous matter. They ordered all playing to cease and instructed the Justices of Middlesex and Surrey that they should forthwith demolish the playhouses, plucking down quite the stages, galleries and rooms that are made for people to stand in, and so to deface them that they might not again be employed to such use.

As for my Lord of Pembroke's men, the Knight Marshal's men were sent to arrest the principal offenders. The company melted away. Gabriel Spencer, Robert Shaa and Ben Jonson were put into the Marshalsea and public cry was made for Nashe; but Nashe disappeared and retired into private life to eat red herrings at Yarmouth, and to sing their praises in *Nashe's Lenten Stuff*. Jonson, just before he was arrested, went over to the Rose, and there compacted to join the Admiral's; and to meet his expenses in the Marshalsea he drew £4 from Henslowe. The Admiral's were keen to have him.

A month later Andrew Wise, the stationer, took in hand to publish Shakespeare's play of *Richard the Second*. He entered his copy on 29th August and contracted with Valentine Sims for the printing. It was, however, considered wiser to omit the Deposition Scene; for anything which seemed even remotely to touch on the succession problem was treasonable matter, especially after the business of Parson's *Conference*. The first copies were on sale at the Sign of the Angel in Paul's Churchyard in September.

At the beginning of October the Council relented, so playing after all could be resumed before Hallowmas. The playhouses had survived, for the drastic order to demolish them was never carried out. The Chamberlain's men, however, were no longer at the Theatre. Their disputes with Master Giles Alleyn still continued, and the twenty-one years' lease had expired. Fortunately they were able to migrate to the Curtain which James Burbage and Brayne had acquired a decade before. On the 8th October Spencer, Shaa and Jonson were released from the Marshalsea, and immediately went over to join Alleyn at the Rose. Three days later the playhouse was opened again, and the Admiral's men, now augmented by the best of Pembroke's, played the *Spanish Tragedy*.

The Chamberlain's men had no cause to feel amiable towards rival companies. *The Isle of Dogs* was a silly adventure at any time but especially in the general uneasiness; and there was poor consolation for two months' idleness even in the thought that the principal offenders had been in gaol ever since. Moreover the Admiral's men were the gainers, for they had profited by the addition of two experienced actors and one promising dramatist.

Parliament had been summoned for the 24th October, which meant that the City would be full, and the autumn and winter season promised to be lucrative, for this time there was no hint of plague. Two days after the formal opening of Parliament there was a sudden great alarm in London. A gentleman arrived at Court with the news that the Spanish fleet was at sea; one of their ships straggling from the main body had been captured and rescued, but not before she had been searched and her papers taken off, by which it appeared that the general rendezvous was Falmouth. Several exciting days followed. All along the south coast the whole forces were mustered, horse and foot; bags of money were sent down into the west; and gentlemen were dispatched to their charges. Parliament met again on the 27th to present the Speaker but was adjourned for a week. No further alarms, however, occurred, and it was learned that the Spanish fleet had indeed come within two days' sail of Plymouth but a storm caught them, destroying fifty ships; the rest turned for home.

Meanwhile the ships of Essex's fleet were coming in from the Islands one by one, in no sort of order. Southampton had behaved with great gallantry, and Essex had bestowed the honour of knighthood upon him for his courage in action. Essex himself landed on the 28th. He immediately offered himself for service in the present emergencies and was gladly accepted. For some days everyone was kept busy, but as the first alarm wore off, the news of the Islands Voyage began to circulate and the Court was again buzzing with a new Essex incident.

Essex returned to Court on 5th November, where he was received without enthusiasm. Accounts of the expedition were various, for the officers were themselves divided into factions. The expedition had not been a success; carracks and valuable plunder had been missed and even his own officers admitted that Essex had not distinguished himself either for prudence or generalship. The Fayal business especially was criticised. Ralegh captured Fayal without waiting for Essex, and Essex, egged on by his more reckless subordinates, chose to regard the action as a direct affront intended to rob him of the renown of the expedition. Whereupon he allowed the Spaniards to escape with their goods while he spent a whole day cashiering Ralegh's officers. There had even been talk of beheading Ralegh for insubordination. My Lord's jealousy to be reputed matchless for magnanimity and honour was doubtless laudable, yet Ralegh, for all his unpopularity, was not only an older and more experienced commander but his action at Fayal was notably gallant and entirely correct. This talk of glory was tolerable from Essex who still had many of the qualities of the romantic knight about him; but his personal officers were not such as to inspire confidence in sober-minded observers, being men of desperate fortunes.

There was the usual scene at Court, for Essex had a genuine grievance. During his absence his rival the Lord Admiral was promoted; on 23rd October the Queen advanced him to be Earl of Nottingham and the patent of his nobility set forth in very honourable terms his great services in '88 and at Cadiz last year, with no more than a bare mention of Essex's share. Moreover by this elevation the new Earl being also Lord Steward of the Household for the Parliament took precedence over Essex on state occasions. Essex therefore was doubly touched in his honour and retired to his bed.

Copies of *Richard the Second* were selling briskly and Wise was looking forward to a new edition. Meanwhile he acquired the manuscript of *Richard the Third*, which he entered on 29th October. The publication of *Richard the Second* was well timed, for Essex's young men were talking high, and affected to see some significant parallels to present times in the story. Bolingbroke departing for banishment, for instance, behaved much as the Lord General as he passed through the streets of London at this time of depressed fortunes:

Ourself and Bushy, Bagot here and Green
Observ'd his courtship to the common people,
How he did seem to dive into their hearts
With humble and familiar courtesy,
What reverence he did throw away on slaves,
Wooing poor craftsmen with the craft of smiles
And patient underbearing of his fortune,
As 'twere to banish their affects with him.
Off goes his bonnet to an oyster-wench;
A brace of draymen bid God speed him well,
And had the tribute of his supple knee,
With 'Thanks, my countrymen, my loving friends';
As were our England in reversion his,
And he our subjects' next degree in hope.

Richard the Second was causing such interest that Shakespeare began to work on a sequel. As before he went back to Holinshed for the story, which he resumed where he had left it two years ago. He read on past the reign of Henry the Fourth and through to the end of Henry V., where the old first part of *Henry VI.* began. It was an interesting story. Moreover if anyone could see reflections of the present in *Richard the Second*, how much nearer came this story of Henry Bolingbroke and the Percies. This Hotspur must have been a man very like my Lord of Essex, flamboyantly brave, incredibly romantic (for an Englishman) in his worship of mere honour, one who had created the legend that he was a man of judgment and trusted no counsel but his own, and yet no one easier led by any hot-head who could present a wild project as an enterprise of honour. Shakespeare grew interested in Hotspur and began to fancy him in various situations. For his behaviour at Court there were ample modern examples; but Hotspur must be shown as a whole man, at home, in Council, on the battlefield.

Then there was that old play of the Queen's men, *The famous victories of Henry V*. It was a poor thing but it had some situations that might be reworked; the robbery at Gadshill, for instance, and the other disreputable adventures of young Prince Henry. One knew well enough the kind of man that hung about a young Prince; there were plenty of them about town at the moment, younger brothers with no more fortune than a good leg and a couple of handsome suits, captains without companies; "afternoon's men" as the phrase went, who spent the time between dinner and dark in gaming, taverns, bawdy houses or plays.

One of these professional captains Shakespeare now began to envisage as the companion in mischief to the young Prince. He called him Sir John Oldcastle, finding the character in the old play; but as Sir John developed he became the gross embodiment of the shadier side of the war. Captains had special opportunities; the pay for the soldiers passed through their hands and by judicious selection of recruits and by manipulation of the muster rolls the captain could line both his purse and his belly. The worst rascalities were in the Irish service where the rebellion was rapidly becoming dangerous. Captains about town spent generously whilst funds lasted upon taverns, harlots and players, and some of them ran to fat. Many were gentlemen of good, and even of noble family and excellent education who preferred the excitement of the wars to a life compounded of farming, hunting, occasional lawsuits in London and the local dignity of Justice of the peace. They were queer characters with flamboyant clothes, hasty tempers, blustering manners, and vocabularies of unfathomable richness; and at the return of the expedition many of them were let loose on the City. Such a personality Shakespeare magnified into Sir John Oldcastle.

He wrote the historical scenes of the play with zest, with no illusions about Hotspur and yet allowing him the glamour of his honour:

> By heaven, methinks it were an easy leap
> To pluck bright honour from the pale-fac'd moon,
> Or dive into the bottom of the deep,
> Where fathom-line could never touch the ground,
> And pluck up drowned honour by the locks;
> So he that doth redeem her thence might wear
> Without corrival all her dignities:
> But out upon this half-fac'd fellowship!

Yet those who had just come back from the Islands were less exalted in these same notions of honour; it was worth very little; it lost the plunder of a garrison at Fayal and five rich carracks at St. Michael's; and anyhow what was the good of honour when a man was dead? There was something to be said for this mood too; and then Shakespeare began to parody himself and to mock his own best speeches.

In the mouth of Sir John honour became a much cheaper affair. All men, soldiers included, owed God a death, but the debt, he argued, was not due yet:

I would be loath to pay him before his day. What need I be so forward with him that calls not on me? Well, 'tis no matter; honour pricks me on. Yea, but how if honour pricks me off when I come on? how then? Can honour set a leg? No. Or an arm? No. Or take away the grief of a wound? No. Honour hath no skill in surgery then? No. What is honour? a word. What is that word, honour? Air. A trim reckoning! Who hath it? he that died o' Wednesday. Doth he feel it? No. Doth he hear it? No. It is insensible then? Yea, to the dead. But will it not live with the living? No. Why? Detraction will not suffer it. Therefore I'll none of it: honour is a mere scutcheon; and so ends my catechism.

This self-parody was a good game. Another scene which would call for some tears in the beholding was that incident of the Prodigal Prince repenting before his father. It was a pretty passage even in Holinshed. He would parody that too, in a play; and the thought of a stage player suggested the great Alleyn. And so when Sir John crowned himself with a cushion, his hacked dagger held sceptrewise, he assumed the port and majesty of Alleyn, discoursing heroical matters in some fusty tragedy:

Weep not, sweet Queen, for trickling tears are vain; . . .

For God's sake, lords, convey my tristful Queen;
For tears do stop the floodgates of her eyes.

And he did it as like one of these harlotry players—over the water at the Rose—as a man could see, with just that thick pathos which only Alleyn could infuse into a lamentable discourse of "eyes, no eyes, but fountains fraught with tears."

This Christmas the Chamberlain's men performed at Court four times and the Admiral's men twice. There was some trouble over *Henry the Fourth.* The original Oldcastle was styled Lord Cobham. He had been burnt a martyr to his Lollard principles and seditious practices in the reign of Henry V., and as a result found a niche in Fox's *Book of Martyrs.* The present Lord Cobham was newly succeeded to the title and was an unpleasant young man, puritanically inclined. Great offence was caused him that one of his name should appear in so fantastic and disreputable a guise on a public stage. The fat knight was therefore transformed into Sir John Falstaff for public occasions; at private performances he remained Oldcastle for a time.

The quarrels at Court between Essex and the Admiral, who was supported by the Cecils, were patched up by Christmas but they were much discussed and added to the general bad temper. Elizabethan gentlemen were ever ready to carp and gird at each other, and there was plenty of matter for the satirist as for the serious-thinking man.

Meanwhile in the early months of 1598 Shakespeare wrote a second part to *Henry the Fourth.* The story was less satisfactory than the former because it gave no very coherent plot, but he could foresee a third play of Henry the Fifth, as the ideal patriot king, and this play would link up the two, showing how the wild young Prince became the true King and confounded the prophets.

Certain passages in the first part were particularly successful and would bear repetition; a scene or two of the Prince and his sick father; Falstaff, naturally, and especially some more parodies of Alleyn. Moreover the Falstaff gang were themselves irregular "humourists," specimens of the odd creatures to be encountered in Paul's Walk or along the Bankside.

This conception of "humours" arose from the venerable theory that all matter, including the physical body, was ultimately compounded of the four principles of earth, air, fire and water, represented in the human body by black bile, blood, bile and phlegm. So long as the elements were balanced, body and mind were healthy; but deficiency or excess reacted upon the temperament and produced a man who was melancholic, sanguine, choleric or phlegmatic. By an easy abuse of scientific terms "humour" was used to denote any mental complex; and anyone who wished to justify eccentric behaviour pleaded the excuse of his "humour." Everyone was suddenly beginning to take an interest in humours, and to label and analyse the vagaries of human aberration. Shakespeare was thus making his own contribution to the gallery of contemporary humours though most satirists were more concerned with types from a higher stratum of society.

He opened his play with a personification of Rumour, painted full of tongues, as his prologue; a lady very familiar to Londoners in these war years:

> Open your ears; for which of you will stop
> The vent of hearing when loud Rumour speaks?
> I, from the orient to the drooping west,
> Making the wind my post-horse, still unfold
> The acts commenced on this ball of earth:
> Upon my tongues continual slanders ride,
> The which in every language I pronounce,
> Stuffing the ears of men with false reports.
> I speak of peace, while covert enmity
> Under the smile of safety wounds the world:
> And who but Rumour, who but only I,
> Make fearful musters and prepar'd defence,
> Whilst the big year, swoln with some other grief,
> Is thought with child by the stern tyrant war,
> And no such matter? Rumour is a pipe
> Blown by surmises, jealousies, conjectures,
> And of so easy and so plain a stop
> That the blunt monster with uncounted heads,
> The still discordant wavering multitude,
> Can play upon it. But what need I thus
> My well-known body to anatomise
> Among my household?

Some new characters were added to the Falstaff gang. The hostess of the first part developed into the voluble Mistress Quickly, with her professional friend Doll Tearsheet; and to Falstaff's company Ancient Pistol was recruited. This ramping swaggerer took his gait, vocabulary and name from the great Alleyn. Pistol was such another as the Count Hermes with his great pistol and terrible oaths; and he stalked in the Boar's Head Tavern, and fetched his stations, and bent his brows with Alleyn's Cutlack gait as he ranted out the more sonorous lines from the plays that were being played just now at the Rose:

These be good humours, indeed! Shall pack-horses,
And hollow pamper'd jades of Asia,
Which cannot go but thirty miles a day,
Compare with Cæsars, and with Cannibals,
And Trojan Greeks? Nay, rather damn them with
King Cerberus; and let the welkin roar.
Shall we fall foul for toys?

On all of which Doll Tearsheet commented: "For God's sake, thrust him downstairs! I cannot endure such a fustian rascal."

In another scene Falstaff was taken out of his way to pass through Gloucestershire to collect the recruits paraded for his inspection by Justice Shallow. This kind of scandal was common at the time; five years before the abuses of the press in Gloucestershire were notorious and had roused the anger of the Council. On that occasion the captain took £10 each from the unwilling recruits; Captain Sir John Falstaff and Master Corporate Bardolf were content to free Mouldy and Bullcalf for £3 the pair. In this instance the captain was a rogue and the justice faithful; as often as not the justices used the Queen's press as a good means of ridding the parish of its undesirables.

Shakespeare's cynical frankness in these scenes was a notable contrast to the patriotic outbursts of *King John;* but the general mood had changed. This war was interminable. Two years ago Englishmen were fighting for a cause and for very life, but now there seemed to be neither glory nor object in the war. The glamour of Cadiz disappeared in ugly scandals about embezzled loot; the Islands Voyage left no one with any sense of glory. Besides, the Spanish war was almost forgotten in the new troubles in Ireland. Rebellion had been steadily growing for the last three years and though troops, money and arms were continually being sent over nothing decisive was ever done. On both sides there was nothing but further treachery. Sir John Norris was sent over in '95. He died of a festering wound in the late summer of '97. The Lord Burgh had been appointed Deputy in the spring of '97, a man who had won a fine reputation for straight dealing as Governor in the Brille. He began with energy, but he fell ill in October and was soon dead; some said that he was poisoned by his own countrymen who feared his honesty. The abuse of the Queen's service was universal and enormous; whilst paymasters and captains grew rich the unlucky soldiers were embezzled of their pay, starved for victuals and clothing, and then preyed on the country. But more and still more men were demanded from the shires and the City, and few ever came back.

As for the more serious parts of the play, the scenes between Prince John and the rebels in the North were necessary to complete the story. Shakespeare kept them as short as he could; he needed space for the long scene between Prince Henry and his dying father. Here the situation came very near to the times. For some months now the wilder followers of Essex had openly boasted that when the time came they would set him on the throne by force and then some heads would fly. Shakespeare was not one of those who had fallen before the glamour of Essex, and especially since Southampton began to play Patroclus to this Achilles; for Shakespeare still felt gusts of bitterness towards Southampton. He realised, too, as most other Englishmen, that Essex and his lawless resolutes were becoming daily more dangerous. They sneered at the Queen. It was easy enough for anyone to say that she was growing old, less able than in the past; and her vanity and meanness were notorious. Nevertheless this last autumn there had come over as ambassador extraordinary from the French King a certain Monsieur de Maisse, and for six weeks he negotiated with her in person. Monsieur de Maisse was no novice; he had served for a number of years as ambassador in Venice and he came prejudiced against the English Court. His verdict upon the Queen was that this was the wisest and most accomplished Princess in the world.

At such times no one could forget the problems of state which might at any moment become everyone's problem, and Shakespeare's own sympathies were abundantly shown in this play. His answer to those who criticised the Queen and would expedite the course of nature was partially given in the bitter cry of King Henry for sleep:

How many thousand of my poorest subjects
Are at this hour asleep! O sleep! O gentle sleep!
Nature's soft nurse, how have I frighted thee,
That thou no more wilt weigh my eyelids down
And steep my senses in forgetfulness?
Why rather, sleep, liest thou in smoky cribs,
Upon uneasy pallets stretching thee,
And hush'd with buzzing night-flies to thy slumber,
Than in the perfum'd chambers of the great,
Under the canopies of costly state,
And lull'd with sound of sweetest melody?
O thou dull god! why liest thou with the vile
In loathsome beds, and leav'st the kingly couch
A watch-case or a common 'larum bell?

As he wrote the play Shakespeare realised that it was not coming out quite as he had planned it. He found that the historical scenes were for the most part rather dull and Falstaff was getting the upper hand; there was too much Falstaff. So the old man was rejected summarily and deservedly. In the epilogue to the play, further instalments were promised; but he disappeared from the history of Henry the Fifth; his heart was fracted and corroborate. Shakespeare had finished with Falstaff after his dismissal.

VI

THE NEW COMEDY

WITH the increasing popularity of the Chamberlain's men, booksellers began to take a greater interest in Shakespeare's plays. Danter published a pirated edition of *Romeo and Juliet* in 1597. Wise acquired the manuscript of the first part of *Henry the Fourth* early in 1598, and entered it on 25th February. Soon after Cuthbert Burby brought out *Love's Labour's Lost*, and for the first time Shakespeare's name appeared on the title page of a play. Wise noted the innovation. Thereafter he also added "By William Shakespeare" to the new editions as they came out: his second edition of *Richard the Third*, his second and third editions of *Richard the Second*, all of which appeared in this year, as well as a second edition of *Lucrece*.

Wise's publications were regular and authorised transactions, but Danter's *Romeo and Juliet* was a theft of the players' rightful copy. As a matter of principle it was generally unadvisable to allow popular plays to get into print for there was no legal right in such property, and the players usually kept their plays in their own hands unless there were good reasons for printing them. There were penalties for the printer who published books without permission of the Stationers' Company but the growing value of Shakespeare's name made piracy worth the risk. The Chamberlain's men, however, were not defenceless. They appealed to their patron and by arrangement with James Roberts, who held the monopoly of printing play bills, they caused *The Merchant of Venice* to be entered in Stationers' Hall so that none but Roberts should have the right to print it. To the entry was added the proviso "that it be not printed by the said James Roberts or any other whatsoever without licence first had from the Right Honourable the Lord Chamberlain." This practice of blocking publication through the Stationers' Company was not new; several of the gentlemen authors, who preferred that their works should circulate amongst their private friends in the more aristocratic form of a manuscript copy, had used it. It was, however, the first occasion that Shakespeare sought to protect the property of his own company.

Shakespeare was now generally recognised as the greatest of English dramatists. This summer a serious-minded young student named Francis Meres completed a vast collection of similitudes, taken from more than a hundred and fifty authors and set out under two hundred headings. Towards the end of his book he added a short "Comparative discourse of our English with the Greek, Latin and Italian poets." Shakespeare was easily his favourite poet, praised as amongst the greatest who had enriched the English tongue, as a lyric poet, as one most passionate to bewail the perplexities of love, as a writer of comedy and tragedy. He added, "As Plautus and Seneca are accounted the best for comedy and tragedy among the Latins, so Shakespeare among the English is the most excellent in both kinds for the stage."

The summer of 1598 was full of excitement. In Ireland the rebellion went from bad to worse; in France the French king made a separate peace with the Spaniards. At the very beginning of July there was an amazing scene at Court. Essex was for having his own nominee, Sir George Carew, sent over to Ireland; the Queen was unwilling and preferred Sir William Knollys. Essex in a temper turned his back in scorn, whereupon the Queen returned him a box on the ear and bade him get him gone and be hanged. Essex withdrew in a passion, and everyone waited to see what would happen. Essex refused to submit or to apologise; the Queen was unwilling to receive him back into favour without submission. Tactful friends on the Council, particularly the Lord Keeper, wrote persuading him that he was doing more than harm to himself and playing into the hands of his enemies, and that policy, duty and religion enforced him to submit to his sovereign. He answered indignantly that princes could err, and subjects receive wrong, and if needs must he would continue to suffer.

A month later old Lord Burleigh died; he had been ailing for some time. He was the last of the statesmen who had stood by the Queen from the beginning of the reign, and the greatest. It was doubly unfortunate for Essex that he should be absent from his place in the Council, though by this time Sir Robert Cecil was almost as firmly established in the Queen's service as his father had been; but as yet he lacked the prestige of his father, and the noble rank of his rivals.

Shakespeare now returned to comedy, rewriting an old play which he called *Much Ado about Nothing*. The plot was twofold, the main story telling how young Claudio wooed Hero, how Claudio was deceived by Don John, the Prince's bastard brother, how he repudiated Hero at the altar, and then how Hero's honour was restored and the marriage completed. The second story was dramatically less important; it told how Benedick, the sworn bachelor, and Beatrice, the predestined old maid, having a sympathetic antipathy to each other were by a trick both brought to think themselves beloved by the other. The story was nominally set in Messina but the characters for all their Italian names were English and the mood very much that of the autumn of '96 when the gallants came back from Cadiz. The play opened with such another home-coming from a campaign in which much glory has been won and few lives lost; and Benedick was shown wearing one of these great Cadiz beards.

Shakespeare found himself more interested in the characters of Benedick and Beatrice than in the main story. They were not dissimilar to the earlier pair of Berowne and Rosaline of *Love's Labour's Lost*, but he handled them more easily, and the thrust and parry of their wit was quicker and more natural. He had learnt the trick of such conversations; they must be written in prose, for verse however light was unavoidably more stilted than normal conversation, and the repartee of two such characters must come quicker even than ordinary talk. There was a good deal of prose in the *Henry the Fourth* plays, but in this play he experimented further with its possibilities. He schemed the plot so that the mutual declaration of love between Beatrice and Benedick should come at a tragic moment, after Hero is repudiated and carried off apparently dead. That scene hitherto was all in verse, rhetorical, emotional, noisy, expressing various passions. Shakespeare closed it with a stanza of verse, alternately rhymed. Then leaving Benedick and Beatrice alone on the stage he continued in a quiet, vibrant prose:

"Lady Beatrice, have you wept all this while?"

"Yea, and I will weep a while longer."

"I will not desire that."

"You have no reason; I do it freely."

"Surely I do believe your fair cousin is wronged."

"Ah! how much might the man deserve of me that would right her."

"Is there any way to show such friendship?"

"A very even way, but no such friend."

"May a man do it?"

"It is a man's office, but not yours."

"I do love nothing in the world so well as you: is not that strange?"

"As strange as the thing I know not. It were as possible for me to say I loved nothing so well as you; but believe me not, and yet I lie not; I confess nothing, nor I deny nothing. I am sorry for my cousin."

"By my sword, Beatrice, thou lovest me."

"Do not swear by it, and eat it."

"I will swear by it that you love me; and I will make him eat it that says I love not you."

"Will you not eat your word?"

"With no sauce that can be devised to it. I protest I love thee."

"Why then, God forgive me!"

"What offence, sweet Beatrice?"

"You have stayed me in a happy hour: I was about to protest I love thee."

"And do it with all thy heart."

"I love you with so much of my heart that none is left to protest."

"Come, bid me do anything for thee."

"Kill Claudio."

He experimented also in the technique of a plot which depended for its effect upon reversal of fortune—a double reversal, for first Hero's marriage was turned to disaster, and then Claudio's distress to marriage. This kind of story could be made effective by surprise. If so, everyone must be kept in ignorance that Hero was innocent, and that she was really alive after her swooning; but such a method needed vast explanations; the resolving of the entanglements of the *Comedy of Errors* took up a long scene at the end. The other method was to sacrifice the surprises and to keep the audience foreknowing and the characters ignorant. It was more effective emotionally. As he plotted the story, everyone knew that Hero would be shamed in the church, unless something intervened; and until the very moment of its happening there was still a chance that Hero would yet be spared. The emotional effect of this kind of irony was far greater than the simpler satisfaction of surprise.

Shakespeare added some low comedy which would appeal to a London audience. Dogberry, Verges and the rest were sober citizens doing their duty by the City and serving their turn on the watch. Young gentlemen who walked abroad by night knew well enough the shortcomings, and the stolid obstinacy, of a London watch. He added also one daring simile touching on the behaviour of Essex:

> And bid her steal into the pleached bower,
> Where honeysuckles, ripen'd by the sun,
> Forbid the sun to enter; take favourites,
> Made proud by princes, that advance their pride
> Against that power that bred it.

Essex was still absenting himself from Court at the end of August when news came of a great defeat in Ireland. Sir Henry Bagnal, the Marshal, in attempting to relieve the fort at the Blackwater marched out of Armagh with an army of 3,500 foot and 300 horse. They came suddenly upon the enemy entrenched in a bog; the vanguard was thrown into disorder, units became scattered and the army broke up into rout. Of the total force 2,000 were casualties with 15 captains. It was the greatest disaster that had happened to English troops during the reign. Ireland, for certain, seemed to be lost.

A few days after this ill news reached London, the funeral of Lord Burleigh was celebrated with becoming pomp; and it was noted that the Earl of Essex, whether because of his own troubles or because of his grief wore the most sorrowful countenance of all the mourners. As yet there was no sign of reconciliation with the Queen.

Southampton also was in trouble. His intimacies with Mistress Vernon could no longer be concealed, for she was seven months with child by him. He came over secretly from Paris, married her, and returned. When the news was carried to the Queen she was so angry that she ordered the new Countess to be imprisoned in the Fleet. The Earl was commanded to return to London forthwith. A week later, however, the Queen and Essex were reconciled.

Throughout the year a steady flow of satires exuded from the press as those who were imitating *Virgidemiarum* sent off their satires and epigrams to be printed. The second part of *Virgidemiarum* and Bastard's *Chrestoleros* were published in April; John Marston's *Satires* in June; his *Scourge of Villainy* in September; a few days later followed Guilpin's *Skialetheia*.

Everard Guilpin was a great admirer of plays, especially those at the Curtain. He too had seen a significance in *Richard the Second* and in his first satire he adapted the passage of Bolingbroke's departure with unmistakable and hostile reference to Essex:

> when great *Felix* passing through the street,
> Vaileth his cap to each one he doth meet,
> And when no broom-man that will pray for him,
> Shall have less truage than his bonnet's brim,
> Who would not think him perfect courtesy?
> Or the honey suckle of humility?
> The devil he is as soon: he is the devil,
> Brightly accoustred to be-mist his evil:
> Like a swartrutter's hose his puff thoughts swell
> With yeasty ambition: *Signor Machiavel*
> Taught him this mumming trick, with courtesy
> To entrench himself with popularity,
> And for a writhen face, and body's move,
> Be barricadoed in the people's love.

Marston's *Scourge of Villainy* attracted most notice, as it well might, by its astounding terms of abuse as he lashed those who most offended his nostrils, perverts, simonists, hypocrites, self-seekers, simpering poets, fantastic gallants, critics, and "humourists" of all kinds:

> I bear the scourge of just Rhamnusia,
> Lashing the lewdness of Britannia,

he began:

> Let others sing as their good genius moves,
> Of deep designs, or else of clipping loves:

Fair fall them all, that with wit's industry,
Do clothe good subjects with true poesy:
But as for me, my vexed thoughtful soul
Takes pleasure in displeasing sharp control.
  Thou nursing mother of fair Wisdom's lore,
Ingenuous Melancholy, I implore
Thy grave assistance: take thy gloomy seat;
Enthrone thee in my blood; let me entreat,
Stay his quick jocund skips, and force him run
A sad pac'd course, until my whips be done.
Daphne, unclip thine arms from my sad brow;
Black cypress crown me, whilst I up do plough
The hidden entrails of rank villainy,
Tearing the veil from damn'd impiety.
  Quake guzzel dogs, that live on putrid slime,
  Scud from the lashes of my yerking rhyme.

The book did not lose in popularity when its readers, in spite of the author's protest that he was not glancing at private persons, began to fit names to Marston's victims.

Ben Jonson was caught up in the new movement. As a classical scholar and an old pupil of Camden he had his theories of dramatic propriety, and pondered the question of style and technique deeply. He agreed with Sidney's *Defence of Poesy* that true comedy had its purpose, a duty to the commonwealth to hold up the mirror to vice and folly, and to show their true deformity. He noted how every intelligent person was daily growing more dissatisfied with the shortcomings of his neighbour, and how this disgust was being translated into Satire.

If the dramatists were to do their work, they must bring this satire on the stage. The first effort in collaboration with Nashe to reform the commonwealth through drama had been most unfortunate. Authority was in no mood for criticism; and Jonson had thereafter endured two months' leisure in the Marshalsea wherein to reflect on the proper function of the dramatist in the State.

Then he began afresh to write a new play which he called *Every Man in His Humour.* Since his release from the Marshalsea in October 1597, with Shaa and Gabriel Spencer, he had been with the Admiral's at the Rose, and was under contract to write for them. But the new play was not given to the Admiral's. Instead Jonson betook himself to Shoreditch and offered it to the Chamberlain's men at the Curtain. The play was suited to their needs admirably. After the success of Falstaff Captain Bobadilla was pretty sure to go down; Cob would fit Kemp's particular talent; and with this new vogue for satire the gentlemen from the Inns of Court would like this play. Moreover Jonson was gaining quite a reputation as a dramatist, and the title was excellent.

Every Man in His Humour was a very neat comedy. Jonson kept to his intention of displaying folly as exhibited in a number of foolish persons of all kinds. There was Lorenzo senior a grave, admirable but slightly overanxious father, who is worried because his son Lorenzo junior spends too much time on poetry. Lorenzo junior has a friend named Prospero, a well-proportioned young wit. To their society two foolish gentlemen attach themselves, Stephano, who is Lorenzo junior's cousin, come up from the country to learn gentlemanly deportment, and Matheo—a townsman who writes fourth-rate poetry. Signior Matheo is troubled with a personal problem of honour and he comes to consult Signior Bobadilla (who passes for a soldier of vast military experience). Bobadilla, to be sure, is not so magnificent in his apartment as when he walks abroad, for he lodges with Cob, a water carrier, to Matheo's surprise, for he has not known the captain hitherto in private life. Matheo enters to find Bobadilla slowly awaking after a heavy night. Matheo is carrying a book—a new copy of the *Spanish Tragedy*, a play which has Bobadilla's very hearty approval: "I would fain see," says he, "all the poets of our time pen such another play as that was. They'll prate and swagger, and keep such a stir of art and devices, when, by God's so, they are the most shallow pitiful fellows that live upon the face of the earth again."

Matheo agrees. "Indeed, here are a number of fine speeches in this book—'O eyes, no eyes, but fountains fraught with tears'; there's a conceit! 'fountains fraught with tears!' 'O life, no life, but lively form of death'—is't not excellent? 'O world, no world, but mass of public wrongs!' O God's me! 'Confus'd and fill'd with murther and misdeeds!'

Is't not simply the best that ever you heard? Ha, how do you like it?"

And Bobadilla replies emphatically, "'Tis *good*."

Jonson then brought the two gulls Matheo and Stephano together in the company of Lorenzo junior, Prospero and Bobadilla. Stephano is introduced to Matheo and Bobadilla and mightily admires their qualities: "My name, sir," he explains, "is Signior Stephano, sir, I am this gentleman's cousin, sir, his father is mine uncle. Sir, I am somewhat melancholy, but you shall command me, sir, in whatsoever is incident to a gentleman."

"Signior," replies Bobadilla with dignity, "I must tell you this, I am no general man; embrace it as a most high favour, for, by the host of Egypt, but that I conceive you to be a gentleman of some parts. I love few words: you have wit: imagine."

"Ay, truly sir, I am mightily given to melancholy."

Whereupon Matheo realising that if his new acquaintance is melancholy he must be a gentleman of fashion and intellect, is anxious for his further acquaintance. "O Lord, sir," he observes, "it's your only best humour, sir; your true melancholy breeds your perfect fine wit, sir. I am melancholy myself divers times, sir, and then do I no more but take your pen and paper presently, and write you your half score or your dozen of sonnets at a sitting." And further he offers Stephano the use of his study.

To which Stephano replies, "I thank you, sir; I

shall be bold I warrant you; have you a close stool there?"—for this piece of furniture was peculiarly devoted to melancholy contemplations.

There were other examples of the humours, such as Thorello the merchant, inordinately jealous of his wife, and Giuliano his brother, a plain downright squire.

Having set out his characters, Jonson with the aid of Musco, a mischievous servant, proceeded to elaborate a plot which arose out of their peculiar humours. Old Lorenzo is moved to action by suspicions of his son, Thorello by jealousy of his wife. Bobadilla, after boasting how he would bastinado Giuliano, is confronted with his victim and himself well cudgelled; and, after a sufficiency of complications, everything is disentangled by Doctor Clement a magistrate in the last act, wherein Jonson wrote a fine speech in defence of poetry which he gave to Lorenzo junior:

> Indeed if you will look on Poesy,
> As she appears in many, poor and lame,
> Patch'd up in remnants and old worn rags,
> Half starv'd for want of her peculiar food,
> Sacred invention, then I must confirm
> Both your conceit and censure of her merit.
> But view her in her glorious ornaments,
> Attired in the majesty of art,
> Set high in spirit with the precious taste
> Of sweet philosophy, and which is most,
> Crown'd with the rich traditions of a soul,
> That hates to have her dignity profan'd

With any relish of an earthly thought:
Oh, then how proud a presence doth she bear.
Then is she like herself, fit to be seen
Of none but grave and consecrated eyes:
Nor is it any blemish to her fame,
That such lean, ignorant, and blasted wits,
Such brainless gulls, should utter their stol'n wares
With such applauses in our vulgar ears:
Or that their slubber'd lines have current pass,
From the fat judgments of the multitude,
But that this barren and infected age,
Should set no difference twixt these empty spirits,
And a true poet; than which reverend name,
Nothing can more adorn humanity.

The speech was a manifest challenge; for the young author was not lacking in boldness, which indeed, with encouragement, would soon develop into arrogance. *Every Man in his Humour* was perfectly in tune with the current mood.

The play was first produced by the Chamberlain's in the middle of September; and at the outset it received an unexpected advertisement. Gabriel Spencer, who had been Jonson's companion in woe over the *Isle of Dogs*, had not forgiven Jonson for leaving the Admiral's and disposing of his best work to the rival house. On the afternoon of 22nd September Spencer waited for Jonson as he came away from the Curtain. Abusive language followed and Spencer challenged him to the field. They fought in Hoxton Fields. Jonson's sword was ten inches shorter than his adversary's and he was wounded in the arm; but he ran Spencer through the right side and left him dead.

A few days later Edward Alleyn, who was away in the country, received a sad letter from his father-in-law—"Now to let you understand news," Henslowe wrote, "I will tell you some but it is for me hard and heavy. Since you were with me I have lost one of my company which hurteth me greatly, that is Gabriel: for he is slain in Hogsden Fields by the hands of Benjamin Jonson, bricklayer. Therefore I would fain have a little of your counsel if I could."

Jonson was arrested. A month afterwards at his trial he was able to plead benefit of clergy and was released with loss of his goods. Thus the Admiral's lost both poet and player.

Ever since the death of old James Burbage, Cuthbert Burbage had been trying to persuade Giles Alleyn, his landlord, to give him a new lease of the ground whereon the Theatre stood. Alleyn was encouraging but vague. Cuthbert was, however, in a dilemma. Under the original lease of 1576 it was agreed that the Theatre buildings should belong to Burbage at the end of his time provided that he removed them before the actual date of expiry. Cuthbert, relying on Alleyn's promises to renew the lease, let the buildings stand. Still nothing was agreed. At the end of September 1598, Cuthbert made a further appeal for settlement. Alleyn presented him with a lease ready drawn. The conditions were so distasteful that Cuthbert refused to sign.

Alleyn now proposed to demolish the Theatre and use the timber for his own benefit: but the Burbages learnt of his intentions.

The problem was discussed by the Chamberlain's Company. There was, clearly, no hope of re-occupying the Theatre, and great danger that the valuable timber and fittings would be lost. The Curtain was a makeshift and not satisfactory. Accordingly the chief sharers of the Company—the two Burbages, Shakespeare, Heminges, Phillips, Pope and Kemp—agreed that they would unite to build and finance a new playhouse in a different neighbourhood. They found a site on the Bankside, south of the Thames, a garden plot in Maiden Lane, not far from the Rose; and they signed a lease to commence on 25th December. To finance the new enterprise it was agreed that the two Burbages should share half the expense, and that the second half should be divided amongst the other five. Shakespeare would thus come to own a tenth share in the playhouse in addition to his share as a member of the Chamberlain's company.

Three days later Cuthbert and Richard Burbage, with Peter Street, a master builder, and a dozen of his workmen armed with swords, bills, axes and other weapons, set about the old Theatre, and quickly tore it down, whilst the widow of James Burbage, a very doughty old lady, looked on and liked well of their proceedings. Alleyn himself was away. Some of his people made protests, which were unheeded. When Alleyn came back from the Christmas holidays the Theatre had vanished; its bones now lay piled on the new site a couple of hundred yards from the Rose playhouse.

It snowed hard on the 28th December and the Thames was frozen over. Next morning Henslowe and the Admiral's men tramped down Maiden Lane. They stared at the pile of timber, thinking gloomily upon the phœnix. They foresaw nothing but troubles.

VII

THE GLOBE

BY the beginning of the year 1599 it had been as definitely decided as anything in Queen Elizabeth's court could ever be that the Earl of Essex should be sent over to Ireland as Lord Deputy, with ample powers and a large army. For his part he gave out that he, and he alone, could solve the problem. His enemies were eager for him to go, for they would benefit whatever the issue. If he did indeed heal the running sore, the country would be relieved of the burden of men and taxes; and if he failed, then his career would be ruined, for his creditors would swarm over him like flies on a carcass. Outwardly the Queen had forgiven him for his behaviour in the previous summer. Opinions were very varied amongst his friends. The wiser realised that away from the Queen mutual ill-feeling would grow; she would be dissatisfied with his achievements however great, and he would feel that he was being insufficiently supported from home. Moreover the Irish war was very different from Cadiz or Rouen and offered no chance of a quick or spectacular victory.

During January and February the army was collected, and two thousand men were sent over from the troops in the Low Countries, though Sir Francis Vere, to the indignation of the Council, was careful to select his worst. It was a difficult time for everyone. Essex demanded more ample powers than the Queen was willing to allow; the date of his departure was constantly put forward; and he became so distracted by the difficulties that he was constantly proclaiming that he would draw out of the business altogether.

In the middle of February, when tempers were generally frayed, a young Cambridge lawyer, a certain Dr. John Hayward, tactlessly published a book called *The first part of the life and reign of King Henry the IV*, but it ended with the first year of the reign and was more concerned with the deposition of King Richard the Second. Moreover it was dedicated to Essex in a Latin epistle which contained some curious and equivocal phrases . . . "*magnus siquidem es, et præsenti iudicio, et futuri temporis expectatione*"; what greater honours could future time hold out—except the Crown? This dedication was followed by an Epistle to the Reader signed A. P. concerning the profitable nature of the faithful records of history. If Dr. Hayward was ignorant of the parallel which had been made between Bolingbroke and my Lord of Essex, he was more of an innocent than most of his readers would allow. The book was bought up eagerly for it was very generally asked why such a work should come out at this of all times. The Archbishop of Canterbury sent for the Wardens of the Stationers' Company and demanded that the epistle dedicated to the Earl should be excised.

Essex's commission for Ireland was signed on 12th March, and all his demands were met, the Queen at the last showing herself very gracious and willing to content him. On 24th March the establishment of his army was passed; it allowed for a considerable staff, 1,300 horse in 26 bands, and 16,000 infantry in 160 bands. Three days later Essex set out. Taking horse in the City, and accompanied with a great number of noblemen and many others, he rode down Cornhill and Cheapside and so into the open country; and as he went great crowds pressed round him, crying out, "God save your Lordship! God preserve your honour." For four miles the Londoners followed him, a few even kept up until the evening; but when they came home their enthusiasm had been dashed. It was calm and fine as the cavalcade set out, but at Islington a great black cloud came down upon them from the north-east, bringing sudden lightning and thunder and a heavy shower of rain and hail. It was a bad omen.

Meanwhile the workmen were busy in Maiden Lane and the new playhouse was rising fast. The company were impatient to enter into possession for the Curtain was small and inconvenient. In these months Shakespeare finished the last play of the series which traced the rise and fall of the House of Lancaster. The story was less attractive than eighteen months ago when he began the first part of *Henry the Fourth*, and he lost interest. As a result he wrote it scene by scene and no longer saw it as a whole play. In any drama of King Harry certain incidents were essential: the King's reformation, his hearty custom of passing disguised amongst his soldiers and enjoying their subsequent embarrassment, the victory at Agincourt, and the blunt wooing of French Kate. These must be brought in. The rest of the play was to be made up of some scenes of martial matters, and the audience would expect more Falstaff. In this they were disappointed. Shakespeare had lost the knack of Falstaff. Moreover Falstaff would inevitably spoil the play. Either he would make King Henry ridiculous as he had pricked the bubble reputation of Hotspur in the first play, or else he must be less than himself. Being unwilling to degrade Falstaff Shakespeare killed him. The rest of his gang, however, could survive until Fortune's furious fickle wheel was ready to roll over them. Bardolph therefore reappeared, and Ancient Pistol, as enthusiastic an admirer of melodrama as ever. To these two Shakespeare joined Corporal Nym, a newcomer. Nym also in far off way had come under the influence of the drama, but he was for this new fashion of the Jonsonian humour, so that when Pistol and Nym spoke in anger they stood, as it were, for the old and the new stagecraft; whilst Pistol ranted Alleyn, slightly muddied, Nym never opened his mouth but a humour dropped out.

"I am not Barbason," he cried; "you cannot conjure me. I have an humour to knock you indifferently well. If you grow foul with me, Pistol, I will scour you with my rapier, as I may, in fair terms: if you would walk off, I would prick your guts a little, in good terms, as I may; and that's the humour of it."

Pistol flashed back:

> O braggart vile and damned furious wight!
> The grave doth gape, and doting death is near;
> Therefore exhale.

In writing the serious scenes Shakespeare was uneasy. Since the successful appearance of *Every Man in his Humour* last autumn Jonson had insistently sneered at the methods of the chronicle play, the three rusty swords that did duty for an army, the lack of unity, the breaking of all rules either of classic propriety or stark commonsense. There was much truth in his jibes. If the sole business of the dramatist was to show an exact image of the times then nothing could be more ridiculous than the attempt to represent mighty courts in this wretched makeshift playhouse. But Jonson was a very cocksure young man with a wonderful eye for little details, who saw everything on the surface and nothing underneath.

Shakespeare knew that most of his audience

would rise to a patriotic drama on a popular hero; yet he was nervous lest some of the intellectuals would titter or mew when the five hired men came on to represent the English army at Agincourt. He therefore made as little of the army as he could, but the difficulty could not be wholly avoided. It could be overcome only by boldness, and so, remembering Bottom's solution for a similar problem, he wrote a prologue, which partly by modest persuasion, partly by sheer oratory, would force the spectators to accept his play in a sympathetic mood:

> O! for a Muse of fire, that would ascend
> The brightest heaven of invention;
> A kingdom for a stage, princes to act
> And monarchs to behold the swelling scene.
> Then should the warlike Harry, like himself,
> Assume the port of Mars; and at his heels,
> Leash'd in like hounds, should famine, sword, and fire
> Crouch for employment. But pardon, gentles all,
> The flat unraised spirits that hath dar'd
> On this unworthy scaffold to bring forth
> So great an object: can this cockpit hold
> The vasty fields of France? or may we cram
> Within this wooden O the very casques
> That did affright the air at Agincourt?

Having opened in this strain, he relied mainly on rhetoric for his effects. It was a return to the epic manner. So *Henry the Fifth* was written as a play of fine speeches rather than of action and subtle characterisation; some were long pieces of description, as the picture of the horrors of a town sacked by angry soldiers, or of France ruined by war and overgrown with weeds. At times inspiration flagged, as in the Archbishop's tedious homily on the Salic Law, but then the Muse was spurred into the swelling strain of

> Once more unto the breach, dear friends, once more;

and,

> O God of Battles, steel my soldiers' hearts,

and,

> This day is called the Feast of Crispian.

And, most moving of all, for no one in his audience could have failed to think of modern instance, King Henry's soliloquy on the utter loneliness of Kingship:

> We must bear all. O hard condition!
> Twin-born with greatness, subject to the breath
> Of every fool, whose sense no more can feel
> But his own wringing. What infinite heart's ease
> Must kings neglect that private men enjoy!
> And what have kings that privates have not too,
> Save ceremony, save general ceremony?
> And what art thou, thou idle ceremony?
> What kind of god art thou, that suffer'st more
> Of mortal griefs than do thy worshippers?
> What are thy rents? what are thy comings-in?
> O ceremony! show me but thy worth:
> What is thy soul of adoration?
> Art thou aught else but place, degree, and form,
> Creating awe and fear in other men?
> Wherein thou art less happy, being fear'd,

> Than they in fearing.
> What drink'st thou oft, instead of homage sweet,
> But poison'd flattery? O! be sick, great greatness,
> And bid thy ceremony give thee cure.

Until young Ben could better that, let him keep his theories within more modest bounds; and that was the humour of it.

Nevertheless *Henry the Fifth* was task work, for Shakespeare was after new experiments with drama. Now that he was unrivalled master of his craft he was less directly influenced by the work of other and younger men, but with the rest of his generation he was becoming absorbed in this problem of human character. Men were made thus and thus; and it needed no biting satire or comedy of humours to display the essential foolishness of a jealous husband, or a Paul's man posing as a hero from the wars, or the gawky son of a country farmer buying his way to gentility. But these methods of chastising folly were not wholly satisfactory, and left the real problems unheeded. The gull who posed as a melancholic, shrouded by his ample cloak and his large black hat, and sitting apart in conspicious privacy, was a familiar object. Davies satirised him; Jonson brought him on the stage. But why should there be this air of prevailing melancholy?

Hitherto Shakespeare had not pondered very deeply upon the problems of character. Instinctively when writing a new play he could visualise the differences—voice, gesture, action, sentiment—that distinguished one man from another, and how the actors in his own company could be persuaded to interpret them. He began to desire something fuller, and to brood over the greater problem of what lay behind these strange vagaries of outward behaviour.

Dr. Hayward's book was selling so well that Wolfe printed off a new edition of 1,500 copies with an epistle apologetical. The Council were alarmed; so the wardens of the Stationers' Company seized the whole edition and delivered the books to the Bishop of London, who caused them all to be burnt.

This affair opened the eyes of the Archbishop to the dangers of the new craze for satires, epigrams and books of all kinds which in pretence of purging the humours of the state actually attacked certain illustrious individuals under feigned names. It was high time to make a conspicuous example. On 4th June therefore a ceremonial bonfire was lit in the Hall of the Stationers' Company, and therein were cast the offending books: Marston's *Pigmalion* and *Scourge of Villainy* went up in smoke, Guilpin's *Skialetheia*, the *Snarling Satires*, the volume of Davies' *Epigrams* and Marlowe's translation of Ovid's *Elegies*, the book of marriage and wiving translated from Hercules and Torquato Tasso, *The Fifteen Joys of Marriage*. A strange incomprehensible allegory called *Caltha Poetarum* was called in, as well as Hall's *Satires* and *Willobie his Avisa*. The controversy between Nashe and Dr. Harvey was brought to an abrupt end, for all their books were called in and a ban laid upon their writings. Moreover it was forbidden hereafter to print any satires, epigrams, or English histories unless approved by some of the Council.

No certain news, but disquieting rumours came from Ireland; and indeed it was forbidden to speak or write of Irish affairs. Letters brought by the post were made known only to the Council, which was taken as a sure sign that the war was going badly. Essex was said to be much discontented, and at Court it was muttered that he and the Queen threatened each other's head.

The Chamberlain's Men this summer suffered the first break in their partnership which had existed for nearly five years. Will Kemp the clown was no longer in sympathy with his fellows. His form of art was old-fashioned and boisterous. The groundlings loved him, and a new jig by Kemp certainly attracted a crowd; but as the art of playing advanced Shakespeare and the others began to take their profession more seriously, and the extemporal merriments of the old clown became irksome and embarrassing. They could well away with jigs and tales of bawdry. So resentment grew on both sides. Kemp sold his shares in the new playhouse and in the company and departed. He was succeeded as clown by Robert Armin.

In July the new theatre was finished; it was the finest playhouse in London. The company debated the question of a suitable name. They decided to call it the Globe, and for its sign Hercules carrying the world upon his shoulders. The motto chosen was *Totus mundus agit histrionem;* upon which theme Shakespeare thereupon composed a little essay in verse which began:

> All the world's a stage,
> And all the men and women merely players:
> They have their exits and their entrances;
> And one man in his time plays many parts,
> His acts being seven ages. . . .

It was too good to lose and so he grafted it into the play that he was now writing.

This new play was a straight dramatisation of a novel called *Rosalynd*, the most popular of all the pastoral romances, which Lodge had written during the ample leisure of a voyage to the Canaries and published in 1590; the fourth edition had appeared in '98. Lodge, with an eye on his public, thought to increase its chances by passing it off as one of the brood of *Euphues*, and drew up a long title—*Rosalynd: Euphues' golden legacy, found after his death in his cell at Silexedra, bequeathed to Philautus' sons, nursed up with their father in England;* he added a brief testament of Euphues. Then he began in the now familiar sing-song manner:

> There dwelled adjoining to the city of Bordeaux a knight of most honourable parentage, whom Fortune had graced with many favours, and Nature honoured with sundry exquisite qualities, so beautified with the excellence of both, as

it were a question whether Fortune or Nature were more prodigal in deciphering the riches of their bounties.

But the time came for Sir John of Bordeaux to die, and to bequeath his possessions and much good advice to his three sons, Saladine, Fernandine and Rosader. When the old man was buried, Saladine began to brood. "Riches," said he, "is a great royalty, and there is no sweeter physic than store," and after a lengthy debate with himself in which conscience was overcome by concupiscence he allowed Fernandine to continue with his studies (for he was a scholar and had no mind but on Aristotle), whilst he forced Rosader to be his page boy. By and by Rosader began to grow up and to demand his rights. Saladine was angry, and commanded his men to bind him and then, said he, "I will give him a cooling card for his choler." Rosader retorted with the garden rake, and the argument was continued by Saladine from the safer eminence of a hayloft, whence he promised restitution.

Then there came to the court of King Torismond a Norman wrestler, who challenged all comers and slew most. Saladine saw his opportunity; having bribed the wrestler not to let Rosader escape alive, he spurred Rosader to maintain the honour of the family. So Rosader went forth to try his fortune. Now amongst the spectators there sat Alinda, the king's daughter, and Rosalynd, the daughter of the banished king Gerismond. Rosader looked at Rosalynd and she at him. The Norman had already killed two brothers, but Rosader was not daunted. They closed. The Norman remembering his reward tried his hardest; but Rosader kept his eyes on Rosalynd, who lent him such an amorous look as might have made the most coward desperate, and so fired Rosader's passionate desires that he overthrew the Norman and crushed the life out of him. Rosalynd was impressed. "And to make Rosader know she affected him took from her neck a jewel and sent it by a page to the young gentleman. The prize that Venus gave to Paris was not half so pleasing to the Trojan as this gem was to Rosader; for if Fortune had sworn to make himself sole monarch of the world, he would rather have refused such dignity than have lost the jewel sent him by Rosalynd. To return her the like he was unfurnished, and yet that he might more than in his looks discover his affections, he stepped into a tent, and taking pen and paper writ this fancy:

Two suns at once from one fair heaven there shin'd.
  Ten branches from two boughs tipp'd all with roses,
Pure locks more golden than is gold refin'd,
  Two pearled rows that nature's pride incloses;
Two mounts fair marble white, down-soft and dainty,
  A snow dyed orb, where love increased by pleasure
Full woefull makes my heart and body fainty. . . ."

How tedious this pastoral stuff could be; and yet it was a good tale, and what a joyous comedy it would make if properly told.

Shakespeare wrote quickly and light-heartedly, letting his fancy play in cynical mood over the old theme of romantic love in an Arcadian forest of Arden. He kept closely to the story of *Rosalynd*, which needed very little alteration, but he wrote his own dialogue, giving it just those slight touches that revealed the artificiality of the original. He even took over most of the names for his characters, and added a few of his own, for he felt the need of a contrast to show up the unreality of these delicate shepherds and shepherdesses. This he provided in a couple of real yokels, William and Audrey. He added also a whetstone for the wits of the gentry, a fool called Touchstone, a motley, material-minded fool who found no amusement in playing with a sheephook:

"And how like you this shepherd's life, Master Touchstone?" asked Corin, the old shepherd.

"Truly, shepherd," he answered, "in respect of itself, it is a good life; but in respect that it is a shepherd's life, it is naught. In respect that it is solitary, I like it very well; but in respect that it is private, it is a very vile life. Now, in respect it is in the fields, it pleaseth me well; but in respect it is not in the Court, it is tedious. As it is a spare life, look you, it fits my humour well; but as there is no more plenty in it, it goes much against my stomach. Hast any philosophy in thee, shepherd?"

"No more but that I know the more one sickens the worse at ease he is; and that he that wants money, means, and content, is without three good friends; that the property of rain is to wet, and fire to burn; that good pasture makes fat sheep, and that a great cause of the night is lack of sun;

that he that hath learned no wit by nature nor art may complain of good breeding, or comes of a very dull kindred."

"Such a one is a natural philosopher. Wast ever in court, shepherd?"

"No, truly."

"Then thou art damned."

"Nay, I hope—"

"Truly, thou art damned like an ill-roasted egg, all on one side."

As no society gathering nowadays was complete without its melancholic, in the forest court of the banished Duke, Shakespeare set a melancholy courtier; and in the portrayal he realised that here was his chance of working out some of the ideas on human character which had been quickening in his mind for the last six months. It would have been simple to make this melancholic a mere humour, with a few long speeches on these degenerate days and plenty of business with the large hat and black cloak—like Chapman's Dowsecer. But this method explained nothing. Why should the old gentleman be melancholy? Doctors of medicine wrote learnedly, and at times wisely, about the causes and symptoms of melancholy, acute indigestion, despised and unsatisfied love, thwarted ambition which led to physical inertia, sedition, suicide, or gross hallucination. But many of the melancholy gentlemen suffered from none of these complaints; they neither kept nor desired mistresses, ate sparingly, slept well, lacked all ambition, and yet they were melancholy.

It was a melancholic of this kind that Shakespeare now determined to create, a man not unlike the famous Count Michel de Montaigne whose essays Florio was translating when Shakespeare and he had lived together in my Lord of Southampton's household; a man who was an epicure of sensations; who had experimented with sensuality in his youth, and had travelled and questioned, always looking for something he knew not what, but only certain that he never found it; and yet still curious to probe the mystery of every newcomer from a fool to a convertite. If such a character was to be seen whole, he must be brought into contact with people of all kinds. Shakespeare became so fascinated with his creature that he led up to his entrance with a long and elaborate account of his moralisings over the wounded deer. In court he claimed the melancholic's privilege to blow on whom he pleased. Orlando he found tedious, for that clean-limbed young lover had but one idea; the seduction of Audrey shocked him; but the pretty youth Ganimed (alias Rosalind) was so interesting that he even enlarged on his own complex melancholy, "compounded of many simples, extracted from many objects and indeed the sundry contemplation of my travels, which, by often rumination, wraps me in a most humorous sadness."

Melancholy put Shakespeare in mind of a very scandalous book, called *The Metamorphosis of Ajax* which John Harington had written three years before. It was intended to be a scientific discourse, yet written after the manner of Rabelais, upon the new invention of a water closet to take the place of the foul-smelling privy. Ajax was the pattern of melancholy, a perfect malcontent, his hat without a band, his hose without garters, his waist without a girdle, his boots without spurs, his purse without coin, his head without wit. By a simple change he became metamorphosed from AJAX to A JAX and so to A JAKES, which was itself a melancholy object, like the melancholy of Moorditch and such unsavoury similes. There had also been a scurrilous Court anecdote on this word. One day a great lady in the Court was informed by her gentlewoman that Master Wingfield was without. She inquired which of the Wingfields it was. The gentlewoman went out again and asked the gentleman his name. He told her "Jaques Wingfield." The nice-minded gentlewoman, not knowing that French Jaques was English James, returned to report, with a blush, that it was "Master Privy Wingfield."

And so Shakespeare called his melancholy old gentleman Jaques; and the play, for lack of a better name, *As You Like It*.

Meanwhile Jonson had been at work for nearly a year on a new comedy which should show the world (or rather the few rare spirits who were capable of understanding) what a comedy should be. The Chamberlain's Men agreed to produce it. It was called *Every Man out of His Humour*. The first play merely depicted the fools as they were; this would scourge them out of their follies, for

Jonson was now taking himself very seriously, not only as *castigator morum* but as teacher of comedy. He began therefore by selecting various specimens of the humours to be demonstrated and drew up a catalogue of their particularities.

As presenter to the play, but taking no part, he invented Asper: he was an ingenious and free spirit, eager and constant in reproof, without fear controlling the world's abuses. One whom no servile hope of gain or frosty apprehension of danger could make to be a parasite, either to time, place or opinion. Asper reappeared in the play as Macilente, a man well parted, a sufficient scholar and traveller, who wanting that place in the world's account which he thought his merit deserved, grew violently impatient of any opposite happiness in another. Macilente was in fact what Asper might well have become had he not been Jonson himself.

There were three specimens of gentle society; Puntarvolo a vain-glorious knight, who affected singularity and his own praise, and indulged in strange performances, resolving in spite of public derision to stick to his own particular fashion, phrase and gesture; Carlo Buffone, a scurrilous and profane jester, a feasthound, a glutton at others' expense, whose religion was railing and discourse ribaldry; and Fastidious Brisk, a neat, spruce, affecting courtier, one that wears clothes well and in fashion, speaks good remnants, swears tersely and with variety and cares not what lady's favour he belies or great man's familiarity. He seeks the favours of Saviolina, a court lady of light wit.

The citizens were represented by Deliro, a man of wealth fit for the Common Council but so besotted on his wife, Fallace, and so rapt with a conceit of her perfections that he lives like a perpetual suitor, whilst all the time she is nothing but a proud mincing peat, who dotes upon the courtier and only wants the face to be dishonest; and by Clove and Orange, an inseparable pair of cockscombs, who will lend money for flattery, whose glory is to invite players and make suppers.

Then there were the countrymen, Sordido, the grasping farmer who believes in almanacks and hopes for foul weather and corn at a great price. He has a son called Fungoso who is a student of the law, and squeezes his father for clothes of the courtier cut. Sordido's brother is another natural clown who is so enamoured of the name of a gentleman that he will have it, though he buy it, and comes up to town every term to learn to take tobacco and see new notions.

The collection was made up with Shift, who learns the latest news from the wars and passes himself as a soldier but whose only accomplishments are taking the whiff, squiring a cockatrice and searching for lenders.

Having assembled his specimens, Jonson proceeded to set them into suitable action. Puntarvolo courts his lady with a strange language culled from romances, and arranges to go travelling with his cat and his dog for coach companions. Macilente is so incensed that he poisons the dog. Carlo Buffone rails on all, and at the end so enrages Puntarvolo that he takes candle and wax and seals up the jester's mouth. Deliro dotes on Fallace, who peevishly despises his humility. Fungoso imitates Brisk's fashions exactly, but is always a suit behind his model, though Fallace falls in love with his clothes and finally disillusions her husband. Sordido is misled by his almanack to expect foul weather and goes to commit suicide at the plenteousness of the harvest, but his servants cut him down and he repents. The others meet suitable retribution.

It was all very like *Every Man in His Humour*, with the difference that the first play was the mirror, the second the magnifying glass of manners. Jonson however was not content to write a comedy, he intended also to give a lecture, with illustrations, upon the art of play writing. He began therefore with an Induction. Asper, Cordatus and Mitis come upon the stage as spectators. Asper is drunk with *sæva indignatio:*

> To see the earth cracked with weight of sin,
> Hell gaping under us, and o'er our heads
> Black, ravenous ruin, with her sail-stretched wings,
> Ready to sink us down, and cover us.
> Who can behold such prodigies as these,
> And have his lips sealed up? Not I: my soul
> Was never ground into such oily colours,

> To flatter vice, and daub iniquity:
> But, with an armed and resolved hand,
> I'll strip the ragged follies of the time
> Naked as at their birth. . . .

At length he notices the spectators, and warns them that he'll not servilely fawn on their applause, but if they'll listen he'll give them music worth their ears. Thence he passes to a long discourse on the theory of the four humours, and asks his friends to note any of the audience who show disgust at his lines:

> O, I would know 'em; for in such assemblies
> They are more infectious than the pestilence:
> And therefore I would give them pills to purge,
> And make them fit for fair societies.

However he must now go in to expedite the play. He leaves with the parting shot:

> Now, gentlemen, I go
> To turn an actor and a humorist,
> Where, ere I do resume my present person,
> We hope to make the circles of your eyes
> Flow with distilled laughter: if we fail,
> We must impute it to this only chance,
> Art hath an enemy called Ignorance.

But there was still more instruction to follow. The earnest Cordatus turns to Mitis to deliver some observations upon the history of Comedy, and the part played in its development by Susario, Epicharmus, Phormus, Chionides, Cratinus, Eupolis, Aristophanes, Menander, Philemon, Cecilius, Plautus, and the rest.

When the play did at last begin Cordatus and Mitis remained upon the stage to comment upon each episode and to show the admirable excellencies of this new comedy.

At the first performance Jonson suffered two disappointments. The play was so long that the players cut it, and the conclusion, introducing the Queen herself upon the stage to resolve all humours in her own person, was ill received. Indeed it aroused the vast indignation of the spectators.

The usual rumours of a coming Spanish invasion had been prevalent in the spring. On 1st August there was another alarm. It was confidently reported that the Spaniards had an armada of 30 galleys and 70 ships at least at the Groin on point of sailing for England. The Council immediately ordered the Queen's ships to be made ready, and from the City were demanded sixteen ships for the defence of the Thames, and 10,000 men, of whom 6,000 were to be trained at once. The landing was expected on the coast of Kent, or else at some place in the Thames. Two days later the enemy's numbers had grown to 70 galleys and 100 ships manned by 30,000 soldiers, and the fleet would be at Brest in three or four days.

On the 5th August a camp was ordered to be raised outside London whither the forces might concentrate. The Lord Admiral was in supreme command with Lord Mountjoy and Sir Francis Vere (who had come over from the Low Countries to report) to assist him. The defence of the City and river was in the charge of the Earl of Cumberland.

In the evening of the following day the Spaniards were reported to have landed in the Isle of Wight and Southampton. There was general panic in London. Women cried out in the streets. The gates were shut and chains laid across the streets. And with fresh rumours the strength of the enemy's fleet grew to 150 ships. As well as 30,000 men, the Archduke was sending another 20,000. The King of Denmark was sending 100 ships. On the North Borders the King of Scots was in arms with 40,000 men. Fighting had already occurred and the Lord Scroop with 200 of his men had been killed.

The Earl of Cumberland's schemes for the defence of the City were heroic, and expensive. He first proposed a bridge of boats at Gravesend. When this was discovered to be impracticable, it was suggested that the passage of the channel should be blocked by sinking hulks in the fairway by Barking Shelf. The engineers pointed out that it would require over 80 ships. The civilians complained loudly that this would be a costly business, and reminded his Lordship that sunken ships half-laden with ballast could not be shifted, which would result in the choking of the river and the permanent ruin of the city.

For the next fortnight training continued. No enemy appeared, and rumours gave way to conjectures. It was a mysterious business and many causes were alleged as that the Queen had been dangerously sick or that a certain great one, now out of the realm, was being reminded that armies could be collected and commanded by others.

On the 23rd August the forces were being dispersed and sent home. Late at night on the 25th the Spanish fleet was reported on the coast of France and messengers posted out to recall the men. Early next morning 3,000 trained men paraded in armour in the streets of London under their captains and the day following 30,000 assembled at Mile End where they were exercised all day. A week later the alarm was found to have been groundless; training ceased; and the men returned to their homes.

The excitement caused by Hayward's *History of Henry the Fourth* and the ban thereafter laid upon English histories greatly stimulated the general appetite for the events of the past. Shakespeare was thus led back to history, and as a prelude to his next play he again read Sir Thomas North's translation of Plutarch's *Lives of the Eminent Greeks and Romans.* The story of Julius Cæsar had always interested him and he was considering it when writing *Henry the Fifth;* he had in fact coupled it with Essex in the last prologue:

But now behold,
In the quick forge and working-house of thought,
How London doth pour out her citizens.
The mayor and all his brethren in best sort,

Like to the senators of the antique Rome,
With the plebeians swarming at their heels,
Go forth and fetch their conquering Cæsar in:
As, by a lower but loving likelihood,
Were now the general of our gracious Empress,—
As in good time he may,—from Ireland coming,
Bringing rebellion broached on his sword,
How many would the peaceful city quit,
To welcome him!

The story, as given in Plutarch's *Lives*, of Cæsar, Brutus and Antony was not easy material for a play; there were too many incidents, and the history was exceedingly complex. To make a good drama it must be vastly simplified. He might have tried a play on the older pattern of the "Life and Death of Julius Cæsar," showing a number of the more exciting episodes in the hero's life, and culminating according to formula in his murder in Act V. Cæsar's story however, unlike most, did not end with his death, or indeed, as Shakespeare realised, from reading the *Lives* of Antony and Octavius Cæsar, until all who had participated in that tragedy were also dead—Cassius, Brutus, Antony, Cleopatra—and young Octavius alone was left to survive.

He found, too, that his interest in the story was less in the great Cæsar than in the murderers, and their characters. It was—as he schemed it—a drama of character waged over Cæsar's body; and here Plutarch gave him most valuable hints, for Plutarch was as interested in personality and motive as in achievement. One passage especially was important.

Cæsar did not trust Brutus overmuch, wrote Plutarch, "nor was without tales brought unto him against him: howbeit he feared his great mind, authority and friends. Yet on the other side also, he trusted his good nature and fair conditions. For, intelligence being brought him one day, that Antonius and Dolabella did conspire against him, he answered that these fat long-haired men made him not afraid, but the lean and whitely-faced fellows, meaning by that Brutus and Cassius. At another time also when one accused Brutus unto him, and bade him beware of him: 'What,' said he again, clapping his hands on his breast, 'think ye that Brutus will not tarry till this body die?' meaning that none but Brutus after him was meet to have such power as he had. And surely (in my opinion) I am persuaded that Brutus might indeed have come to have been the chiefest man of Rome, if he could have contented himself for a time to have been next unto Cæsar, and to have suffered his glory and authority, which he had gotten by his great victories, to consume with time. But Cassius, being a choleric man, and hating Cæsar privately more than he did the tyranny openly, he incensed Brutus against him. It is also reported that Brutus could evil away with the tyranny, and that Cassius hated the tyrant . . ."

Here then was the motive of the drama; the story was to be simplified into a clash of personality between Brutus and Cassius with Cæsar, and later with Antony. Shakespeare therefore went through his

Plutarch to separate those episodes which were relevant to the theme. In the *Life* of Cæsar he found that Antony offered the crown to Cæsar; that Flavius and Marullus tore the diadem from Cæsar's image; the incitements to Brutus to awake; the omens and portents; Calpurnia's forebodings; Artemidorus' warning; the murder of Cæsar; the death of Cinna the poet; the revenge of Cæsar's death; and the appearance of his ghost before Philippi. From the *Life* of Brutus he noted that Brutus was properly learned in the Latin tongue, and was able to make long discourse in it; besides that he could also plead very well in Latin. "But for the Greek tongue, they do note in some of his epistles, that he counterfeited that brief compendious manner of speech of the Lacedæmonians. As, when the war was begun, he wrote unto the Pergamenians in this sort, 'I understand you have given Dolabella money: if you have done it willingly, you confess you have offended me; if against your wills, shew it then by giving me willingly . . .' These were Brutus' manner of letters, which were honoured for their briefness." Shakespeare found also the characters of Brutus and Cassius, how Brutus was incensed against Cæsar; Cassius' arguments to bring him into the conspiracy; Portia's speeches with her husband, and her behaviour before the murder; Brutus' sparing of Antony; Brutus' speech after Cæsar's death; Antony's funeral oration for Cæsar; the triumvirate; Antony's testimony of Brutus "that he thought, that of all them that had slain Cæsar, there was none but Brutus only that was moved to do it, as thinking the act commendable of itself; but that all the other conspirators did conspire his death for some private motive or envy, that they otherwise did bear unto him. Hereby it appeareth that Brutus did not trust so much to the power of his army as he did to his own virtue, as it is to be seen by his writings." A few pages later he took the account of the quarrel between Brutus and Cassius; Cassius' epicureanism; Cassius' and Brutus' opinions about the battle of Philippi; Cassius' fatal error and death at the hands of Pindarus; the second battle of Philippi; Lucilius' fidelity; Brutus' suicide; Portia's death.

The *Life* of Antony yielded further details of the funeral oration, proscription, and the honourable burial given to Brutus' body.

On the whole Plutarch served Shakespeare well, and with such clear indications of character and episode, there remained only to assemble the play and to fill out the scenes. In one respect, however, Plutarch was disappointing. His *Life* of Julius Cæsar was somewhat cold, and though he related a number of anecdotes and sayings of Cæsar's weaker side there was not much which revealed the greatness of the man in the last months of his life. Shakespeare found some difficulty in imagining a character who was so far from his own experience, so that he fell back upon the convention of stage tyrants, who were normally accustomed to lard their discourse with "sentences" and to speak pompously of themselves in the third person:

> No, Cæsar shall not; Danger knows full well
> That Cæsar is more dangerous than he.
> We are two lions litter'd in one day,
> And I the elder and more terrible:
> And Cæsar shall go forth.

Jonson came to hear the play with the sneer that a man who knew little Latin and less Greek was ill-fitted to write upon a Roman theme. This stiff Cæsar amused him, but when Cæsar turned aside the petition of Metellus Cimber with "Cæsar did never wrong but with just cause," he broke into laughter. Shakespeare altered the passage.

These two reacted curiously on each other. In Jonson's presence Shakespeare's genius was rebuked; he recognised Jonson's greater book learning—nor was he allowed to forget it—but his wit was nimbler and he could sail round Jonson and get in his shot long before the heavier vessel had time to train his guns, for all the world like one of our English ships circling a Spanish galleon. Jonson for his part was conscious of another kind of superiority. He sneered at Shakespeare's assumption of gentility, but with a sense (which he seldom admitted) that the man had an open and free nature, and was indeed *generosus*.

Hereafter the Chamberlain's Men parted company with Jonson. They had heard more than enough of his theories of comedy and his outspoken gibes at their art. He was becoming insufferable with conceit at the flattery of the young gentlemen of the Inns of Court. He made a nuisance of himself in the theatre. On the afternoons when his plays were being performed he would sit conspicuously in the gallery, and wince and writhe when the actors failed to give the exact effect to his lines upon which he insisted at rehearsal, so that spectators were distracted and the players irritated. And when the play was over he would stroll to exchange courtesies and compliments with the gallants sitting in the Lords' rooms over the back of the stage. Then everyone would rise and peer at him; and one would nudge another and whisper, "That's Jonson; that's he, that's he that pens and purges humours and disorders."

So Jonson left the Chamberlain's with a sense of injury. If they did not appreciate him at the Globe, the Admiral's would gladly have him back. Two minutes' walk and he was at the Rose, where the Admiral's indeed had work for him, but not to write about the humours. They set him to collaborate with Dekker on a stage version of the tragic story of Page of Plymouth which, ten years before, had horrified all England. It was the familiar tragedy of the miseries of enforced marriage. Eulalia Glandfield, a young woman of Tavistock, was in love with her father's manager, one George Strangwidge, but her parents, on leaving Tavistock and going to live in Plymouth, decided that it would be more convenient to themselves if the girl married a wealthy old widower called Page. Eulalia found married life with the old man so loathsome that she plotted with her true love to make away with him. They hired two assassins and in the night Page was strangled. Eulalia pretended that her husband's death was sudden and natural, but inquisitive neighbours found signs of a struggle; Eulalia, Strangwidge and the two accomplices were arrested and duly hanged. The murder was horrible and provided good copy for a pamphlet and three ballads, but general sympathy was, on the whole, with the girl. It was a good dramatic story.

The play was finished on 8th September and Jonson and Dekker shared £8 between them. Meanwhile they had drawn Chettle into partnership to dramatise the tragedy of Robert the Second, King of Scots.

Jonson did not remain long with the Admiral's and at the end of September he betook himself off where his parts would be better appreciated. The partnership with Dekker was brief, but both men had abundant time to take stock of the other's little failings.

Irish news continued scanty. Essex was more lavish than ever with his knighthoods. At Rouen and Cadiz, he had knighted by the dozen and score, in Ireland by the half hundred, so that it was much noted that in his eight years of military service—during which he had never continued in the field for six months together—he had made more knights than were in all the realm besides. Nothing, however, was heard of any decisive actions against Tyrone, and it was generally known that at Court his failures had called down stinging rebukes from the Queen.

In the middle of September Cuffe, Essex's secretary, came over with letters which he presented to the Queen in person. He answered her criticisms and to some extent satisfied her but the reports of Essex's discontent showed that he was in a dangerous and rash temper. A few hours later a captain arrived at Court with a private letter for the Queen. He brought the news that Essex, after a long conference in private, had concluded a truce with Tyrone. The captain was sent back with all speed with the Queen's angry repudiation. A week later without warning Essex himself suddenly rode into Westminster with some of his followers. They crossed with their horses by the ferry and spurred on to Nonsuch. Without waiting to change his clothes or wash his face of the mud of travel Essex passed up through the presence and the privy chambers, and into the Queen's bedchamber. It was 10 o'clock in the morning. The Queen was still at her toilet. She received him graciously, and dismissed him to change his clothing. He returned at 11 and remained in private talk till afternoon. Then he went away to dinner where he discoursed to an admiring audience of courtiers and their ladies.

After dinner the Queen's mood changed. When Essex returned to her presence she began to ask questions, and dismissed him to make his explanations to the Council. Late that night he was commanded to keep his chamber. Next afternoon he was closeted in private with the Council. After two hours' questioning the Lords of the Council reported to the Queen. The Queen's command came back that Essex should remove from Court and be committed to the charge of the Lord Keeper, and later he came to York House by coach.

A great fear fell upon the City at this sudden turn.

The Admiral's men soon began to suffer from their competitors at the Globe where the Chamberlain's had the advantage of the new house and a fine range of successful plays, including Jonson's two comedies of humours, the two parts of *Henry the Fourth*, the new *Henry the Fifth* and *As You Like It*. The rivalry between the two companies was keen even when they had been separated by the river and the city, now the Admiral's men watched the people passing them by on their way to the Globe, and listened to the applause given to those detestable Falstaff plays. At this crisis it occurred to someone that there might be further profit in the story of Falstaff; not Falstaff himself but the original Oldcastle who had been so hastily renamed. A play treating of the real Oldcastle would have a twofold chance of success; it would attract some who expected another version of Falstaff and please others who had been disgusted by Shakespeare's gross misrepresentation of the Protestant martyr. It might even harm the Chamberlain's by raising the old ill feeling.

The story was parcelled out amongst Munday, Drayton, Wilson and Hathaway. By the 16th October they had the first part ready, and were at work on the second. Rehearsals began at once.

All through the autumn the affairs of the Earl of Essex were the chief topic of conversation in the taverns. Many rumours came from those who hung about the Court. The Queen was known to be highly indignant; the Attorney General had been summoned to Court; the Lord Keeper, the Lord Treasurer and Master Secretary were closeted with the Earl for three hours, but no one knew what passed; and no one visited him, even his servants were afraid to meet in public lest offence should be taken. Meanwhile his particular friends, the Earls of Southampton and Rutland, avoided the Court and passed away their time in going to plays every day.

On 1st November the Admiral's men announced the first performance of *The first part of the true and honourable history of the life of Sir John Oldcastle, the good Lord Cobham*. The quartet of authors had done their work well. In so hasty a compilation fine verse was scarcely to be expected, but otherwise the mixture of elements was well blended, full of noise, movement, bawdry and heroics. They borrowed generously from Shakespeare. The play opened with a good rousing riot scene between the faction of Lord Powis and Lord Herbert, introducing a couple of comic Welshmen. The villain of the piece was the Bishop of Rochester, and Bankside audiences had no love for Bishops. Henry the Fifth reappeared in kingly dignity, but still able to relax and to go disguised amongst his people. Comedy was provided by the disreputable parson Sir John of Wrootham who trailed his wench after him, robbed purses on Shooter's Hill, diced and quarrelled with the king unawares, and was pardoned in the true Harry manner. Oldcastle himself was shown in a long series of exciting adventures, falsely accused, forgiven, again accused and thrown into the Tower, whence he escaped by forcing the Bishop to part with his cloak; and at the end, he was released to flee for safety into Wales.

The performance began with the usual prologue wherein the company self-righteously congratulated themselves that here was no tampering with history or the reputation of a blessed Protestant martyr:

> The doubtful title, gentlemen, prefix'd
> Upon the Argument we have in hand,
> May breed suspense and wrongfully disturb
> The peaceful quiet of your settled thoughts.
> To stop which scruple, let this brief suffice:
> It is no pamper'd glutton we present,
> Nor aged councillor to youthful sin,
> But one whose virtue shone above the rest,

A valiant martyr, and a virtuous peer;
In whose true faith and loyalty express'd
Unto his sovereign, and his country's weal,
We strive to pay that tribute of our love,
Your favours merit. Let fair Truth be grac'd
Since forg'd invention former time defac'd.

It was a great success, and Henslowe, who had been very anxious, disbursed a free gift of ten shillings to be distributed amongst the authors as a special mark of his delight.

In November the Earl of Derby turned theatre manager and at great cost revived the company of the Children of Paul's. The choir boys of St. Paul's had not attempted to compete with the professional players for the last nine years, since the Marprelate affair. One of the first plays to be produced at their revival was an old drama called *Histriomastix*, which was brought up to date by Marston. It was an old-fashioned academical piece with innumerable personifications of the kind popular with young gentlemen of the University, which showed in symbolical manner how the plenteous reign of Peace was destroyed by War, and followed by Famine, till Peace returned. Peace, Plenty, Envy, War, Ambition, Honour, Fury and the rest came on as characters, and their effects were illustrated in a number of little realistic scenes. Amongst the parasites of Peace appeared the players of Sir Oliver Owlet, with Master Posthaste, their poet, whose history bore a remarkable resemblance to that of Poet Munday. These players waxed insolent, but when War was in the ascendant they were pressed as soldiers, and presumably died for their country. As commentator to this medley, from time to time the philosophic Chrysoganus appeared to brood over the follies of mankind. Marston, at this moment, was so firm an admirer of Jonson that Chrysoganus immitated Macilente's manner almost to flattery.

Marston's next play for the Children of Paul's followed shortly after; it was called *Antonio and Mellida*. The argument concerned two Italian Dukes and their children. Andrugio, Duke of Genoa, and his son Antonio had been defeated by Piero, Duke of Venice; both were fugitives and found themselves on the Venetian shore with a price of 20,000 double pistolets on their heads. Antonio and Piero's daughter Mellida love each other; and Antonio seeks her, disguised as an Amazon. The play centred round Piero's court, which included amongst the courtiers some examples of the courtier-like humours, such as Balurdo, who was the fashionable ass with a yellow taffeta doublet cut upon carnation velour, a green hat, a blue pair of velvet hose, a gilt rapier, and an orange tawny pair of worsted silk stockings. The most important of them was Feliche, a happy malcontent, who stood aside, observing and commenting on the folly of others, and rejoicing to see himself "nor fair, nor rich, nor witty, great, nor fear'd." The first part of the play ended with a happy conclusion. Andrugio boldly enters the court of his enemy to offer his own head for the promised reward; Piero, apparently overcome by this noble courage, embraces him as an ally and agrees to the betrothal of Antonio and Mellida.

In the sequel, the comedy turned into dismal tragedy; it was called *Antonio's Revenge.* Even connoisseurs of the tragic scene can hardly have been prepared for the direful contrast, although the prologue began:

The rawish dank of clumsy winter ramps
The fluent summer's rein; and drizzling sleet
Chilleth the wan bleak cheek of the numb'd earth,
Whilst snarling gusts nibble the juiceless leaves
From the nak'd shudd'ring branch; and pills the skin
From off the soft and delicate aspects.
O now, methinks, a sullen tragic scene
Would suit the time with pleasing congruence.
May we be happy in our weak devoir,
And all part pleased in most wish'd content!
But sweat of Hercules can ne'er beget
So blest an issue. Therefore, we proclaim,
If any spirit breathes within this round,
Uncapable of weighty passion,
(As from his birth being hugged in the arms,
And nuzzled 'twixt the breasts of happiness)
Who winks, and shuts his apprehensions up
From common sense of what men were and are,
Who would not know what men must be—let such
Hurry amain from our bleak visaged shows:
We shall affright their eyes. But if a breast
Nail'd to the earth with grief; if any heart
Pierc'd through with anguish pant within this ring;
If there by any blood whose beat is choked

And stifled with true sense of misery;
If ought of these strains fill this consort up—
Th' arrive most welcome. O that our power
Could lackey or keep wing with our desires,
That with unused paize of style and sense,
We might weigh massy in judicious scale.
Yet here's the prop that doth support our hopes:
  When our scenes falter, or invention halts,
  Your favour will give crutches to our faults.

After this dismal preparation, Piero immediately shows his fearful nature. The scene opens with his entry, unbraced, his arms bare and bloody, a dripping poniard in one hand, and a torch in the other. Strotzo his minion follows. In one night's work Andrugio has been poisoned; Feliche stabbed to death and hanged in the window of Mellida's chamber to bring her chastity into question.

Piero's motive is revenge, which has been swelling for nearly a generation. Years ago he and Andrugio had been rivals in love for the Lady Maria, and Andrugio won. Mellida is cast into prison to await her trial. Piero now woos his former love which rouses the ghost of Andrugio to denounce her and reveal the truth to Antonio, demanding vengeance. Accordingly Antonio leads aside little Julio, Piero's son, there cuts the child's throat, letting the hot blood drip over Andrugio's tomb. Antonio next disguises himself as his mother's fool that he may watch events unhampered. Mellida is brought to trial and declared innocent but when she is falsely told that her Antonio is dead, she swoons and is carried out to die of a broken heart.

Vengeance is now ready for Piero. Antonio, Pandulfo (the father of Feliche), and Alberto his friend, plot together. On the eve of his marriage Piero commands a masque and a banquet. The plotters contrive to get Piero alone. They bind him in a chair, pluck out his tongue and triumph over him: then they show him the limbs of Julio carved up in a dish; and at last when the vengers are glutted with Piero's anguish they slay him. All this while the ghost of Andrugio was looking on from aloft; now it can descend satisfied that the debt is fully paid.

Those who liked plays of blood, horror and vengeance were well suited in this tragedy. The intimate little theatre had certain advantages over the playhouses, and Marston made full use of its possibilities; in particular it could be darkened, so that a new form of tragedy, nocturnal and dismal, now came into being. The tragedy was played in darkness to an accompaniment of flickering torches.

In the first part of the play Marston again paid Jonson the compliment of imitation. He prefaced *Antonio and Mellida* with an Induction in which the actors discussed their parts. Jonson, however, was not pleased. Marston's tumid style made him queasy, and imitation annoyed him. Marston's name also was added to the large catalogue of Jonson's dislikes.

The year drew to an end. At Court there was no sign that the Queen was relenting towards the Earl of Essex, who was reported to be very ill. He grew so much worse in December that his recovery seemed hopeless. The Queen was distressed, and by her command eight of the best physicians were sent to hold a consultation upon him. They reported that the principal remedy for his illness was a quiet mind and a change of air. Public prayers were offered for him in some of the city churches, to the annoyance of the Council; and the false rumour went round that he was dead.

This Christmas both Chamberlain's and Admiral's men played at Court, the latter offering *Old Fortunatus* which Dekker had just completed for them. For their performance he wrote a special prologue and epilogue in honour of the Queen.

So the century ended in general gloom and uncertainty.

VIII
THE LOST LEADER

HENSLOWE and Alleyn soon realised that the old Rose could not compete with the new Globe, for the Chamberlain's were stealing their audience. The only solution was to cut their losses and move away to a new neighbourhood. On the 22nd December Alleyn bought a thirty-three years' lease of a piece of ground about forty yards square in the parish of St. Giles without Cripplegate, between Whitecross Street and Golding Lane. Here they prepared to erect a new playhouse, and as they meant to rival the Globe as near as might be, they called in Peter Street to build the house for them.

On 8th January, 1600, they drew up and signed a detailed contract. The house was to be square, unlike the Globe which was octagonal, measuring 80 feet outside, built of timber on a brick foundation. There were three stories, the first twelve, the second eleven, and the top nine feet in height, and in breadth 12 foot 6 inches, but the two upper stories jutted forward ten inches over the lower, with four divisions for the gentlemen's rooms, and contrived in all respects like those at the Globe. The yard within was 55 feet square. The stage itself was 43 feet wide, and extended to the middle of the yard, being protected above by a shadow, or roof, covered with tiles. Details of the fittings and decorations were also to be as at the Globe, except that all the principal and main posts of the frame and stage were to be square and wrought pilaster-wise, with carved proportions called satyrs at the top of each. The cost was agreed at £440, which did not include the painting.

Meanwhile Alleyn sought the approval of his patron; and on the 12th January the Earl of Nottingham signed a general letter to the justices, officers and ministers, and all other whom it might concern, requiring them to permit his servant to proceed in the effecting and finishing of the new house without any let or molestation. Alleyn had made out a very good case for the new house and his arguments were embodied in the letter: the Rose was very inconvenient for the people in wintertime, and the Queen was most favourably disposed towards him.

Nevertheless there was considerable opposition. The Lord Willoughby and other gentlemen of the parish of St. Giles without Cripplegate petitioned the Council against the new Theatre, and on 9th March an order was sent to the justices of Middlesex to see that the intended building should be stayed, and if any had been begun then to have it defaced. The building, however, proceeded without interruption. Henslowe and Alleyn met the complaint by organising a support in the neighbourhood. They promised to contribute handsomely to the relief of the poor, insomuch that a counterpetition signed by twenty-seven of the leading inhabitants, including the constable and two overseers of the poor, was presented. They prayed that the playhouse might continue, for three reasons: the place chosen was convenient and so far from any person or place of account that none could be annoyed; the erectors had promised a very liberal portion of money weekly for the relief of the poor; and lastly they would be contented to accept this means of relief of their poor because the parish could not relieve them, nor had the justices of the shire taken any steps to help them as directed by the late Act of Parliament.

The Council therefore relented, and on 8th April another order was signed by the Earl of Nottingham, Lord George Hunsdon and Sir Robert Cecil that the building should be allowed to proceed. The permission, however, was rather a mark of the Queen's personal regard for Alleyn than an official approval of stage plays. A week before, John Wolfe the stationer, who was beginning to build a playhouse in East Smithfield, was called before the justices and bound over in £40 not to proceed without special permission of the Council.

Early in the year, Kemp provided a sensation. He bet that he would dance a morris from London to Norwich, and like other adventurers on a distant voyage he laid out money to be paid threefold on his return. On 10th February, accompanied by Thomas Sly, his taborer, William Bee his servant, and George Sprat appointed as referee to see fair play, he set out from the house of the Lord Mayor just before 7 o'clock in the morning. A great mob followed him to Bow, where he made his first halt; thence to Ilford, and after a further rest to Romford by moonlight. Here he rested for two days. By the end of the week he reached Braintree but went back to rest over the week-end at Chelmsford. In the second week, much hampered by bad roads, he came on the Saturday to Bury, which he entered at the same time as the Lord Chief Justice and proved the greater attraction to the crowd. A great fall of snow delayed his progress for the next five days, but by Wednesday 4th March he was at the gates of Norwich after nine days on the road, but he broke off his dancing so that he might make a more impressive entry on the Saturday.

Then he went back to St. Stephen's Gate. A vast crowd from the city and the country turned out to watch. At the gate a welcome in rhyme in the name of the citizens was given him by one Thomas Gilbert. In the city the Mayor appointed wifflers to make a way for him through the press, and with great difficulty he pushed his way through to the market place where the City waits with their instruments struck up. On he went towards the Mayor's house, and to take a short cut he fetched a leap over the wall of St. John's Churchyard. The

Mayor with his worshipful brethren and many knights, ladies and gentlemen were waiting to give him a great welcome at the end of his journey.

Kemp was amply rewarded for his labours. The Mayor presented him with £5, and a pension of 40s. yearly for the rest of his life; he was admitted a freeman of the Merchant Adventurers; and his buskins which he wore were nailed up in the Guildhall as a trophy, to show the measure of his great jump.

Kemp came back to London very well satisfied with himself to collect his bets. Some paid up honestly, others avoided him; but as a whole the dance had been an enormous triumph, a more than nine days' wonder. His success, however, did not improve his relations with the rest of the Chamberlain's men; but it encouraged him to plan a far more adventurous journey. He determined to dance over the Alps to Rome.

On 8th April Jonson's *Every Man out of His Humour* was entered and some weeks later was on sale at Sarjeant's Inn gate in Fleet Street. When the Chamberlain's Men looked into the printed copy they found that Jonson had touched the play up since they had first played it. He had added some up-to-date topicalities—a reference to Kemp's dance to Norwich and some parodies of Marston's fustian in the mouths of Clove and Orange. He also made an unkind hit at Shakespeare's gentility, for in that scene where Sogliardo detailed the quarterings of the coat of arms newly bought from the heralds the motto was given "Not without mustard."

The Children of Paul's were by this time well established, and attracting the better kind of spectator, for a gentleman could be sure of his company in the singing school, and not choked with the stench of garlic or pasted to the barmy jacket of a brewer. As yet, however, their comedies were somewhat antiquated, for they had not attempted to keep in advance of the fashion of the moment.

In the late spring Marston finished a new comedy for the Children, called *Jack Drum's Entertainment or the Comedy of Katherine and Pasquil*. It was a comedy of intrigue with a variety of complications. Sir Edward Fortune had two daughters, Camelia and Katherine. Katherine was constant in her love for Pasquil, but her elder sister chameleoned from Brabant junior, a courtier, to John Ellis, a rich but boorish yeoman. Katherine was pursued by Mamon a usurer who hired Mounsieur John fo de King to murder Pasquil, but Mounsieur told Pasquil who pretended to be dead; whereupon Katherine, thinking him murdered indeed, went mad. Pasquil then met Mamon, forcibly took away his bonds and destroyed them, which sent the usurer mad. But the shock of the loss of his mistress sent him mad too, until both lovers were cured by the sight of each other. Sir Edward had a man called Jack Drum who was in love with Winifred, his daughter's maid.

Mounsieur John was exceedingly lecherous and made love to Winifred. She told him that if he would carry her away in a sack to his own chamber he should have his own will; but when he opened the sack out jumped Jack and beat him soundly. Mounsieur, however, was not entirely without his consolations, for Brabant senior, who was overfond of practical jokes, introduced the Frenchman to his own wife, telling him that she was a courtesan, and truly expecting that she would send him hurriedly about his business. But the joke misfired, and the play ended with Brabant being crowned with horns.

There was some attempt in this unlikely farce to write comedy according to the new pattern, and Marston took the opportunity of slipping in a couple of jibes at Jonson in revenge for Clove and Orange. It was one of Marston's more pleasing traits, wherein he differed notably from Jonson, to affect an excess of modesty and to criticise himself. When Brabant junior asked:

> Brother, how like you of our modern wits?
> How like you the new poet Mellidus?—

who might reasonably be identified with the author of *Antonio and Mellida*—Brabant senior answered with the brief criticism:

> A slight bubbling spirit, a cork, a husk.

But Brabant senior a few moments later was himself censured as one of these bumbast wits:

That are puffed up with arrogant conceit
Of their own worth; as if Omnipotence
Had hoised them to such unequal'd height,
That they surveyed our spirits with an eye
Only create to censure from above;
When, good souls, they do nothing but reprove.

There were several excitements in June. The Queen's treatment of Essex was severely criticised, especially since he was being punished without trial or demonstration of his guilt. It had long been rumoured that he would be brought before the Star Chamber, and at last on 8th June he was formally charged with disobeying his direct instructions whilst in Ireland. The case was opened by Coke the Attorney General, and expounded by the Solicitor General and Francis Bacon; and from 9 in the morning till 8 at night Essex was obliged to submit to rhetorical denunciations of his actions.

He behaved with extraordinary discretion and patience, and for the first part of the trial he knelt at the table's end without offering to stand. At length, however, the Archbishop moved that he might stand, and then that he might lean; and at last he was allowed to sit. When the learned counsel had finished, the members of the Council proposed their verdicts. The Lord Keeper Egerton was for drastic punishment, imprisonment in the Tower, a great fine, and dismissal from his high offices. The Lord Treasurer Buckhurst would omit the fine, and the Lord Admiral would omit the Tower. Sir Robert

Cecil spoke wisely and gravely. The decision rested with the Queen and Essex returned to his keeper. He submitted himself so patiently to the triumphs of his adversaries that many of the spectators were moved to weeping at this piteous spectacle of the humiliation of one who so short a time before was Fortune's minion.

On the 22nd of the month a harsh and drastic order reached the magistrates of Middlesex and Surrey from the Council. The order began by reciting the new objections recently made to Alleyn's new house and the old complaints of the disorders caused by stage plays, how they were the occasion of the idle, riotous, and dissolute living of great numbers of people, which were now become formulæ in correspondence between the City and Council. Nevertheless their Lordships recognised that plays were not evil in themselves, and since her Majesty took pleasure in them such persons as were meetest in that kind to yield her Majesty recreation needed playhouses to keep them in exercise. In order, therefore, that the abuses might be put down and the moderation retained, it was commanded that two houses only should be allowed for the use of common stage plays. Alleyn was to occupy his new house on condition that the Curtain was either ruinated or put to some other use, and the Lord Chamberlain's men were permitted to remain in the Globe. It was further ordered that because plays were too frequent and called the people daily from their work to misspend their time these two Companies should be allowed to play twice a week and no oftener. The Council added a third clause pointing out that their orders would be of little effect unless the magistrates enforced them; and to this end they were straightly charged to see to their execution, and to commit to prison the owners of playhouses and players who disobeyed the order.

This was a severe blow to the Lord Chamberlain's Men, for although these harsh orders of the Council were usually mitigated after a few months, or allowed to lapse into disregard, this was no time to risk trouble in the Star Chamber, nor to offend their patron who was a prominent member of the Council.

Three weeks later the Council returned to the matter of Dr. Hayward's book. First Hayward himself was examined, and admitted that the Archbishop's speech supporting deposition was of his own framing and not to be found in any chronicle. The Attorney General then declared that the book was intended to reflect on the present times, for its theme was a king, censured for misgovernment, and a Council for corrupt dealings, causing the nobles to become discontented and the commons to be overtaxed, so that the King is deposed and subsequently murdered. The Council accepted his view and Hayward was lodged in the Tower. Next it was the turn of Wolfe the printer who could only plead that he had got nothing out of the book except a few copies and a fortnight's imprisonment. Then the Bishop of London's chaplain, the Reverend Samuel Harsnett, was brought up for examination: how came he to allow such a book to be passed for the press? He pleaded, with much regret, that a gentleman of the Bishop's household had brought him the manuscript, without epistle, or dedication, and passed it off as a mere flourish of wit, and he had allowed it without reading.

The printers' sharks were again on the prowl this summer and at the beginning of August the Chamberlain's Men once more endeavoured to protect their rights through James Roberts. On the 4th he entered in the Stationers' Register *As You Like It*, *Henry the Fifth*, *Every Man in his Humour* and *Much Ado about Nothing*. They were only partially successful. Jonson had sold a fair copy of *Every Man in his Humour* to Burby and Burre who entered it on the 11th. Burby and Millington also acquired—"conveyed" the wise called it—a very bad version of *Henry the Fifth* which they printed without seeking permission of the Stationers' Company. In the circumstances the Chamberlain's Men thought it best to let *Much Ado* go, and as before Wise, in partnership with Aspley, was allowed to publish it.

The same partners were also given the *Second Part of Henry the Fourth*. They adorned their edition with a full-mouthed title page "The Second part of Henry the Fourth, continuing to his death, and coronation of Henry the Fifth. With the humours of Sir John Falstaff and swaggering Pistol. As it hath sundry times been publicly acted by the Right Honourable the Lord Chamberlain, his Servants. Written by William Shakespeare." After all the troubles which had befallen Dr. Hayward's unfortunate book it was thought prudent to prune the text of some speeches which might seem to glance too obviously at recent events. Such, for instance, were Lady Percy's words of lament for the dead Hotspur:

> He had no legs that practis'd not his gait;
> And speaking thick, which nature made his blemish,
> Became the accents of the valiant;
> For those that could speak low and tardily,
> Would turn their own perfection to abuse,
> To seem like him: so that, in speech, in gait,
> In diet, in affections of delight,
> In military rules, humours of blood,
> He was the mark and gloss, copy and book,
> That fashion'd others. And him, O wondrous him!
> O miracle of men! him did you leave,—
> Second to none, unseconded by you,—
> To look upon the hideous god of war
> In disadvantage; to abide a field
> Where nothing but the sound of Hotspur's name
> Did seem defensible: so you left him.
> Never, O! never, do his ghost the wrong
> To hold your honour more precise and nice
> With others than with him: let them alone.
> The marshal and the archbishop are strong:
> Had my sweet Harry had but half their numbers,

Today might I, hanging on Hotspur's neck,
Have talk'd of Monmouth's grave.

Or the Archbishop of York's recital of the grievances of his party:

Briefly to this end: we are all diseas'd;
And, with our surfeiting and wanton hours
Have brought ourselves into a burning fever,
And we must bleed for it: of which disease
Our late king, Richard, being infected, died.
But, my most noble Lord of Westmoreland,
I take not on me here as a physician,
Nor do I as an enemy to peace
Troop in the throngs of military men;
But rather show a while like fearful war,
To diet rank minds sick of happiness
And purge the obstructions which begin to stop
Our very veins of life. Hear me more plainly:
I have in equal balance justly weigh'd
What wrongs our arms may do, what wrongs we suffer,
And find our griefs heavier than our offences.
We see which way the stream of time doth run
And are enforc'd from our most quiet sphere
By the rough torrent of occasion;
And have the summary of all our griefs,
When time shall serve, to show in articles,
Which long ere this we offer'd to the king,
And might by no suit gain our audience.
When we are wrong'd and would unfold our griefs,
We are denied access unto his person
Even by those men that most have done us wrong.

Almost 170 lines which might cause offence were thus excised.

On 26th August Essex was summoned to York House, where the Lord Keeper, the Lord Treasurer and Sir Robert Cecil informed him that he was now at liberty, except that it was the Queen's pleasure that he should not enter the Court without leave. Essex left London for a few weeks; but the real crisis of his affairs was at hand. Of the many favours which the Queen bestowed upon him, the farm of the tax on sweet wines was one of the most valuable. The grant would expire at Michaelmas. It was the touchstone of his fate. If the Queen renewed it, then it would be clear that she intended ultimately to restore him to favour; but if not, then it would be a sure sign and prelude of his ruin. Essex began to ply her with letters in a strain likely to touch her heart—"Haste paper to that happy presence, whence only unhappy I am banished! Kiss that fair correcting hand which now lays plaster to my lighter wounds, but to my greatest wound applieth nothing!"

It was almost a year since Essex came so suddenly into the Queen's presence, and since then the Realm was existing without his active assistance. In Ireland Lord Mountjoy was steadily driving the rebels back. The soldiers were now disciplined and forgot to run away when the Irish appeared. The contrast between Mountjoy's quiet determined competence and Essex's noisy ineptitude was indeed very marked.

In September a new company of boy players appeared. The success of the Paul's Boys had aroused the envy of Henry Evans who was Lyly's partner in the management of the former Blackfriars playhouse in the '80's. Evans consulted Nathaniel Giles, who had been Master of the Children of the Chapel Royal since July 1597, and the two agreed to set up a new company of Children. The private playhouse which old James Burbage had erected at such cost in '96 was still empty, and no small embarrassment to Richard who was unable to use it after the Council's inhibition but was still obliged to find the rent. The three, therefore, came to terms and an agreement was signed on 2nd September whereby Evans took out a lease of the property for twenty-one years, and to satisfy any doubts that Burbage might have of the value of his bond Evans's son-in-law, Alexander Hawkins, gave security in a bond of £400.

Evans and Giles now began to collect a company of boys. The choir consisted only of twelve; at least eighteen or twenty were needed for a company of boys. Giles, as choir master, had power to impress boys, and the partners proceeded, by virtue of this power, to take up boys for their company. In this way they added to their company such bright children as Nathan Field, one of Mulcaster's pupils, and Salathiel Pavy, an apprentice.

As Michaelmas drew nearer Essex's anxiety increased. A week before the farm of wines expired he wrote again to the Queen, saying plainly, but tactlessly, that if the grant was not renewed, his creditors would close in upon him. Shortly afterwards Bacon happened to be in her company. She observed sarcastically that of late the Earl of Essex had written some very dutiful letters, and that she had been moved by them; but what she took to be the abundance of his heart turned out to be but the preparation of a suit for the renewing of his farm of sweet wines. Essex came back to London at the beginning of October to await the issue.

Meanwhile Essex's friends brought to bear such pressure as they could on those who might influence the Queen. Essex had many friends. Most of the professional soldiers, especially those without companies, were violently of his party; the Puritans regarded him as their champion; in London the citizens always greeted him with applause and demonstrations of affection; all who had cause to dislike the government at a time of depression and heavy taxation made him the symbol of their discontent; and he had, too, the great advantage that he could pass as the national hero depressed, slighted and kept away from the Queen by the sinister intrigues of more crafty politicians.

But if Essex had many noisy friends he had as many enemies. Some, such as Ralegh, hated him personally. The chief members of the Council knew from ample experience that Essex was a difficult colleague and a bar to their own private interests. Sir Robert Cecil, the Secretary, was most in the

Queen's confidence. Outwardly, at least, he behaved with astonishing generosity and patience towards his rival, in spite of many provocations and bitter words. And among the people at large there were many who felt that the interests of the commonwealth were vaster than the private grievances of my Lord; sober men perceived that if his ambitious courses were not checked, tumults and civil wars would follow, and the vast hordes of vagabonds and masterless men would be ready to break into disorder and rapine if the social order should once be disturbed.

These views were common, and some expressed them in writing. A certain William Fulbeck compiled *An Historical Collection* of the continual factions and massacres of the Romans during the period when the history of Livy ceased and Tacitus began. Fulbeck wrote with a threefold purpose. History, he said, revealed the great mischiefs of discord and civil dissension; it showed the cause, which was nothing else but ambition; and declared the remedy, which was to live humbly in the light of the commonwealth with one's equals and not to plot against superiors in dark conventicles. No commonwealth, he declared, could be without men of aspiring humours, and when sovereigns were murdered, as Cæsar was by Brutus, they found occasion straightway for tumults, knowing that anarchy bred confusion and that the best fishing was in a troubled stream. Fulbeck's book was entered on the 10th October.

Two more of Shakespeare's plays came out in the autumn. Fisher published *A Midsummer Night's Dream* and Heyes *The Merchant of Venice.* There was no good reason for withholding them further, and especially since the season was so poor.

The Queen kept her counsels until the end of October. Then it was announced that she would henceforth retain the farm of sweet wines in her own hands. Essex submitted to the decision and prayed only that he might come to Court and kiss her hands; it was refused. It was a sad descent into bathos for one who eighteen months before had gone forth with such bravery and high hopes. Amongst his own followers who had set so much hope on his good success, it bred a feeling of nausea and disillusion, as if the Universe were in disintegration, and all the old standards overrooted and befouled.

Essex retired into the country. He did not remain for long in a mood of humble submission, and soon began to listen to his followers, and not least to Cuffe. This Cuffe was a scholarly person in habits and dress, and spoke with a blunt rudeness, which passed for integrity, but he was secretly ambitious and hoped, through his master, to advance his own fortunes. When Essex appeared in the Star Chamber and admitted his guilt, Cuffe sharply upbraided him as low-spirited and faint-hearted. Essex was annoyed and dismissed him. In the late autumn

Southampton came back to London from the Low Countries, and once more attached himself to his friend. Cuffe approached Southampton and by his mediation was restored to Essex's favour. Then he began again to work on his master and to rouse his passions, which was indeed not difficult for he was infuriated by a remark which the Queen let fall that an unruly horse must be abated of his provender that he may the easier be managed. Cuffe said that it was now clear that the Queen and his enemies were resolved to thrust him down into the extremity of poverty, and once he became a poor man, and neglected by the Queen, he would soon be slighted by all men, forsaken by his friends, and insulted by his enemies.

In the middle of December there was trouble at the Blackfriars Theatre. Under cover of Giles' patent as Master of the Children of the Chapel, Evans and his partner Robinson continued to impress boys to serve in their company. On the 13th December they were so rash as to kidnap a boy named Clifton as he was on his way to school. The boy's father was a gentleman, and as soon as he heard of it, he went to the playhouse and demanded the release of his son. Evans and Robinson treated him contemptuously. When he said that he would complain to the Council, they answered that he could complain where he would, as they had authority enough to take a nobleman's son if they wished. And to annoy Clifton they thrust an acting part into the boy's hand and told him to learn it by heart or he would be whipped. Clifton complained to Sir John Fortescue and two days later the boy was released. The incident was not allowed to pass.

Essex came back to London for Christmas, and it was at once obvious that strange things were in preparation at Essex House. All comers were welcomed. The noblemen of his party—Southampton, Worcester, Rutland, Sussex and Bedford—spent the days with him, as well as his old captains and gallants of ill repute, and many Puritans and preachers, whose sermons attracted great crowds. Their doctrine too was much noted for they preached boldly that the superior magistrates had power to restrain even kings themselves. Essex's own words were unguarded and wild, and when carried to the Queen inflamed her anger. One speech especially was unforgivable; he said that now she was an old woman her mind was as crooked as her body. It was clear that some vast upheaval was at hand. The general alarm was increased when an earthquake shook London four days before Christmas.

This mood was reflected in a remarkable poem written by John Norden the topographer. Norden placed his faith in Essex; and at his departure for Ireland had put out in print a prayer for his good success. Now he published a poem on the mutability of the Universe, called *Vicissitudo rerum*, in which he set out his theory of the Universe, and the interdependence of the whole heavenly system, and the four elements upon whose balance of mutual antipathy order resisted chaos. But the burden of Norden's lament was that order was passing, the Universe was growing tired, worn down by ageing Time:

> We at the present see *Time's* changing state,
> And *Nature's* fearful alterations,
> As if *Time* now did preach the Heaven's debate,
> And *Stars* to band in dismal factions,
> Strange *signs* are seen, divine probations,
> That some *effect* will follow of *admire*,
> Too late, when come, to say it will retire.
>
> The *Sun* and *Moon* eclipsed ne'er so much;
> *Comets* and strange *impressions* in the *air:*
> The *tides* and swelling *floods* were never such:
> The *Earth* doth tremble, Nature doth impair,
> Hideous monsters now possess the chair,
> Where erst Dame Nature's true begotten seed
> Sat truly graced in her proper weed.
>
> Such changes never have been seen of yore,
> In *Countries* and in *Kingdoms*, as of late,
> *Manners*, and *Lawës*, and *Religion's* lore
> Never were prized at so mean a rate:
> Such are the changes of this *Earth's* estate
> It may be said, Time's wings begin to fly,
> Now couching low, that erst did soar so high.

In such a general confusion of distressful moods Shakespeare set about a play for private performance on the story of Troilus and Cressida. It was originally one of the many episodes in the legend of the siege of Troy, and the most popular, which had been retold again and again, so that Cressida was passed into a synonym for light of love, and Pandarus her uncle had given his name to all go-betweens. Shakespeare, however, chose to make his plot twofold; he took over the winning and losing of Cressida from an older play, and he added to it the story of Achilles' quarrel with Agamemnon.

There had been a spate of plays on classical stories in the last eighteen months; the Admiral's men alone had produced *Brute*, *Troy's Revenge*, *Agamemnon*, *Orestes' Furies*, and a version of *Troilus and Cressida* by Dekker and Chettle. Moreover the zeal for stories of Greece and Rome was not entirely disinterested; the problems, personal and national, of the past bore on present difficulties.

Interest in the Troy story was intensified by the publication in the summer of 1598 of Chapman's translation of *Seven Books of the Iliades of Homer, Prince of Poets*. To this book Shakespeare naturally referred for the story of the wrath of Achilles, and turning over the title leaf he came upon this dedication—"To the most honoured now living instance of the Achilleian virtues eternized by divine Homer, the Earl of Essex, Earl Marshal, etc."

Reading further in the dedicatory epistle he found this apostrophe—"Most true Achilles (whom by sacred prophecy Homer did but prefigure in his admirable object) and in whose unmatched virtues shine the dignities of the soul, and the whole excellence of royal humanity; let not the peasant-common politics of the world, that count all things servile and simple, that pamper not their own sensualities, burying quick in their filthy sepulchres of the earth, the whole bodies and souls of honour, virtue and piety, stir your divine temper from perseverance in godlike pursuit of Eternity." So Chapman identified Achilles with my Lord Essex, and Shakespeare, whatever he might have intended, found the present significances of the story of Achilles thrust under his eyes. He read on. Chapman insisted on the parallel: as the former Achilles had Homer to eternise him, so "help then renowned Achilles to prefer and defend your grave and blameless Prophet of Phœbus from the doting and vicious fury of the two Atreides—Arrogancy and Detraction."

Chapman writing these words in the spring of '98 was truer prophet than he knew, for this modern Achilles was sulking in his tents, with his Patroclus and his Thersites.

Shakespeare was thus forced to see the old stories as reflections of his own time, and as he wrote he unpacked his mind of the perilous stuff which was becoming the obsession of himself and those, who, like himself, were queasy at Time's alterations.

The story of Troilus and Cressida could be made romantic; Chaucer made it so; but Shakespeare was in no mood for romance. There was no marriage of two minds here.

Shakespeare wrote the first acts of his play at

white heat. His Troilus was lust mad, and Cressida a natural whore, holding out until she might have him at the very summit of his passion:

> Yet hold I off. Women are angels, wooing:
> Things won are done; joy's soul lies in the doing:
> That she belov'd knows nought that knows not this:
> Men prize the thing ungain'd more than it is:
> That she was never yet, that ever knew
> Love got so sweet as when desire did sue.
> Therefore this maxim out of love I teach:
> Achievement is command; ungain'd, beseech:
> Then though my heart's content firm love doth bear,
> Nothing of that shall from mine eyes appear.

Then Shakespeare transferred his scene to the Grecian camp with the generals in council. Everything falls out wrong; hopes are failing, checks and disasters grow in the veins of the highest reared actions. Agamemnon, as chief in command, regards these things as the protractive trials of Jove to find persistive constancy in man. Nestor follows with the old man's complacent sentiment that ill fortune is the test of valour. And then Shakespeare through the mouth of Ulysses unbosomed himself of the present bitterness. All these troubles come because men refuse to conform themselves to the pattern of the Universe:

> The heavens themselves, the planets, and this centre
> Observe degree, priority, and place,
> Insisture, course, proportion, season, form,
> Office, and custom, in all line of order:

And therefore is the glorious planet Sol
In noble eminence enthron'd and spher'd
Amidst the other; whose med'cinable eye
Corrects the ill aspects of planets evil,
And posts, like the commandment of a king,
Sans check to good and bad: but when the planets
In evil mixture to disorder wander,
What plagues, and what portents, what mutiny,
What raging of the sea, shaking of earth,
Commotion in the winds, frights, changes, horrors,
Divert and crack, rend and deracinate
The unity and married calm of states
Quite from their fixure! O! when degree is shak'd,
Which is the ladder to all high designs,
The enterprise is sick. How could communities,
Degrees in schools, and brotherhoods in cities,
Peaceful commerce from dividable shores,
The primogenitive and due of birth,
Prerogative of age, crowns, sceptres, laurels,
But by degree, stand in authentic place?
Take but degree away, untune that string,
And, hark! what discord follows; each thing meets
In mere oppugnancy; the bounded waters
Should lift their bosoms higher than the shores,
And make a sop of all this solid globe:
Strength should be lord of imbecility,
And the rude son should strike his father dead:
Force should be right; or rather, right and wrong—
Between whose endless jar justice resides—
Should lose their names, and so should justice too.
Then everything includes itself in power,
Power into will, will into appetite;
And appetite, an universal wolf,
So doubly seconded with will and power,
Must make perforce an universal prey,

> And last eat up himself. Great Agamemnon,
> This chaos, when degree is suffocate,
> Follows the choking.
> And this neglection of degree it is
> That by a pace goes backward, with a purpose
> It hath to climb. The general's disdain'd
> By him one step below, he by the next,
> That next by him beneath; so every step,
> Exampled by the first pace that is sick
> Of his superior, grows to an envious fever
> Of pale and bloodless emulation:
> And 'tis this fever that keeps Troy on foot,
> Not her own sinews. To end a tale of length,
> Troy in our weakness lives, not in her strength.

And all this since:

> The great Achilles, whom opinion crowns
> The sinew and the forehand of our host,
> Having his ear full of his airy fame,
> Grows dainty of his worth, and in his tent
> Lies mocking our designs.

This long debate in the Grecian camp was followed by a patch of quick dialogue between Thersites, Ajax and Achilles, and then paralleled by another council in Priam's court where Priam and his sons discuss the seven-year-old question of Helen. Hector is for sending her back; "she is not worth what she doth cost the holding." But Troilus, his passion still unquenched, is for the romantic solution; when Paris

> Brought a Grecian queen, whose youth and freshness
> Wrinkles Apollo's, and makes stale the morning,

they were for keeping her, it were base now to let her go. Hector still urges a quiet consideration of right and wrong, but Troilus touches his weakness with:

She is a theme of honour and renown
A spur to valiant and magnanimous deeds,
Whose present courage may beat down our foes
And fame in time to come canonise us,

and Hector is won over.

After this passage of high sentiment the stage is given to Thersites' scurrilous comments on all and sundry, and upon the heroic argument to snarl:

Here is such patchery, such juggling, and such knavery! all the argument is a cuckold and a whore; a good quarrel to draw emulous factions and bleed to death upon. Now, the dry serpigo on the subject! and war and lechery confound all!

The generals come to visit Achilles who still treats them with contempt, and their comments were not without significance:

Things small as nothing, for request's sake only,
He makes important; possess'd he is with greatness,
And speaks not to himself but with a pride
That quarrels at self-breath: imagin'd worth
Holds in his blood such swoln and hot discourse,
That 'twixt his mental and his active parts
Kingdom'd Achilles in commotion rages
And batters down himself: what should I say?
He is so plaguy proud, that the death-tokens of it
Cry 'No recovery.'

Shakespeare was now ready for the meeting of Troilus and Cressida, and as this was the climax of the story, he led up to it deliberately. At last Pandarus places Troilus ready and then he leads in Cressida with greasy chuckles of satisfaction, like some bawdy farmer introducing a stallion to his filly. The chat of the lovers is in light prose, charged with double suggestion, but it swells into verse as the pair swear true constancy to each other, to be interrupted by Pandarus who shoves them into a chamber with a bed in it; and the curtains are drawn over the consummation.

In the Grecian camp it is agreed that Cressida shall be exchanged for Antenor and restored to her father. Then the generals, seeing Achilles in his tent, pass by him with deliberate coldness. Achilles stays Ulysses for an explanation; and again Shakespeare used the character for his own essay on Time's mutabilities:

> Time hath, my lord, a wallet at his back,
> Wherein he puts alms for oblivion,
> A great-siz'd monster of ingratitudes:
> Those scraps are good deeds past; which are devour'd
> As fast as they are made, forgot as soon
> As done: perseverance, dear my lord,
> Keeps honour bright: to have done, is to hang
> Quite out of fashion, like a rusty mail
> In monumental mockery. Take the instant way;
> For honour travels in a strait so narrow
> Where one but goes abreast: keep, then, the path;
> For emulation hath a thousand sons,

That one by one pursue: if you give way,
Or hedge aside from the direct forthright,
Like to an enter'd tide they all rush by
And leave you hindmost;
Or, like a gallant horse fall'n in first rank,
Lie there for pavement to the abject rear,
O'errun and trampled on: then what they do in present,
Though less than yours in past, most o'ertop yours;
For time is like a fashionable host,
That slightly shakes his parting guest by the hand,
And with his arms outstretch'd, as he would fly,
Grasps in the comer: welcome ever smiles,
And farewell goes out sighing. O! let not virtue seek
Remuneration for the thing it was;
For beauty, wit,
High birth, vigour of bone, desert in service,
Love, friendship, charity, are subjects all
To envious and calumniating time.
One touch of nature makes the whole world kin,
That all with one consent praise new-born gawds,
Though they are made and moulded of things past,
And give to dust that is a little gilt
More laud than gilt o'er-dusted.
The present eye praises the present object.

Early next morning, Troilus must away; but before he has bidden farewell to Cressida, Æneas is at hand with the message that Cressida must be sent to her father. Cressida is, for a time, wild with grief for the first night has been too brief; but she parts calmly, a little resentful at Troilus' insistence that she shall be true to him, and goes off with Diomedes. In the Greek camp she greets the warriors with easy familiarity, kissing them in turn and calling from Ulysses the bitter comment:

> There's language in her eye, her cheek, her lip,
> Nay, her foot speaks; her wanton spirits look out
> At every joint and motive of her body.
> O! these encounterers, so glib of tongue,
> That give a coasting welcome ere it comes,
> And wide unclasp the tables of their thoughts
> To every tickling reader, set them down
> For sluttish spoils of opportunity
> And daughters of the game.

The indecisive combat between Ajax and Hector follows and the Greeks entertain their enemies for the night.

Shakespeare went further in this purgation of his pent-up emotions, and in the Cressida story he erupted those disgusts at bodily love, and lust, and faithlessness which from time to time would come over him with an overpowering sense of physical nausea. After supper Diomedes slips away from the company. Ulysses and Troilus follow to watch as Cressida lightly gives Troilus' love gift to his new bedmate:

> Let it not be believ'd for womanhood!
> Think we had mothers; do not give advantage
> To stubborn critics, apt, without a theme
> For depravation, to square the general sex
> By Cressid's rule.

After the culmination of this bitterness the conclusion of the play was huddled up in confused alarums. Patroclus is slain and his body taken to Achilles who at last is roused. Hector, wearied with the fighting, lays aside his sword and helm, and while he is resting Achilles and his myrmidons come upon and kill him in cold blood: and this was your most true Achilles.

At any other time Shakespeare would have ended the play on a tragic level, with an eulogy, dignified and noble for dead Hector, a note of pity and sadness. The theme of this play was not the death of a hero but lechery and incontinent varlets. So he left it to Pandarus to have the last word, a rueful comment on his own trade.

IX

TUMULTUOUS INTERLUDES

IN the winter Jonson finished another play which the Children at Blackfriars acted. It was called *Cynthia's Revels*, and was the most elaborate portrayal of the humours that he had yet attempted, but all ancient rules and common practice in the making of a comedy were neglected. In form the play was after Lyly's model, a gallimaufry of mythology, flattery of Queen Elizabeth, and satire of the foolish amusements and habits of the gentlemen and ladies about the Court; and, being intended solely for the delight of a very select audience, it was full of topical quips.

Jonson again opened with the now fashionable device of the Induction. Three of the children came on, in their own persons, and one of them in spite of opposition gave a brief outline of the plot. It was a very necessary concession to the spectators who would otherwise have found some difficulty in following such story as there was. The boys then mimicked some of the antics of fashionable spectators, and the prologue was at last allowed to have his condescending say. Jonson made no plea for patient hearing; the audience, not the poet, was on trial;

for he knew, and said in so many words, that his poesy afforded

Words above action: matter above words.

But although the plot was chaotic some of the scenes and character sketches were subtle and elaborate. Some had already appeared in slightly different guise in *Every Man out of His Humour*. In their new reincarnations they were more acutely delineated, nearer to identifiable persons, for as Jonson progressed with his portrayal of the humours his method was changing from the construction of a type to the description of real people who were themselves typical. Anaides in the new play was described as one who had two essential parts of a courtier, pride and ignorance: "Marry, the rest come somewhat after the ordinary gallant. 'Tis Impudence itself, Anaides; one that speaks all that comes in his cheeks, and will blush no more than a sackbut. He lightly occupies the jester's room at the table, and keeps laughter, Gelaia, a wench in page's attire, following him in place of a squire, whom he now and then tickles with some strange ridiculous stuff, uttered, as his land came to him, by chance. He will censure or discourse of anything, but as absurdly as you would wish. His fashion is not to take knowledge of him that is beneath him in clothes. He never drinks below the salt. He does naturally admire his wit that wears gold lace or tissue; stabs any man that speaks more contemptibly of the scholar than he. He is a great proficient in all the illiberal sciences, as cheating, drinking, swaggering, whoring, and such like, never kneels but to pledge healths, nor prays but for a pipe of pudding-tobacco. He will blaspheme in his shirt. The oaths which he vomits at one supper would maintain a town of garrison in good swearing a twelvemonth. One other genuine quality he has which crowns all these, and that is this: to a friend in want, he will not depart with the weight of a soldered groat, lest the world might censure him prodigal, or report him a gull: marry, to his cockatrice, or punquetto, half a dozen taffeta gowns, or satin kirtles, in a pair or two of months, why they are nothing."

It may have been that Jonson was still practising the austere critical creed of your true satirist who spared the person and chastised the folly; but Marston thought otherwise and recognised himself in the character.

Asper reappeared as Crites, "a creature of a most perfect and divine temper: one in whom the humours and elements are peaceably met, without emulation of precedency. He is neither too fantastically melancholy, too slowly phlegmatic, too lightly sanguine, or too volubly choleric, but in all so composed and ordered, as it is clear Nature went about some full work; she did more than make a man, when she made him. His discourse is like his behaviour, uncommon but not unpleasing; he is prodigal of neither. He strives rather to be that which men call judicious than to be thought so; and is so truly learned that he affects not to show it. He will think, and speak his thought, both freely; but as distant from depraving another man's merit as proclaiming his own. For his valour, 'tis such, that he dares as little to offer an injury as receive one. In sum, he hath a most ingenuous and sweet spirit, a sharp and seasoned wit, a straight judgment, and a strong mind. Fortune could never break him or make him less. He counts it his pleasure to despise pleasures, and is more delighted with good deeds than goods. He doth neither covet nor fear; he hath too much reason to do either; and that commends all things to him." It was an obvious and intentional Portrait of the Artist—by Himself; and the play reached its climax when Crites was presented by Arete to Cynthia who accepted his labours with gracious words:

With no less pleasure than we have beheld
This precious crystal work of rarest wit,
Our eye doth read thee, now instil'd our Crites;
Whom learning, virtue, and our favour last,
Exempteth from the gloomy multitude.
With common eye the Supreme should not see:
Henceforth be ours, the more thyself to be.—

—a symbolical forecast of the beatification of Saint Ben which was inevitable once the Queen should see his comedy. The Epilogue was in the same temper as the Prologue, and ended with the boast:

By God, 'tis good, and if you like't, you may.

Unfortunately *Cynthia's Revels* was labour lost. Jonson's ambition of making a direct appeal to the Queen for her favours was thwarted. The play was not allowed to appear at Court, and he was obliged to content himself with private performance at the Blackfriars, and such celebrity as he might win from publication.

After Christmas the Council's apprehensions increased. In the New Year, Sir Thomas Egerton, the Lord Keeper, sent his son to salute Essex and to say, from his father, that his good offices with the Queen were frustrated by the Earl's action in allowing his house to be visited by so many captains of ill repute and by his encouragement of all comers which caused him to be suspected of aiming at popularity. Essex replied haughtily that he saw no reason to reject those who came in good will to visit him.

The Council therefore once more took up the matter of Hayward's *Henry the Fourth*, and on 22nd January a new examination was held in the Tower. The Attorney General had collated the book with the available authorities and found a number of statements for which he could find no historical warrant. Hayward was now pressed for his sources, and made some surprising admissions. The epistle, though signed A. P., was, he declared, his own writing and though he spoke generally of the lessons of history, he did not intend any particular application to present times. He admitted, however, that he had foisted into the reign of Henry IV. a passage concerning Henry II. from Fox's *Acts and Monuments;* but he justified it on the ground that it was lawful for a historiographer to insert any passage from previous histories even if no other historian had mentioned it. As for his descriptions of Bolingbroke's courteous manners, he acknowledged that the details were of his own invention though he had found in Hall and other writers that Bolingbroke was of a popular behaviour. It was all very suspicious.

Events now moved very quickly. On Friday, the 6th February, Lord Mounteagle, Sir Charles and Sir Joscelin Percy, and three more of Essex's particular followers came to the Globe. They asked that *Richard the Second* should be played on the following afternoon. The players answered that it was so old a play and so long out of use that they would have small or no company at it. The gentlemen, however, were importunate and when promised 40s. the players agreed. On the Saturday afternoon therefore *Richard the Second* was put on. A number of Essex's followers were present: Lord Mounteagle, Sir Christopher Blount, Sir Gelly Merrick, Essex's Steward, Sir Charles Percy, Captain Thomas Lee and others. Essex himself and Cuffe his secretary were absent, for he had just received a summons, delivered in person by Master Secretary Herbert, to appear before the Council and to explain his intentions. He refused to come, declaring that it was unsafe, for his life was threatened.

Next morning about 10 o'clock the Lord Keeper, the Earl of Worcester, Sir William Knollys and the Lord Chief Justice appeared before the gate of Essex House. They were admitted, but without their servants. As they entered the court an excited crowd surged round them. The Earl of Essex himself was there with the Earls of Rutland and Southampton, Lord Sandys, Lord Mounteagle and a great gathering of knights, gentlemen and others. The Lord Keeper delivered his message that they were sent from the Queen to understand the cause of the present assembly and to let them know that if they had any particular cause of grief they should have hearing and justice. This arrival of the Councillors was quite unexpected and a great clamour arose in the court. Essex led them into the house and to his book chamber where he ordered them to be held till his return.

With a party of about two hundred men Essex now left his house and moved towards the City, intending to make for Fenchurch Street for the house of Sheriff Smyth, who had promised to join him with a thousand men of the train bands. As he entered the City he began to cry out: "For the Queen! For the Queen! A plot is laid for my life." The citizens crowded out of their houses to watch his company as they passed, but none offered to arm or to join them.

Meanwhile the alarm had been given at Whitehall. A barricade of carts was hastily erected, and a little army collected under the command of the Lord Admiral. Lord Thomas Burleigh with Garter King of Arms hurried to the City and proclaimed Essex and his complices to be traitors; and in other parts the proclamation was repeated by the Earl of Cumberland and the Knight Marshal.

Essex's hopes were soon disappointed. When he reached Sheriff Smyth's house, the Sheriff withdrew quietly by the back door and offered his services to the Lord Mayor. Essex appealed to the citizens, crying out that England was being betrayed to the Infanta, and imploring them to arm. No one came over to his side; instead his own company began to diminish as enthusiasm cooled into prudence. After considerable wavering, he determined to go back to his house and bargain for his own freedom with his hostages.

Essex and his company therefore left Fenchurch Street and passed down again through the City, but when they came to the west gate of St. Paul's the chains were across the street, and a band of pikes and musketeers waiting to oppose him. Essex drew his sword and commanded Sir Charles Blount to set upon them, which he did resolutely and slew one but was himself taken. The musketeers replied with a volley. Seeing that further action was helpless, Essex and such followers as remained went down to the river and took boat to Essex House, which he proposed to defend to the last. When they arrived, they learnt that the Councillors had been released.

The royal forces closed in, and the Lord Admiral posted his men so that the house was surrounded on the landward sides. Then with his own troops he seized the garden by the Thames. Cannon were brought up from the Tower and set ready to force a breach. There was for some time desultory sniping from both sides and a few casualties, but the position within was hopeless. It was now dark night, and between eight and nine o'clock. The Lord Admiral being ready to begin the battery sent Sir Robert Sidney to summon the rebels to yield. The Earl of Southampton answered him boldly, declaring that if the Admiral would give them hostages for their safety they would appear before the Queen; if not, they would die fighting. The Lord Admiral sent back that conditions would not be discussed with rebels, but knowing that the Countess of Essex, the Lady Rich and their gentlewomen were within—for indeed they filled all places with their shrieking and lamentations—he granted that they might come forth; and he allowed the defenders an hour's respite to fortify the place of their departure.

Before the hour was past Essex's mind was again wavering. Lord Sandys, who was elderly, was for fighting to the end; but Essex began to think of surrender, and sent out that he would yield upon conditions. The Admiral again returned that he would not discuss conditions. There was no further resistance.

At ten o'clock that night all the noblemen came out and, falling upon their knees, delivered up their swords to the Lord Admiral.

As for the Queen, the rebellion left her unmoved. She ate her dinner as on any other day. Even when a false report was brought that the City had revolted with Essex she took no more notice than if it had been a fray in Fleet Street. Indeed she could hardly be restrained from going forth to outdare the rebels by her own presence.

Both sides had been taken somewhat unawares. The Council were still ignorant whether the rebellion was a sudden act of folly or whether some vast movement was not still to be expected in the counties. There were many prisoners in the various prisons; examinations were immediately begun and the truth of the matter was soon sifted out.

Four days after the rising there was a new sensation. Captain Thomas Lee, who was in Essex's inner councils in Ireland and had already shown himself to be a desperate man, conceived the plan of seizing the Queen's person and forcing her to sign an order for Essex's release. He mentioned his purpose to Sir Henry Neville, the ambassador to Paris, and Sir Robert Cross, another military man, but they divulged it. That evening Lee was seized in the Palace as he lurked about the door of the privy chamber; he was tried and condemned to death three days later. On Sunday the 15th—a week after the rising —the preachers in every pulpit were told what to say, and interpreted their instructions according to their own sympathies and advantages. They made much of the parallel with Richard the Second. At the Paul's Cross sermon there was a vast congregation, who expressed loud applause for the Queen's delivery.

Coming so soon after the latest examination of Hayward, the Council took a very serious view of the playing of *Richard the Second*. Two of the prisoners were examined concerning the affair, and on the 18th, Augustine Phillips, one of the Chamberlain's company, gave his version on oath. The players were considered to be innocent and no action followed; nor indeed was it likely that the Lord Chamberlain's own servants would intentionally take the part of one in disgrace with the Court.

Essex and Southampton were tried in Westminster Hall next day before the Lord Treasurer, the Lord High Steward and twenty-five of their peers, being charged with the plot to surprise the Court, their coming in arms into London to raise rebellion, and defending his house against the Queen's forces. It was not a dignified occasion, and from 9 in the morning till nearly 7 at night the prisoners wrangled with the Queen's learned counsel and their judges whilst their fellow noblemen smoked their pipes and refreshed themselves with beer and biscuits. Both Earls were condemned to death. The day after the trial Essex was visited by his chaplain, the Reverend Abdy Ashton, who played upon his feelings to such effect that he underwent a complete revulsion, and learning from the facts which came out in the trial that his followers had revealed much, he too gave up many secrets to the Council. He was spared for a few days.

On Shrove Tuesday—the 24th February—the Lord Chamberlain's men were summoned to play at Court. Very late that night the Earl of Essex was warned to prepare for death in the morning. The Queen signed the warrant for Essex's execution, and did not again change her mind. He met his fate bravely, confessing his guilt and the justice of his sentence, and prompted by the divines who accompanied him, behaved with great piety to the end. The sentence of death on Southampton was held over, and he remained a prisoner in the Tower.

Eight days later the five principal rebels were brought to trial. They were Sir Christopher Blount, Sir Charles Danvers, Sir John Davies, Sir Gelly Merrick and Henry Cuffe. They were all condemned. Cuffe and Merrick were quartered at Tyburn on the 13th; Danvers and Blount were beheaded on Tower Hill on the 18th. There were no further executions.

Although Essex's guilt and the justice of his death were amply shown to the world there was a very strong feeling in his favour. No one dared show it openly, but the Council were greatly annoyed by the ballads and lewd rhymes which were constantly brought to them, insomuch that early in April a proclamation was made offering a reward of £100 for information that would lead to an arrest.

These tragical events intensified the general disillusion. It was discernible in Marston's next play for the Children of Paul's, which was another comedy, called *What You Will*. The plot was in germ not unlike the story of Ulysses. Albano, merchant of Venice, went to sea leaving behind his doting, clinging wife Celia to a lonely bed. News came that he was drowned. Immediately the widow was pestered with suitors, and began to favour one Laverdure, a Frenchman. The other wooers to thwart the Frenchman disguised a perfumer as Albano. The news moreover was false, and at the climax of the complications the true and false Albanos confront the widow and all ends happily.

It was a good lively story and Marston, realising by this time that even a comedy of intrigue needed live characters and real emotions, infused it with not a little of himself and his own problems, and disgusts. To give variety and suitable comment, he added to the party Quadratus the epicure, and Lampatho Doria the disillusioned agnostic, fresh from seven years spent in futile sophistries at the University; for Marston himself, like many other outward cynics, was at heart an idealist, floundering to find balance between the real and the ideal.

When Jacomo, one of Celia's suitors, entered, unbraced and slovenly, showing all the conventional signs of the rejected lover, Quadratus rounds on him with a tirade on love:

> Love! Hang love.
> It is the abject outcast of the world.
> Hate all things; hate the world, thyself, all men;
> Hate knowledge; strive not to be overwise:
> It drew destruction into Paradise.
> Hate honour, virtue; they are baits
> That 'tice men's hopes to sadder fates.
> Hate beauty: every ballad-monger
> Can cry his idle foppish humour.
> Hate riches: wealth's a flattering Jack;
> Adores to face, mews 'hind thy back.
> He that is poor is firmly sped;
> He never shall be flattered.
> All things are error, dirt and nothing,
> Or pant with want, or gorged to loathing.
> Love only hate, affect no higher
> Than praise of Heaven, wine, a fire.
> Suck up thy days in silent breath,
> When their snuff's out, come Signior Death.

Later Quadratus and Lampatho, with Simplicius an empty-headed gallant, accompany Laverdure as he visits the pedant who is to marry him to Celia. They come on the pedant instructing his pupils in Latin grammar. When the others have gone Lampatho is moved to confide to Quadratus his disgust with Simplicius and with himself:

> In Heaven's handiwork there's naught,
> None more vile, accursed, reprobate to bliss,
> Than man; and 'mong men a scholar most.

The cause of Lampatho's melancholy was mainly doubt, for he had hoped by learning to find some solution for his intellectual problems, but he ends worse than he began:

> The whoreson sot is blest,
> Is rich in ignorance, makes usance on't,
> And every day augments his barbarism.
> So love me calmness, I do envy him for't.
> I was a scholar: seven useful springs
> Did I deflower in quotations
> Of cross'd opinions 'bout the soul of man.
> The more I learnt, the more I learnt to doubt:
> Knowledge and wit, faith's foes, turn faith about.

The vapid voice of Simplicius interrupts him for a moment; then he resumes:

> Honest epicure. Nay, mark, list. Delight,
> Delight, my spaniel slept, whilst I baus'd leaves,
> Toss'd o'er the dunces, pored on the old print
> Of titled words, and still my spaniel slept.
> Whilst I wasted lamp-oil, bated my flesh,
> Shrunk up my veins; and still my spaniel slept.
> And still I held converse with Zabarell,
> Aquinas, Scotus, and the musty saw
> Of antic Donate; still my spaniel slept,
> Still went on went I; first *an sit anima*,
> Then, and it were mortal. O hold, hold! at that
> They're at brain-buffets, fell by the ears amain
> Pell-mell together; still my spaniel slept.
> Then whether 'twere corporeal, local, fix'd
> Extraduce; but whether't had free will
> Or no, ho philosophers
> Stood banding factions all so strongly propp'd

I stagger'd, knew not which was firmer part;
But thought, quoted, read, observ'd and pried,
Stuff'd noting-books; and still my spaniel slept.
At length he waked and yawn'd and by yon sky,
For ought I know he knew as much as I.

The appearance of the real Albano, as yet undiscovered, at the second nuptials of his own wife gave Marston an opportunity for a speech on the contrast between true and modern love:

If love be holy; if that mystery
Of co-united hearts be sacrament;
If the unbounded goodness have infused
A sacred ardour, if a mutual love,
Into our species, of those amorous joys,
Those sweets of life, those comforts even in death,
Spring from a cause above our reason's reach;—
If that clear flame deduce his heat from heaven;—
'Tis like his cause, eternal, always One.
As is th' instiller of divinest love,
Unchanged by time, immortal maugre death!
But O, 'tis grown a figment, love a jest,
A comic poesy! The soul of man is rotten,
Even to the core;—no sound affection.
Our love is hollow-vaulted—stands on props
Of circumstance, profit, or ambitious hopes!
The other tissue gown, or chain of pearl,
Makes my coy minx to nuzzle 'twixt the breasts
Of her lull'd husband; t'other carkanet
Deflowers that lady's bed. One hundred more
Marries that loathed blowze;—one ten pound odds
In promised jointure makes the hard palm'd sire
Enforce his tender daughter's tender lips to start
At the sharp touch of some loath'd stubbed beard;

The first pure time, the golden age, is fled.
Heaven knows I lie; 'tis now the age of gold,
For it all marreth, and even virtue's sold.

Marston also, like Shakespeare, nauseated by the disharmony of the Universe, concentrated his disgust in a loathing of sex and sensuality.

Marston kept his annoyance with Jonson out of the play except for an occasional significant speech, but the insults of *Cynthia's Revels*, and Jonson's gross arrogance were becoming intolerable. He answered them in a brief induction which should show that others too had their own critical standards. Atticus, Doricus and Philomuse sit chatting on the stage until the candles are lit. They fall to discussing those spectators who carp at plays, and Philomuse breaks out with abuse in the Jonsonian manner, but Doricus interrupts him:

Nay, nay, nay.
Heaven's my hope, I cannot smooth this strain;
Wit's death, I cannot. What leprous humour
Breaks from rank swelling of these bubbling wits?
Now out upon't, I wonder what tight brain,
Wrung in this custom to maintain contempt
'Gainst common censure; to give stiff counter-buffs,
To crack rude scorn even on the very face
Of better audience. 'Slight, is't not odious?
Why, hark you, honest, honest Philomuse
(You that endeavour to endear our thoughts
To the composer's spirit), hold this firm:
Music and poetry were first approv'd
By common sense; and that which pleased most,

Held most allowed pass: know, rules of art
Were shaped to pleasure, not pleasure to your rules;
Think you that if his scenes took stamp in mint
Of three or four deem'd most judicious,
It must enforce the world to current them,
That you must spit defiance on dislike?
Now, as I love the light, were I to pass
Through public verdict, I should fear my form,
Lest ought I offer'd were unsquared or warp'd.
The more we know, the more we want:
What Bayard bolder than the ignorant?
Believe me, Philomuse, i' faith thou must,
The best, best seal of wit, is wit's distrust.

And to point a moral Marston next made Philomuse describe his play as neither comedy, tragedy, pastoral, moral nocturnal or history, "but even *What You Will*, a slight toy, lightly composed, too swiftly finished, ill plotted, worse written, I fear me worse acted, and indeed *What You Will.*"

At home the excitement caused by the rebellion gradually subsided. In Ireland the Lord Mountjoy was making good progress and winning great respect from the professional soldiers for his competence and integrity, but there was a strong expectation that the Spaniards were about to send help which would be no small embarrassment to the Queen's forces. In the Low Countries also, a new danger threatened, for at the end of June the Archduke of Austria began to invest Ostend. Sir Francis Vere took over command of the defence with a force of English soldiers, and soon began to make vigorous counterattacks on the enemy and to beat them off with heavy loss; but more large drafts of reinforcements were continually demanded from home for both campaigns.

Jonson did not take kindly to Marston's protest. He was infuriated. Would these wretched poetasters never learn to recognise their betters? They taxed him with impudence, self-love and arrogance because they thought his merit as small as their own. The envious dogs must be taught to know their master. Hitherto he had been too gentle. He had chastened manners, not men; now they should feel the lash. He would bring their humours on the stage.

When the report of the coming event was announced to the Chamberlain's men, they took counsel. Jonson had sneered casually at players in *Cynthia's Revels*, but, more important than words, this quarrel was drawing away the better part of their audience at the Globe to the private houses. It had been a bad winter. The trouble over *Richard the Second* fortunately blew over without disastrous consequences, but with no performances in Lent the year had been very lean. At the Fortune also the prospects were poor, and few new plays were being produced this year. The Chamberlain's men therefore called in the aid of Dekker: Jonson was writing a play which would attack the players; would he answer Jonson? Dekker was ready enough, for he too was a sufferer in this poor season. Jonson heard of the new enemy and thrust him in with the others.

After fifteen weeks gestation only, the prodigy was brought forth, and *Poetaster or his Arraignment* was then put on by the Children at Blackfriars. The scene was Rome, in the reign of Augustus, and the theme that when wits and arts were at their height in Rome, Virgil, Horace and the rest of those great master spirits had no want of detractors. It was a brilliant notion, for it gave Jonson ample opportunities of displaying his vast classical reading; and further, much of his story was already written for him, needing only translation or adaptation.

This time he condescended to write a play after accepted modes. The plot was double. The first part showed the story of Ovid's amour with Julia and his banishment from Rome; in the second Horace was pursued by various bores and parasites, falsely accused before the Emperor, and at last triumphantly vindicated. A certain Captain Tucca (another of the Bobadil family) acted as go-between for the two stories.

The play opened with Envy appearing from darkness to damn the author. Thence, after a defiant prologue, to young Ovid composing, which gave an opening for a translation of some forty lines from the *Elegies*. Ovid senior enters with Captain Tucca and Lupus, a magistrate, and two others. He upbraids his son for wasting his time. It is even suggested that he may be writing plays, and these players are an idle generation who do much harm in a state. Why, Tucca complains, "an honest decayed commander cannot skedler, cheat nor be seen in a bawdy house but he shall straight be in one of their wormwood comedies. They are grown licentious, the rogues: libertines, flat libertines. They forget they are i' the statute, the rascals; they are blazoned there; there they are tricked, they and their pedigrees; they need no other heralds, I wis—" *Non sanz droict* still stuck in Jonson's throat.

In the second act the fashionable crowd of Ovid's friends, with the inevitable wealthy citizen and his wife, appear. The real business of the play began in the third act. Horace is taking the air when Crispinus comes upon him. Horace, as everyone knew, was Jonson, and Crispinus, Marston. It was a witty dramatisation of the famous satire:

Ibam forte via Sacra, sicut meus est mos,
Nescio quid meditans nugarum, totus in illis . . .

where Roman Horace told how a bore fastened upon him and drove him almost to lunacy. Rescue comes at last when Crispinus is arrested for debt, and Horace slips away. At this juncture Tucca appears and goes bail. A player passes by. Tucca stops him, makes him promise a supper, and introduces him to Crispinus, and asks what plays are afoot, for he would fain bring his cockatrice to see a play if he knew when there were a good bawdy one; "but they say you ha' nothing but humours, revels and satires, that gird and fart at the time, you slave."

"No, I assure you, Captain," answers the actor,

"not we. They are on the other side of Tiber. We have as much ribaldry in our plays as can be, as you would wish, Captain. All the sinners i' the suburbs come and applaud our action daily."

Tucca then insists that two of the boys shall give an imitation of stage players. This done, he returns to the matter of the supper and warns the player not to bring any of his objectionable fellows, such as Poluphagus your eating player, or Æsop your politician: but Frisker the zany may come, and Mango, but he must not beg rapiers or scarves.

At this point the presence of Demetrius is noticed, a very simple honest fellow, a dresser of plays about the town—Dekker in fact—whom the players have hired to abuse Horace and bring him into a play, for it will get them a huge deal of money, and they have need of it for this winter has made them poorer than so many starved snakes.

The fourth act returns to Ovid, Julia and his friends. They parody the gods in a licentious banquet, but are interrupted by the Emperor Augustus himself. Ovid is cast into banishment, and the act concludes with a dialogue of passionate farewell between Ovid below and Julia above at her chamber window.

In the fifth act Augustus and his Court meet to do honour to poets, and not least to Horace. Virgil is introduced and persuaded to read a portion of the *Æneid* (translation by Jonson) but the reading is suddenly interrupted by the incursion of Lupus,

Captain Tucca, Crispinus and Demetrius, the actor and the lictors, and various knights. They have discovered a dangerous plot, and the evidence is a mysterious emblem found in Horace's study. Horace soon turns the charge aside. The Emperor is then persuaded to order the trial of Crispinus and Demetrius as Horace's detractors. The evidence is in their own writings, and here Jonson quite brilliantly parodied the slavering style of Marston and Dekker's trotting measure:

Ramp up, my genius; be not retrograde:
But boldly nominate a spade a spade.
What, shall thy lubrical and glibbery Muse
Live, as she were defunct, like punk in stews?
Alas! that were no modern consequence,
To have cothurnal buskins frighted hence.
No; teach thy Incubus to poetize;
And throw abroad thy spurious snotteries
Upon that puft-up lump of barmy froth
Or clumsy chilblain'd judgment; that with oath
Magnificates his merit; and bespawls
The conscious time, with humorous foam, and brawls
As if his *organons* of sense would crack
The sinews of my patience. Break his back,
O poets all, and some: for now we list
Of strenuous vengeance to clutch the fist.

The Muse of Demetrius was more homely:

Our Muse is in mind for th' untrussing a poet,
I slip by his name, for most men do know it.
A critic, that all the world bescumbers
With satirical humours, and lyrical numbers:

And for the most part himself doth advance
With much self-love, and more arrogance.
And, but that I would not be thought a prater,
I could tell you he were a translator.
I know the authors from whence he has stole,
And could trace him too but that I understand 'em not full
and whole.
The best note I can give you to know him by
Is that he keeps gallants' company;
Whom I would wish in time should him fear,
Lest after they buy repentance too dear.

The offenders are found guilty. Horace administers an emetic pill which in a brief space relieves Crispinus' congested verbosities, and up come the offending words into Horace's basin "retrograde," "reciprocal," "incubus," "glibbery," "lubrical," "defunct," "magnificate," and a host more, and, with a final heave, "obstupefact." Crispinus and Demetrius are made to swear that they will not henceforward malign, traduce, or detract the person or writings of Quintus Horatius Flaccus, and the play ends with a final word of encouragement to Horace from Cæsar Augustus, and the conclusion that

Envy will dwell where there is want of merit
Though the deserving man should crack his spirit.

Poetaster aroused considerable indignation. Professional soldiers suspected that their reputations were being touched. Lawyers too were angry. The players especially were indignant; Jonson's pretence that he had avoided particular individuals was too thin. It was not however only the actual words which galled them so much, as Jonson's condescending superiority to the quality. The coxcomb had forgotten, for all his air of learning, that within these four years he was himself a player, and second rate at that; and before a bricklayer. Shakespeare and the Chamberlain's men urged Dekker to get on with the work. They also arranged that the Children of Paul's should put the play on privately.

Dekker was soon ready with his play; it was named *Satiromastix, or the untrussing of the Humorous poet*. He had no store of lines from Horace barbed with double meanings, but there was ample mud on the Bankside. The only plot on hand was a partly finished drama of *The Life and Death of King William, surnamed Rufus with his lascivious wooing of Celestine, bride of Sir Walter Terrill;* he had also some scenes of low comedy concerning the wooing of an ancient and not overscrupulous widow, Mistress Miniver, with her rather dubious set of friends, Sir Rees ap Vaughan, Sir Quintilian Shorthose, Sir Adam Prickshaft and other gentry, rather in the vein of the *Shoemaker's Holiday*. The Rufus story should have been tragic, but as there was no place for Jonson by the side of a dead king, Dekker brayed the two stories together and bodged up a happy ending. Then he proceeded to deal with Jonson, taking over into *Satiromastix* English Horace, Crispinus, Demetrius, and Captain Tucca, who fitted well into Mistress Miniver's set.

In such a medley of centuries and countries it was quite unnecessary to observe any rules of decorum. Horace was introduced in the first act. The curtain was drawn aside, and there he sat in his study, the candle burning by him, books lying confusedly about. The poet was composing an epithalamium, but inspiration flagged. Asinius Bubo, Horace's faithful satellite enters, and the verses—so far as the Muse has marched—must be read to him. Dekker used his experiences of Jonson in '99 to good effect, and reproduced faithfully his mannerisms, his little repetitions of phrase, his "prithee, how, how?"; his abuse of his enemies; his magazine of epigrams, carefully prepared but discharged with an air of spontaneity; his trick of fishing for praise with a modest "Nay, prithee, good Asinius, deal plainly, do not flatter me, come, how—?"

Dekker admitted the identity of Marston and himself with Crispinus and Demetrius and brought them into his own play, with considerable effect; for they are sweet gentlemanly faced men who very mildly protest at Horace's arrogant indignation that particular men should take offence at his general censures. Captain Tucca, however, is not so squeamish. In Dekker's version he is a mixture of Jonson's Tucca, Simon Eyre, and Falstaff, with a rich vocabulary and considerable indignation with Horace, whom he plentifully bescumbers with reminiscences and nasty epithets: "thou thin-bearded hermaphrodite," "my Saracen's head at Newgate—," "ha' seen thy shoulders lapped in a player's old cast cloak, like sly knave as thou art; and when thou ran'st mad for the death of Horatio, thou borrowedst a gown of Roscius the stager (that honest Nicodemus), and sent'st it home lousy, did'st not?"

Horace in revenge writes epigrams upon Tucca which so annoy the Captain and his friends that they carry him off to Court to arraign him before King William; and here Tucca grows very eloquent. "Thou hast no part of Horace in thee," he cries, "but's name and his damnable vices. Thou hast such a terrible mouth that thy beard's afraid to peep out. But look here, you staring Leviathan, here's the sweet visage of Horace. Look, parboiled face, look: Horace had a trim long beard, and a reasonable good face for a poet (as faces go nowadays). Horace did not screw and wriggle himself into great men's familiarity, impudently, as thou dost; nor wear the badge of gentleman's company, as thou dost thy taffety sleeves, tacked to only with some points of profit. No, Horace had not his face punched full of eyelet-holes, like the cover of a warming pan. Horace loved poets well and gave coxcombs to none but fools, but thou lov'st none, neither wise men nor fools, but thyself. Horace was a goodly corpulent gentleman, and not so lean a hollow-cheeked scrag as thou art. No; having the copy of thy countenance, by this I will learn to make a number of villainous faces more, and to look scurvily upon the world, as thou dost."

They crown him with nettles and make him swear to behave himself in future with more discretion and modesty; and the episode is closed by the King with the words:

Our spirits have been well feasted. He whose pen
Draws both corrupt and clear blood from all men,
Careless what vein he pricks, let him not rave
When his own sides are struck. Blows blows do crave.

Jonson was bitterly hurt and for some time kept silent, which was taken as sure proof that he admitted defeat. At last he wrote an apologetical dialogue between Nasutus, Polyposus and the Author, which the Children pronounced at the Blackfriars. Weary and misunderstood, for these three years provoked by their petulant styles on every stage, he had but thought to try if shame could win upon them. He named no names. As for Ovid's remarks about the Law, they were his own words:

Non me verbosas leges ediscere, non me
Ingrato voces prostituisse foro.

As for the players:

it is true, I tax'd 'em,
And yet but some; and those so sparingly,
As all the rest might have sat still, unquestion'd,
Had they but had the wit, or conscience,
To think well of themselves. But impotent they
Thought each man's vice belong'd to their whole tribe:
And much good do't 'em. What th' have done 'gainst me,
I am not mov'd with. If it gave 'em meat,

> Or got 'em clothes, 'tis well; that was their end.
> Only amongst them, I am sorry for
> Some better natures, by the rest so drawn,
> To run in that vile line.

Here, he concluded, he would leave the monsters to their fate, and since the Comic Muse had proved so ominous, he would try if Tragedy had a more kind aspect; whereat the gusts of inspiration began to blow. "Leave me," said he; "there's something come into my thought,

> That must and shall be sung, high and aloof,
> Safe from the wolf's black jaw, and the dull ass's hoof."

Nasutus tiptoed away in reverence.

This apology was only once spoken, and thereafter forbidden. Authority was in no mood for further public squabbling at this time. Nor were the proprietors of the Blackfriars anxious to make another appearance in the Star Chamber. Jonson therefore parted company with the Children. His quarrel with the players was with the Chamberlain's men. The Admiral's perhaps would welcome him back. When he applied at the Fortune they had indeed work for his tragic Muse. It was high time that the *Spanish Tragedy* should be redecorated and brought up to date. On 25th September Jonson drew 40s. from Henslowe for his additions to the old play. So the whirligig of time brought its perfect revenges to the sportive ghost of melancholy Kyd.

The long-expected coming of the Spaniards to

Ireland took place in October. Three thousand soldiers were landed at Kinsale; and they brought with them artillery and stores, and many women and children. Then they set about fortifying Kinsale until Tyrone should collect his forces and unite to destroy the English. In a few weeks Lord Mountjoy had drawn his trenches round Kinsale and waited the issue with considerable anxiety, for his men would be outnumbered if the Irish joined with the Spaniards, and his men were in no condition to endure the miseries of trench warfare in the winter.

At the end of the month Parliament assembled. Its main business, as usual, was to provide for the huge costs of the war which were rapidly mounting. The assembly was less docile than usual. Many of the members were young men, infected with the general discontent of the time. They objected particularly to the growing abuse of the Queen's prerogative of granting monopolies in various commodities as a reward for service. When the Queen learnt that the grievance was genuine, she sent for the Speaker and expressed great indignation that her grants had been abused. He was told to convey to the House that the matter would be immediately remedied; and the proclamation was issued three days later. On 30th November the Queen received a large deputation of members who came to return thanks. She spoke to them affectingly of her love for her people. "To be a King," she said, "and wear a crown is more glorious to them that see it than it is a pleasure to them that wear it."

Another controversy came to a head this autumn. For many months there had been troubles amongst the Catholic priests. Wisbech Castle was used as a place of internment for prisoners, and for the better regulating of their spiritual life, an archpriest was appointed from Rome. Blackwell the archpriest was not a Jesuit, but he was under the influence of the Jesuits, a tactless, tyrannical man who demanded entire submission from the seculars. Before long the bitterest feud broke out between the secular and the Jesuit priests, for the seculars complained that most of the troubles which came upon Catholics arose because the Jesuits meddled in politics and engineered plots and attempts from abroad to assassinate the Queen. As the archpriest refused to listen to their complaints they began to appeal for the general support of the faithful. When Doctor Bancroft, Bishop of London, realised that this feud was likely to cause a split amongst the Catholics, he began to support the seculars. He obtained privileges for them and arranged for their books to be printed. The first books of the controversy were reasonably dignified, but late in the autumn there appeared four which gave the Bishop great satisfaction, particularly one inappropriately called *A sparing discourse of our English Jesuits*, for indeed it spared very little. It was particularly hot against the Jesuit doctrine of equivocation which caused intense dislike in England, for by condoning perjury it cut away the foundation of the English system of law.

Parliament broke up in time for Christmas. During the holidays, the Lord Chamberlain's players acted thrice at Court. At Cambridge the Christmas play at St. John's College was called *The Return from Parnassus:* it was full of comment and reference to the stage and its affairs. Jonson, said one of the young men, was the wittiest fellow of a bricklayer in England; to which another retorted, "A mere empiric, one that gets what he hath by observation, and makes only nature privy to what he indites; so slow an inventor that he were better betake himself to his old trade of bricklaying; a bold whorson, as confident now in making a book as he was in times past in laying of a brick."

As for Shakespeare:

> Who loves not Adon's love or Lucrece rape?
> His sweeter verse contains heart-throbbing line,
> Could but a graver subject him content,
> Without love's foolish lazy languishment.

A little later they brought Burbage and Kemp upon the stage to give a lesson in acting. This mimic Kemp had little use for the dramatic efforts of University men—few of them pen plays well: "They smell too much of that writer Metamorphosis, and talk too much of Proserpine and Jupiter. Why, here's our fellow Shakespeare puts them all down; aye, and Ben Jonson too. O that Ben Jonson's a pestilent fellow; he brought up Horace giving the poets a pill, but our fellow Shakespeare hath given him a purge that made him bewray his credit." And this was the verdict of young men upon the whole controversy.

X

THE TRAGEDY OF HAMLET

THE tragedy of the decline and fall of Robert, Earl of Essex, had roused more excitement and emotion than any event since the defeat of the Great Armada in '88; and Shakespeare, to whom one of the protagonists had meant so much, was stirred even more profoundly than most. Here was true tragedy, exuberance and waste, hubris and nemesis.

Shakespeare wrote little in the early months of the year, but in the late autumn he took up the old tragedy of *Hamlet* and rewrote it. The company had owned a play on the Hamlet story for the last dozen years and more. Originally it was a rival piece to *The Spanish Tragedy.* That play told the story of how the father of a murdered son took vengeance on the murderers. In *Hamlet* a son revenged his murdered father. It was constantly being put on and brought up to date. It had been acted during the temporary amalgamation at Newington Butts in '94, and again in '96 at the Theatre. The play pleased the wiser sort as well as the groundlings, for it touched on problems of policy and philosophy which were beyond the comprehension of the multitude.

Shakespeare now revised it so completely that there was little, if anything, left of the original dialogue. The motivation and construction had also been immeasurably improved. It was still, however, a play of revenge and there was an etiquette to be observed in such themes. In *The Spanish Tragedy* the plot was divided into three sections,—how Horatio was murdered; how Hieronimo discovered the murderers; and finally how he took an adequate and artistic revenge. Playgoers expected something rare in such dramas, for vengeance was not a matter of an eye for an eye; to be wholly satisfactory the victim should pay fuller measure than he gave in this world and perish everlastingly in the next, being cut off at some moment when there would be no opportunity for him to make his peace with Divine Providence, so that his damnation could be satisfactorily ensured. Hieronimo's ghastly dramatic revenge was a very artistic business; so too was the dreadful end of Piero in Marston's play of *Antonio's Revenge*. Kyd stressed the infernal aspect of vengeance, opening his play with the appearance of the ghost of Don Andrea and of Revenge herself, who at the close withdraws to drag off her victims to Tartarus:

> For here, though death hath end their miseries,
> I'll there begin their endless Tragedy.

Such personification was very crude and antiquated, and Shakespeare did away with it. A greater effect could be produced more naturally by suggestion.

The first scene was always a problem, and in *Hamlet* he evolved an opening which would create in the spectators the right mood, a feeling which was compounded of horror and foreboding, so that when the plot began to move they would understand that the Court of Denmark was pervaded by the faint stench of some unseen putrefaction. He opened the play with a sentry on guard anxiously waiting his relief, and jumping at the sound of approaching footsteps:

"Who's there?"
"Nay, answer me; stand, and unfold yourself."
"Long live the king!"
"Bernardo?"
"He."
"You come most carefully upon your hour."
" 'Tis now struck twelve; get thee to bed, Francisco."
"For this relief much thanks; 'tis bitter cold,
And I am sick at heart."
"Have you had quiet guard?"
"Not a mouse stirring."
"Well, good-night."
"If you do meet Horatio and Marcellus,
The rivals of my watch, bid them make haste."
"I think I hear them. Stand, ho! Who's there?"
"Friends to this ground."
"And liegemen to the Dane."
"Give you good-night."

They fall to talk of a mysterious *thing* which appears, and Horatio refuses to believe them. Then it does appear, in the same figure, like the King that is dead, and naturally they wonder what it means. Horatio declares that it portends some strange eruption in the State of Denmark; and very likely. There are all the signs of a war afoot, and he knows the Court gossip: young Fortinbras's actions are suspicious.

After this scene of orchestral overture, the story had now to move forward, and certain explanations were necessary. Shakespeare chose a method which he had already used several times. The new King Claudius presides over his first Council, and as is very natural on such occasions, begins by recapitulating the events immediately leading up to their meeting. The ambassadors are despatched to Norway. Laertes, the son of Polonius who is the chief Councillor about the Court, is given leave to go to Paris. Then Claudius turns to Hamlet, who has hitherto remained silent but conspicuous in his black, to ask him to reconsider his intention to go back to Wittenberg. Claudius and the court withdraw; Hamlet is left alone to utter the first of several soliloquies.

Shakespeare's broodings over human character first reached a fulness in *Hamlet*. He had been gradually developing his ideas on the analysis of character. Jaques was an experiment. In *Julius Cæsar* the character of Brutus was displayed rather more fully than the others, and Brutus's conflicting motives were to some extent revealed before the meeting of the conspirators; but in *Hamlet* he went much further than ever before in anatomising a mind. Self-revelation in the conditions and conventions of the little Elizabethan theatre could best be accomplished by soliloquy. He had used soliloquies often enough but hitherto they were direct, intended to convey to the audience a piece of information, either that the speaker was playing a deceitful part, or to let them know what was happening or about to happen, or else set pieces of declamation. Thus Prince Hal explained that he was far less in Falstaff's pocket than the fat knight supposed, or Benedick chattered about love and bachelors, or, earlier, Richard Crookback came forward to declare bluntly that he was determined to be a villain. In *Hamlet* for the first time Shakespeare elaborated the soliloquy to show a character exploring his own complex mentality. Such self-analysis was not entirely new in English literature. In the novels of the euphuists the artificial ladies and gentlemen would meander off into soliloquies on love and duty for pages on end, but rather for the sake of pretty parallels of image and sentence thus produced than for any deeper psychological cause. Montaigne had analysed his own emotions. More recently in English, Sir William Cornwallis in his two remarkable little books of *Essays* sat describing his own moods hour by hour.

In the first soliloquy Shakespeare revealed Hamlet's mind brooding disgustedly over the shock of his mother's remarriage. She and his father had doted upon each other almost indecently, and now she was committing incest, posthaste, with a man who had no physical attraction. In this state Horatio and Marcellus and Bernardo come upon him with the strange tale of the apparition, and he is eager to watch with them. Here at last is something to be done, a relief for one night from Claudius's interminable carousing.

This scene was followed by a passage between old Polonius and his two children, Laertes and Ophelia. Laertes, parting from his sister, warns her to beware of Hamlet, for princes however they may love must marry by policy. Polonius comes upon them, bestows a catalogue of precepts upon Laertes and hurries him off; to those who had read the famous ten precepts which the late Lord Burleigh composed for his son the episode was uncommonly like parody.

Hamlet's next soliloquy was delivered after the arrival of the players and the recitation of the Hecuba speech. The player's passionate enunciation has profoundly stirred him, reminding him that he has done nothing, and can do nothing but curse. But the incident puts an idea into his head. He will cause the players to play something like the murder and then he will know for certain; for the ghost might indeed have been a devil or an illusion; such illusions were a common symptom in the advanced stages of melancholy; and those who wrote treatises on the subject gave strange examples of hallucination. Shakespeare used this soliloquy with triple intention; it showed the intensifying of Hamlet's mood of disgust, explained his delay, and revealed his mind working towards the next stage in the drama.

Again after the play scene, Shakespeare revealed the movement of Hamlet's mind. As Hamlet, now keyed up for vengeance, passes on his way to see his mother, he comes upon Claudius at prayer. He draws his sword and approaches stealthily:

> Now might I do it pat, now he is praying;
> And now I'll do't; and so he goes to heaven;
> And so am I reveng'd. That would be scann'd;
> A villain kills my father; and for that,
> I, his sole son, do this same villain send
> To heaven.

But as he raises his arm for the stroke, there comes back to him the murder which is about to be revenged, the other murder in the garden, and the ghost's most bitter complaint:

> Thus was I, sleeping, by a brother's hand
> Of life, of crown, of queen, at once dispatch'd;
> Cut off even in the blossoms of my sin,
> Unhousel'd, disappointed, unanel'd,
> No reckoning made, but sent to my account
> With all my imperfections on my head.

These were the words which throbbed in Hamlet's mind in the unspoken beats of the unfinished blank verse line. He lowers his sword and continues:

> Why, this is hire and salary, not revenge.
> He took my father grossly, full of bread,
> With all his crimes broad blown, as flush as May;
> And how his audit stands who knows save heaven?
> But in our circumstance and course of thought
> 'Tis heavy with him. And am I then reveng'd,
> To take him in the purging of his soul,
> When he is fit and season'd for his passage?

There was no hell-fire here. Hamlet must wait to take his uncle:

> At gaming, swearing, or about some act
> That has no relish of salvation in't;
> Then trip him, that his heels may kick at heaven,
> And that his soul may be as damn'd and black
> As hell, whereto it goes.

Up to this point the play followed the pattern of revenge drama. The first part showed how the duty of vengeance was laid upon Prince Hamlet; the second how Prince Hamlet proved his uncle guilty; and a third should follow to show how Hamlet took vengeance. Shakespeare now set his plot in a new direction and began a second revenge play. Hamlet goes to his mother and, as before when his emotions were aroused, his mind erupts his disgust at sex, and particularly at his mother's sexuality, and his detailed broodings over her marriage with his uncle. As prelude to this violent scene Polonius injudiciously utters a cry and is despatched; and hereby the filial duty of vengeance is laid upon Polonius' son Laertes.

Hamlet is now packed off to England to be murdered quietly and disappears from sight. At the Danish Court Ophelia's mind gives way under her sorrows and she goes mad. Laertes having heard confused rumours of his father's death, returns at the head of a mob of Danes to demand revenge. Claudius pacifies him, when letters come from Hamlet that he is landed in Denmark, and is alone. Claudius makes up his mind quickly. He works upon Laertes' emotion and easily persuades him to undertake Hamlet's murder under the guise of a seeming accident. Whilst they are discussing the details the Queen enters with the news that Ophelia is drowned.

The plot was now ripe for the consummation of both revenge themes; and as he would have the final episode in the play a unity in itself Shakespeare began the last act leisurely and with comedy. The sexton and his mate set about digging a grave for Ophelia. The nice point whether or not she should be given Christian burial touches professional interest, but death is all in their day's work and a man must labour in his vocation. Hamlet and Horatio come upon him; and as the sexton flings up skulls and bones from the earth Hamlet perceives that this is but another aspect of the futility of existence. "Here's fine revolution and we had the trick to see't," he remarks, "Did these bones cost no more the breeding but to play at loggats with them?" The lesson is brought home to him when the sexton produces a skull of a man whom they both had known, Yorick the King's jester:

> Alas! poor Yorick. I knew him, Horatio; a fellow of infinite jest, of most excellent fancy; he hath borne me on his back a thousand times; and now, how abhorred in my imagination it is! my gorge rises at it.

Then comes the funeral of Ophelia which Shakespeare staged very simply, making his solitary priest to follow, instead of leading, the coffin. The sudden quarrel between Laertes and Hamlet abruptly changed the emotion of the scene from sorrow to passion, and when the curtain closed over the grave the last episode of the play was ready to begin.

Shakespeare was almost reluctant to let the play end. He began the last scene with Hamlet and Horatio in conversation and the explanation of Hamlet's return. Then he prolonged the suspense and again lowered the emotion to comedy by bringing on the overdressed young Osric with his fashionable jargon and affected ways—Shakespeare could teach even Jonson a thing or two in sketching a court ape, and that in a couple of gestures without the tedious mechanism of Jonson's introductory descriptions. The challenge which Osric bore accepted, the whole court was brought upon the stage to watch the combat between Laertes and Hamlet. The end came quickly as Fate pricked off her victims, first the Queen, then Claudius stabbed by Hamlet, Laertes, and last of all Hamlet himself; so that all plots met in one centre.

But as in all his tragedies Shakespeare diffused the intensity of tragic emotion before dismissing his audience, for it was not his method to leave a tragic theme until he had shown how life was continued. Before Hamlet was dead the roll of drums was heard, heralding the approach of Fortinbras and his army. So Hamlet was carried pompously to his burial to the sound of a dead march, and when the stage was emptied the play ended with a peal of cannon.

Hamlet was full of reminiscence and passing comment on men and events. In the old play which he rewrote Shakespeare found that Ophelia was made to throw herself from a cliff; but the title of the play put him in mind of a tragedy of his youth. In the winter after he was fifteen a girl of Tiddington, about a mile from Stratford, fell into the water and was drowned at a spot where the Avon's banks in summer are overhung by willows and thickly crowned with wild flowers. He embalmed the memory of the place and the event in an elaborate dirge for Ophelia:

> There is a willow, grows aslant a brook,
> That shows his hoar leaves in the glassy stream:
> There with fantastic garlands did she come
> Of crow flowers, nettles, daisies and long purples. . . .

It was not surprising that the story of twenty years ago should have come to him, for the girl's name was

Katharine Hamlet. This, however, was an old, sentimental memory.

Hamlet's advice to the players before they acted his plays was a natural opportunity for observation on the rivalries of the Chamberlain's men with other companies, and Shakespeare used it to state the dramatic creed of his own company and for an attack, hardly disguised, upon Alleyn and his hyperbolical methods:

"Speak the speech, I pray you, as I pronounced it to you, trippingly on the tongue; but if you mouth it, as many of your players do, I had as lief the town-crier spoke my lines. Nor do not saw the air too much with your hand, thus; but use all gently: for in the very torrent, tempest, and—as I may say—whirlwind of passion, you must acquire and beget a temperance, that may give it smoothness. O! it offends me to the soul to hear a robustious periwig-pated fellow tear a passion to tatters, to very rags, to split the ears of the groundlings, who for the most part are capable of nothing but inexplicable dumb-shows and noise: I would have such a fellow whipped for o'er-doing Termagant; it out-herods Herod: pray you avoid it."

"I warrant your honour."

"Be not too tame neither, but let your own discretion be your tutor: suit the action to the word, the word to the action; with this special observance, that you o'erstep not the modesty of nature; for anything so overdone is from the purpose of playing, whose end, both at the first and now, was and is, to hold, as 'twere, the mirror up to nature; to show virtue her own feature, scorn her own image, and the very age and body of the time his form and pressure. Now, this overdone, or come tardy off, though it make the unskilful laugh, cannot but make the judicious grieve; the censure of which one must in your allowance o'er-weigh a whole theatre of others. O! there be players that I have seen play, and heard others praise, and that highly, not to speak it profanely, that, neither having the accents of Christians nor the gait of Christian, pagan, nor man, have so strutted and bellowed that I have thought some of nature's journeymen had made men and not made them well, they imitated humanity so abominably."

Then he set about Kemp. Kemp had fulfilled his plan of dancing to Rome but the trip was a failure, and in September, 1601, he was back in London. The Chamberlain's men had no room for him. He was now bringing prosperity to Worcester's men who were playing at the Rose:

"And let those that play your clowns speak no more than is set down for them; for there be of them that will themselves laugh, to set on some quantity of barren spectators to laugh, too, though in the meantime some necessary question of the play be then to be considered; that's villainous, and shows a most pitiful ambition in the fool that uses it. And then you have some again that keep one suit of jests as a man is known by one suit of apparel; and gentlemen quote his jests down in their tables before they come to the play, as thus: 'Cannot you stay till I eat my porridge?' and 'You owe me a quarter's wages'; and, 'My coat wants a cullison'; and 'Your beer is sour'; and blabbering with his lips, and thus keeping in his cinquepace of jests, when, God knows, the warm clown cannot make a jest unless by chance, as the blind man catcheth a hare. Masters tell him of it."

Earlier, on hearing of the players' arrival Hamlet glanced at the stage war and the disastrous competition of the children:

"What players are they?"

"Even those you were wont to take delight in, the tragedians of the city."

"How chances it they travel? their residence, both in reputation and profit, was better both ways."

"I think their inhibition comes by the means of the late innovation."

"Do they hold the same estimation they did when I was in the city? Are they so followed?"

"No, indeed they are not."

"How comes it? Do they grow rusty?"

"Nay, their endeavour keeps in the wonted pace: but there is, sir, an aery of children, little eyases, that cry out on the top of question, and are most tyrannically clapped for't: these are now the fashion, and so berattle the common stages,—so they call them,—that many wearing rapiers are afraid of goose-quills, and dare scarce come thither."

"What! are they children? who maintains 'em? how are they escoted? Will they pursue the quality no longer than they can sing? will they not say afterwards, if they should grow themselves to common players,—as it is most like, if their means are no better,—their writers do them wrong, to make them exclaim against their own succession?"

"Faith, there has been much to-do on both sides: and the nation holds it no sin to tarre them to controversy: there was, for a while, no money bid for argument, unless the poet and the player went to cuffs in the question."

"Is it possible?"

"O! there has been much throwing about of brains."

"Do the boys carry it away?"

"Ay, that they do, my lord; Hercules and his load too."

Again in the play scene, wishing to emphasise the difference between acting and ranting, Shakespeare made his players produce their play in the Alleyn manner. Their drama was written in hyperbolical and bombastic language, prefaced by an inexplicable dumb-show which is quite beyond Ophelia's comprehension, and the murderer before he gets to business must overact his emotions, gesticulating and mowing over the sleeping victim.

On Essex and his tragedy there were passing comments:

> The single and peculiar life is bound
> With all the strength and armour of the mind
> To keep itself from noyance; but much more
> That spirit upon whose weal depend and rest
> The lives of many. The cease of majesty
> Dies not alone, but like a gulf doth draw
> What's near it with it; it is a massy wheel,
> Fix'd on the summit of the highest mount,
> To whose huge spokes ten thousand lesser things
> Are mortis'd and adjoin'd; which, when it falls,
> Each small annexment, petty consequence,
> Attends the boisterous ruin. Never alone
> Did the king sigh, but with a general groan.

And even more significant, in the incident where Laertes broke in upon the King; for here the scene was very close to what might have happened on the 8th February, a few months before had Essex broken through to the Presence in Whitehall:

> Let him go, Gertrude; do not fear our person:
> There's such divinity doth hedge a King,
> That treason can but peep to what it would,
> Acts little of his will.

But not only did he comment; Shakespeare put more of himself in *Hamlet* than ever before. Of late years, as his comprehension deepened he was infusing even the most trivial story with his own experience and using the drama as a vessel for his most intimate thoughts. *Hamlet* was full of them, on sorrow, on drunkenness, on sleep and death and life, on true courage and nobility, on fate, on mortality and faith and love, on the Universe. In this final version it was written in settled dejection, and though he could still admit that man was the beauty of the world, it was an outward perception of no avail to lift the smothering weight from off his breast. This thought was brought home to him by a passage in a little book that came out in the autumn of 1601, written by a certain William Parry and entitled *A new and large discourse of the Travels of Sir Anthony Shirley*. It was an astounding narrative, for Shirley had journeyed over Europe to Italy, thence by ship to Antioch, and so to Aleppo down the Euphrates to Babylon, across to the Tigris and into Persia where he stayed for some time in the Court of the Sophy at Kasvin. Thence, being appointed special ambassador of the Sophy, he went by the Caspian Sea to Moscow and at last, after many adventures, left Archangel and returned to Italy by the Baltic and Germany.

Parry had something to say of travel and the lofty conceptions which it bred. "To see," said he, "those resplendent and crystalline heavens overcanopying the earth, invested most sumptuously in height of Nature's pride with her richest livery, the particularities whereof, were they described according to the truth of their nature, it might breed a scruple in natural man whether Man were, for transgression, ever unimparadised or no." But to Hamlet in his dejection, "It goes so heavily with my disposition, that this goodly frame the earth, seems to me a sterile promontory, this most excellent canopy the air, look you, this brave o'erhanging firmament, this majestical roof fretted with golden fire, why it appeareth nothing to me but a foul and pestilent congregation of vapours. What a piece of work is a man, how noble in reason, how infinite in faculties, in form and moving, how express and admirable in action, how like an angel in apprehension, how like a god: the beauty of the world; the paragon of animals; and yet, to me, what is this quintessence of dust?"

XI

END OF AN EPOCH

AT the beginning of the year 1602 good news came to London from both theatres of war. In Ireland Lord Mountjoy defeated Tyrone with great slaughter when he came up to relieve Kinsale; twelve hundred Irish dead were counted on the field, and eight hundred wounded, of whom many died, and the rest were hanged. The English losses were reported as one killed and eight wounded.

In Ostend Sir Francis Vere once more rebuffed the Archduke. Just before Christmas through shortness of men, munitions and supplies, Sir Francis realised that he could not hope to hold out against the assault which the enemy were obviously about to deliver. He was thus forced to play for time, and to gain respite he offered to parley with the enemy. The Archduke sent over officers to negotiate, but by various pretexts Sir Francis put them off till Christmas Eve when he received them at his headquarters, feasting them that night and promising to open discussions next morning. When morning came, the long expected reinforcements had arrived in harbour, and the Spaniards were sent back with Vere's regrets that in the circumstances he could not in honour proceed with the negotiations.

Three days later a furious bombardment was opened. Vere made every preparation possible, but he could only muster twelve hundred fit men to resist an army of ten thousand. That night the enemy came on, and endeavoured to storm the defences at all points. Assault and defence were desperate, but the defenders held fast, and at last the Spaniards retreated leaving two thousand dead before the ramparts, and a vast quantity of arms, material and booty.

So the defence against the sea and the enemy went on, whilst the stoutest and bravest soldiers of the Low Countries, Spain, England, France, Scotland and Italy, eagerly contended for a barren plot of sand, and found there, as it were, one common sepulchre, and an eternal monument to their valour. Here, if ever, was an example of true manhood; and Shakespeare, much moved by these stirring events, added yet another passage to *Hamlet:*

> Examples gross as earth exhort me:
> Witness this army of such mass and charge
> Led by a delicate and tender prince,
> Whose spirit with divine ambition puff'd
> Makes mouths at the invisible event,
> Exposing what is mortal and unsure
> To all that fortune, death and danger dare,
> Even for an egg-shell. Rightly to be great
> Is not to stir without great argument,
> But greatly to find quarrel in a straw
> When honour's at the stake. How stand I then,
> That have a father kill'd, a mother stain'd,

Excitements of my reason and my blood,
And let all sleep, while, to my shame, I see
The imminent death of twenty thousand men,
That, for a fantasy and trick of fame,
Go to their graves like beds, fight for a plot
Whereon the numbers cannot try the cause,
Which is not tomb enough and continent
To hide the slain? O! from this time forth,
My thoughts be bloody, or be nothing worth!

In the middle of January news came that the Spaniards in Kinsale had surrendered upon honourable terms.

Another of Shakespeare's plays appeared early in the year. John Busby, who printed *Henry the Fifth* in 1600, had obtained a version of *The Merry Wives of Windsor* which he entered on 18th January, and immediately transferred to Arthur Johnson. The text which Johnson produced was quite as bad as *Henry the Fifth.*

The Merry Wives of Windsor had been another command performance. The Queen was so delighted with Falstaff that she ordered Shakespeare to continue him for another play and to show him in love. Shakespeare produced the play in a fortnight.

These command performances were always embarrassing; and as before, he turned over the old playbooks until he came upon a comedy of jealousy which could be converted into some kind of setting for Falstaff. Some of the old favourites reappeared. Falstaff was still squired by a Pistol, a Nym and a Bardolph. Justice Shallow and Mistress Quickly returned, but, like Bottom's companions after the dream, they had forgotten their former existence. Mistress Quickly *rediviva* of Windsor was more respectable than the quondam Quickly, and now acted as housekeeper to a French doctor, one Dr. Caius. The Justice had forgotten the recent friendship with Sir John and was for bringing him up before the Council for riotous behaviour. Bardolph and Pistol were wofully bated but Corporal Nym was more stuffed with humours than ever.

For all his haste in this play Shakespeare tried his hand, for the first time, at a play of contemporary manners, his own version of a comedy of humours, but without the moral purpose which Jonson claimed for himself; and he worked in similar situations and characters. Justice Shallow was provided with a nephew in Master Slender who was cousin-german to Stephano, and the jealous Ford was of Thorello's kindred; Sir Hugh Evans, however, parson and schoolmaster, was entirely Shakespeare's own.

The plot was full of loose ends. It began with a scene between Justice Shallow, who has a promising grievance against Falstaff, but Shallow and his affairs are quite forgotten in a quarrel between the Welsh parson and the French doctor which is patched up by the Host. The real business of Falstaff as lover then goes forward. He imagines that Mistress Ford is in love with him and thereby provokes the dame and her gossip, Mistress Page, to vengeance. The rest of the play, except for occasional digressions into the affairs of Anne Page, is taken up with Falstaff's intrigue. The knight, who is far from being at home amongst Windsor citizens, is sadly baffled, twice thinks that he has reached his goal but each time Ford comes back and Sir John is bustled out of the house, first in a basket of dirty linen and then disguised as a witch.

As with *A Midsummer Night's Dream* children were made available for the players, and so the final scene of Falstaff's ignominy was set at Herne's Oak where Falstaff was bidden to disguise himself as Herne the Hunter with a buck's head upon him, and was there pinched and burnt for his lecherous desires by the children dressed up as fairies.

It was not a great play, but it was full of rollicking scenes which moved so fast that even if Sir John Falstaff seemed to have lost his old knack of getting out of scrapes there was at least the consolation that his discomfiture was all very good fun. Falstaff in love, even by royal command, could hardly be expected to behave like an Arcadian shepherd; nor was he of the build for a romantic lover.

On the 2nd February the Chamberlain's men performed Shakespeare's latest comedy in the hall of the Middle Temple. It was called *Twelfth Night or What You Will*. His last comedy, if it could be called so, was *Troilus and Cressida*, a play which purged by its excess of bitterness. The new play presented a well-known story of how a sister and a brother, separated by shipwreck, each supposed the other dead until after various strange chances they were reunited; but Shakespeare in these weeks recaptured a mood which had deserted him for years and escaped from bitter realities into a land of fancy and true love. In *Troilus* he showed love as an emotion so vile that men pretended it was noble; earlier, in *As You Like It*, he had been ironic at the romantical hyperboles of young people who wished to mate; never a man, said Rosalind, died for love. Nevertheless women could die for love sometimes; and a few months after *As You Like It* was written there was a notable and pathetic example. In the early summer of 1599 one of the Maids of Honour who waited on the Queen was named Margaret Ratcliffe. Her brother Sir Alexander Ratcliffe, a gallant and experienced soldier, was serving in Ireland under Essex. In June the report came that he was killed in action. The love between brother and sister was well known, and the Queen herself undertook to break the news. Thereafter Margaret Ratcliffe pined away, refusing food sometimes for two days together. She lived until the autumn and then on 12th November she died of grief. The Queen caused the body to be opened, and it was found well and sound except for certain strings striped all over the heart. The lady was buried as a nobleman's daughter in Westminster Abbey. Her pathetic death was much talked of, and Ben Jonson wrote a poor epigram upon her:

M arble, weep for thou dost cover
A dead beauty underneath thee,
R ich as nature could bequeath thee:
G rant then no rude hand remove her.
A ll the gazers on the skies
R ead not in fair heaven's story,
E xpresses truth, or truer glory,
T han they might in her bright eyes.

R are as wonder was her wit;
A nd like nectar, ever flowing:
T ill Time, strong by her bestowing,
C onquered hath both life and it;
L ife whose grief was out of fashion
I n these times. Few so have rued
F ate in a brother. To conclude,
F or wit, feature and true passion,
E arth thou hast not such another.

The tale which Shakespeare translated into *Twelfth Night* was very popular; it had been told in half a dozen or more collections of tales, and there was an English version in Barnabe Riche's *Farewell to Military Profession.* His story was called "Apolonius and Silla." Apolonius was a young Duke of Constantinople, of great possessions, who made an expedition against the Turk. On his return his ship was driven to Cyprus where he was worthily entertained by Pontus, the Duke and Governor of that Island. Pontus had two children, Silvio and Silla. Silla, his daughter, fell deeply in love with Duke Apolonius, but he was too greatly occupied with his own martial thoughts to notice her encouraging glances. When Apolonius had gone Silla persuaded Pedro her servant to pass her off as her sister, and make the voyage to Constantinople. At sea the captain of the galley was so much attracted by his passenger that he began first to woo and then to threaten her; but Silla's chastity was saved, for a great storm arose, and after a long tossing the ship was cast on shore, Silla riding the waves on a chest of the captain's clothes. Being thus cast alone on a foreign shore, Silla bethought her of the dangers which might happen to an unprotected woman, and being still as fervent as ever to have a sight of her Apolonius she dressed herself in the captain's clothes, took the money which she found in the chest, and assumed her brother's name of Silvio. So she made her way to Constantinople, presented herself to the Duke, and craved his service; and in a short time the supposed Silvio was well advanced in his favour.

Now there was present in Constantinople a wealthy widow called Julina, as wealthy as she was beautiful; to this lady Duke Apolonius became a suitor, and who must be the constant messenger of his love but his Silvio. Julina being thus continually visited by this handsome young courtier fell in love and declared her passion.

By this time the real Silvio, who guessed the reason of Silla's flight, and her destination, was come to Constantinople, and there, as he was taking the air, the Lady Julina met him, and mistaking him for his disguised sister, she called him by name, and invited him to her house. Silvio was surprised to hear himself invited by name but realising that it would be a point of great simplicity if he should forsake that which Fortune so favourably proffered, he accepted her invitation for supper on the following evening at her palace. Supper being ended, Julina would not let her guest go home, and, when the servants were in bed and quiet, she came to Silvio and spent the rest of the night with him till morning.

When Silvio began to ponder the adventure, he felt sure that there had been a mistake and thought it more discreet to continue his journey. The Duke continued to press his suit. Julina told him that she was now married; and when his servants began to report how kindly she used to receive Silvio, the Duke in anger caused his former favourite to be thrust into a dungeon. At length Julina, perceiving by developments that her reputation was in hazard, went to the Duke. Silvio was called before them and protested innocency, to Julina's and the Duke's growing indignation; but when Julina taunted Silvio with having gotten her with child, the unfortunate girl realised that things were now in such a pretty tangle that she must give up her secret. She therefore led Julina aside and revealed her sex. Whereat the Duke was so amazed at her devotion that he appointed the marriage day and wed Silla with great triumph.

The fame of this strange and wonderful matter was soon spread abroad through all Greece, and so came to the ears of the real Silvio who hastened back to Constantinople, where after explanations had passed between the Duke and himself he returned to Julina. "And thus, Silvio having attained a noble wife, and Silla, his sister, her desired husband, they passed the residue of their days with such delight as those that have accomplished the perfection of their felicities."

The story was not more fantastic than the others which Shakespeare had turned into comedy. Its theme, which was common to many plays and innumerable pleasant discourses, was that a maid in love will endure anything to win her man. Shakespeare, however, in transmuting the story into drama, changed the stress, making less of the love story of the Duke and the Countess, and elevating the theme of the love between sister and brother, so that the climax of the play was the reunion of Viola and Sebastian. Moreover he converted the widow into a Countess, also mourning the loss of a dead brother.

Then he began to plot the auxiliary story which was necessary in any play and he plundered some of the types of the comedy of humours: a gull, a waggish servant—but a woman not a man, a tippling knight of the kind that often attached himself to a great house, a Puritan. Ranging back over the last eighteen months Shakespeare remembered two notable incidents in which a Puritan was involved. The first was the great case of Darrell the exorcist which was a matter for controversy for four years.

It was long one of the practices of the Jesuits in the northern counties to claim the power to drive out evil spirits from those possessed. In 1596, however, one John Darrell, a Puritan preacher, began to win a reputation as an exorcist. His first case was the notorious episode of Thomas Darling, "the Boy of Burton." Darling was taken with fits and hallucinations, and would see green angels standing in the window and similar manifestations. A local witch was suspected and duly condemned. In the later stages of the case Darrell was brought in to see the boy and declared him to be possessed with an unclean spirit. Next day Darrell set about an exercise of prayer, and after a lengthy wrestle with the Evil One the boy was suddenly and strangely cured.

In March 1597 there was a most sensational case in Lancashire where seven persons in the family of Master Nicholas Starkie of Cleworth were all possessed, Master Starkie's son and daughter, three young girls living in the house, and two women of thirty years and more. A man witch named Hartley was accused and hanged, but as the manifestations continued after his death, Darrell was pressed to come. At first he refused the invitations but at length consented, and with George More, another preacher, he set about the evil spirits. The battle was long and fierce; from seven in the morning till three in the afternoon they prayed continuously, and then, as if Satan was much disturbed by their fasting and prayer, all seven victims suddenly began to bell and roar in fearful manner trying to cry down the voices of the preachers. This contest continued for nearly two hours, and the preachers were almost exhausted; but Satan gave in first, and the possessed were suddenly quietened in a deathlike stillness. When they came to, all declared that the evil spirit had passed out of them.

There was a similar case at Nottingham in the November, when a boy called Sommers was also afflicted. Again Darrell was successful, and the people of Nottingham asked him to remain amongst them as their preacher. Unfortunately a great controversy now broke out. The boy Sommers confessed that he was a fraud. Darrell preached violently against him, but the dispute became so violent that in March 1598 the Archbishop of York ordered a commission of inquiry to be held. Sommers was brought before them, and directly after he had sworn that all his previous manifestations were counterfeit, he was seized with a great fit and wallowed up and down the chamber where the inquiry was being held. The same thing happened at the next meeting. Darrell was thus triumphantly vindicated.

The Archbishop of Canterbury grew alarmed, for manifold inconveniences might follow if a Puritan preacher should gain such a hold on the imaginations of the people. Darrell was therefore summoned before the Ecclesiastical commission and imprisoned at Lambeth. The boy Darling was also brought to London, and lodged by himself in the Bishop of London's house. Here, by sundry suggestions, including a visit to a public execution, he was persuaded to confess that he too had counterfeited. When he was set at liberty, he was allowed to visit Darrell, and immediately withdrew his confession.

Darrell in the eyes of his supporters was thus once more vindicated and was by many looked on as a martyr in the cause of truth. He and More remained in prison for several months. He was again brought before the commissioners in May, 1599. When he was confronted with the confessions of the possessed, especially Darling's, he retorted that they had been extorted by fraud and violence and that such strange manifestations could not have been counterfeited.

Accordingly the Bishop of London, who was a great believer in the press, set Mr. Harsnett, his chaplain, to work to write up the case against the exorcists, and in the autumn of 1599 his book, *A discovery of the fraudulent practises of John Darrell*, appeared. It set out the evidence in great detail. Darrell's friends were indignant, and retorted with pamphlets in his defence, impugning the justice of the proceedings. The most important answer however came from Darrell's assistant More, who in 1600 published a long and detailed account of the Lancashire possessions, his main object being to confute the Jesuits who were denouncing the Puritan exorcisms as fraudulent, though they had themselves won over one of the possessed women and were exhibiting her in the country.

Shakespeare determined to make some use of this controversy and he submitted his Puritan to a charge of possession and a feigned exorcism. More's book was full of interesting details. When the Starkie children saw the preachers reach out for a Bible they began to mock them, crying out, "Reach them the bibble-babble, bibble-babble." The girl's evil spirit was apparently the spirit of pride, for she would talk to it and demand fashionable and worldly clothing, a smock and a petticoat of silk, and a French farthingale, and cork shoes of red Spanish leather, and hose of orange colour for these were in the fashion.

The other incident that furnished Shakespeare with ideas was a case in the Star Chamber which caused a good deal of merriment in the winter of 1601. In 1596 Sir Thomas Posthumus Hoby married, as her third husband, Margaret widow of Thomas Sidney, a lady who in her own right possessed considerable property at Hackness in Yorkshire, whither they went to live. Sir Thomas, however, was not well suited to the hearty life of a Yorkshire county gentleman. He was very small, and his neighbours used to call him "the little knight that useth to draw up his breeches with a shoeing horn"; he was litigious; and both he and his wife were puritanical. He was therefore not popular with other gentlemen his neighbours. In August 1600 a party of them, who had been out hunting, came to his mansion at Hackness and invited themselves for the night. Sir Thomas, who had previously sent word that they would not be welcome, sat grudgingly with his guests at supper, when they entertained each other in discourses of horses and dogs (sports unto which Sir Thomas never applied himself), partly in lascivious talk and great oaths, partly in inordinate drinking of healths (an abuse never practised by Sir Thomas). After supper Sir Thomas had their chambers made ready, and came to conduct them thither himself, but they answered that they would finish their game of dice first. Hoby descended to the hall to family prayers, and when the strains of a psalm mounted upwards, the revellers began to stamp with their feet and to make other rude noises. Next morning at breakfast, when they called for more wine, Sir Thomas sent for the key of the cellar to prevent it. They then fell again to play, and shortly after, one of his servants came out and told them peremptorily that their play was offensive to Lady Hoby and willed them to depart the house. Hoby meanwhile had shut himself in the study. The leader of the party therefore craved admittance to Lady Hoby and took his leave. They then left the mansion with many noisy threats and much abuse, even calling its master a scurvy urchin and a spindle-shanked ape.

Sir Thomas petitioned the Council for redress, and after the usual passing to and fro of complaints and answers, the case came before the Star Chamber in January 1602. There was good matter for a play in this story.

There were other casual topicalities in the play, especially in the scene where Feste brought Olivia's message to Viola.

> "To see this age!" said he. "A sentence is but a cheveril glove to a good wit: how quickly the wrong side may be turned outward!"
>
> "Nay, that's certain; they that dally nicely with words may quickly make them wanton."
>
> "I would therefore my sister had had no name, sir."
>
> "Why, man?"
>
> "Why, sir, her name's a word; and to dally with that word might make my sister wanton. But indeed, words are very rascals since bonds disgraced them."

To the audience of lawyers in the Middle Temple these quips were reminiscent of the raging controversy over equivocation and, too, of a very unsavoury case which occupied the Star Chamber in the summer of 1600. A certain Mistress Fowler, very well known about the city, leaving the society of her husband, turned prostitute, and employed her own brother to act as her bawd and pander. At length she became the mistress of a self-styled Captain Haynes. The three worthies then plotted to have the wronged husband put out of the way and caused charges of high treason to be framed against him. It was only after Master Fowler had lain six months in the Tower that the sordid business was brought to light. All three were suitably punished, to the scandalised amusement of the town.

At the conclusion of the same scene Shakespeare went out of his way to give a compliment to Armin the company's clown. One of Armin's particular accomplishments was to compose extempore verses. He would ask the audience to suggest a subject, and thereupon would produce a poem out of his head. Shakespeare had used this habit in *As You Like It*, for when Rosalind appeared with Orlando's verses, all rhyming with her name, Touchstone (played by Armin) retorted with a few more of his own. Armin had published a collection of these trifles in 1600 during the lean weeks caused by the Council's inhibition on playing, and one of the pieces was on the Fool:

> True it is, he plays the fool indeed;
> But in the play, he plays it as he must;
> Yet when the play is ended, then his speech
> Is better than the pleasure of thy trust:
>   For he shall have what thou that time has spent,
>   Playing the fool thy folly to content.
>
> He plays the wise man then, and not the fool,
> That wisely for his living so can do:
> So doth the carpenter with his sharp tool,
> Cut his own finger oft, yet lives by 't too.
>   He is a fool to cut his limb, say I,
>   But not so with his tool to live thereby. . . .

Armin ended this extempore effort with a quip which ran:

> A merry man is often thought unwise,
> Yet mirth in modesty's lov'd of the wise:
> Then say, should he for a fool go?
> When he's a more fool that accounts him so?
> Many men descant on another's wit,
> When they have less themselves in doing it.

Shakespeare, at leisure, produced a revised version:

> This fellow's wise enough to play the fool
> And to do that with craves a kind of wit.
> He must observe their mood on whom he jests,
> The quality of persons, and the time,
> Not, like the haggard, check at every feather
> That comes before his eye. This is a practice
> As full of labour as a wise man's art;
> For folly that he wisely shows is fit;
> But wise men folly-fall'n, quite taint their wit.

It was an encouragement to Armin, and pointed the contrast between the new comedian and the old Clown at the Rose.

Having thus collected the materials for his comedy, Shakespeare began to work on the detail of the plot. Amongst those who criticised plays there had been a good deal of talk of art and construction; and he had himself erred by paying too little attention to the niceties of plot making. In this play he showed that he too could construct a flawless plot when he wished. He set the play in a land of fancy which he called Illyria, opening with a scene that would suggest the tone and atmosphere in which the comedy was conceived—musical, fantastical, melancholy. It began with music, and the curtains were drawn to reveal the Duke Orsino brooding on love.

He returned to this mood after this noisy interlude of the drunken knights, with its promise of mirth to come, in a scene full of musical melancholy, wherein Cesario, falling in with Orsino's broodings, in the safety of disguise defended womankind from the Duke's easy generality that the love of woman was but appetite:

> "My father had a daughter lov'd a man,
> As it might be, perhaps, were I a woman,
> I should your lordship. . . ."
> "And what's her history?"
> "A blank, my lord. She never told her love,
> But let concealment, like a worm i' the bud,
> Feed on her damask cheek: she pin'd in thought,
> And with a green and yellow melancholy,
> She sat like Patience on a monument,
> Smiling at grief. Was not this love indeed?"

It was a palinode for Cressida.

To contrast with this scene of lyrical expectation, he then resumed the plot of the Puritan's undoing.

It was customary to end a comedy with a jig, but Shakespeare was unwilling to spoil the effect of his play. He ended, as he began, in music, giving the clown a little song, which was in effect a miniature jig, of the frivolity of man's life:

When that I was and a little tiny boy,
  With hey, ho, the wind and the rain;
A foolish thing was but a toy,
  For the rain it raineth every day. . . .

A great while ago the world begun,
  With hey, ho, the wind and the rain;
But that's all one, our play is done,
  And we'll strive to please you every day.

Twelfth Night was but a toy, or what you will; but how pleasant a change from this snarling business of setting the world to rights.

In public life an air of anxious expectancy was developing. Now that Essex was dead and his followers were without a cause, the question of the succession became simpler. For some years the claims of James of Scotland were gradually becoming stronger, and in this year it was noted that many of the nobility were in communication with some of the great men in the Scottish Court. There were other claimants. Some were for the Lady Arabella. The Jesuits would have put the Infanta of Spain on the throne, but there was no general support for a Spanish princess. Essex indeed had tried to bring Sir Robert Cecil into odium by proclaiming that the Secretary stood for the Infanta, a lie which was very decisively rebutted at the trial. Cecil was quietly playing his own hand, but not for a Catholic. However, for the present, the Queen was in excellent health, though her temper was somewhat uneven.

This March Shakespeare was the subject of a table jest, which ran that when Burbage played Richard the Third, a citizen's wife fell in love with him, and invited him to come to her that night, and to give the name of "Richard the Third." Shakespeare overheard the conversation, and supplanted his partner by arriving first. When the message came that Richard the Third was at the door, he sent back word that William the Conqueror came before Richard the Third.

Prosperity was returning to the public theatres now that the restrictions of the last two years were relaxed, and in May Shakespeare further strengthened his position at Stratford by the purchase of 107 acres of land at Stratford for which he gave £320.

In July the Chamberlain's men had reason to suspect that a pirated copy existed of *The Tragical History of Hamlet, Prince of Denmark.* Roberts therefore was approached, and as before forestalled printing by entering his copy in the Stationers' Register on the 26th July.

As the year wore to its close, it was obvious that the great change was imminent. The Queen's health was failing, and her temper was becoming more difficult; but Christmas at Court was very gay, with plays, bear baiting and much dancing.

At the beginning of March 1603, however, the Countess of Nottingham, who was one of the Queen's oldest friends, died, and thereafter the Queen seemed almost suddenly to leave go of her hold upon life. She complained much of aches and pains, lost interest in affairs of state, and grew very melancholy. She suffered too from sleeplessness. The Council were alarmed, but for a few days the danger seemed to have passed. Then she grew worse. The Council began to take precautions. Commanders of garrisons were warned to be ready for emergency; rogues about the City were pressed as soldiers and shipped off to the Low Countries; watches in the City were strengthened.

On the 19th March the Lord Mayor and justices of Middlesex and Surrey were commanded to restrain stage plays until new direction should be given. There would be no more playing before Queen Elizabeth.

For the Chamberlain's Men and for Shakespeare it was the end of a chapter. They had played together now for more than eight years, forming an unique fellowship of players, dramatist, and an audience trained into harmony. It was only eleven years since the scenes of brave Talbot first roused the enthusiasm of Londoners; less than ten since Marlowe died, and *Venus and Adonis* was printed. Ten years was a short time in which to create so full a company as peopled such plays—*Richard the Third*, *The Two Gentlemen*, *The Errors*, *The Shrew*, *Love's Labour's Lost*, *Richard the Second*, *Romeo and Juliet*, *Midsummer Night's Dream*,

King John, *The Merchant*, the two parts of *Henry the Fourth*, *Much Ado*, *Henry the Fifth*, *As You Like It*, *Julius Cæsar*, *Troilus and Cressida*, *The Merry Wives*, *Hamlet*, *Twelfth Night*.

Shakespeare was now thirty-eight. His years in London had been full of maturing experiences; the early days under Alleyn, when he was excited and enthusiastic, and took *The Spanish Tragedy* and *The Jew of Malta* for the finest of dramas; the friendship with Southampton—it promised so largely and ended in disappointment and humiliation; his passion for the dark woman which brought him bitterness and disgust—but she taught him much. There had been compensations; for a playwright, more than all other artists, has his reward in the contagious applause of his audience. Now he had achieved a great reputation, and recognition, and prosperity in material things.

But more than these, as Shakespeare grew older his vision expanded; he could now comprehend the unending diversity of God's creatures. He was still moulding his philosophy and discovering his own religion. The old Catholic faith in which his father died and lived was little more to him than a sentimental regret; for the new parson, he had neither affection nor respect. His belief was mainly agnostic; but yet at times he could perceive a dim purpose in the intricate pattern of life, the craftsmanship of a divinity that shaped men's ends, a special providence in the fall of a sparrow, realising that the ripeness of life consisted neither in eating and drinking, nor in the slavery of passion, nor in thinking too precisely upon the event.

On Sunday the 23rd of March the chapel at Richmond was crowded, and there were few who could refrain from weeping when the preacher offered fervent prayer for the Queen's recovery; but she was speechless now and past hope.

Very early the next morning, those who lived at Richmond were awakened by the rumbling of the coaches of the nobility as they passed through the darkness to Whitehall. About ten o'clock, the Council and the noblemen came out of the palace, and at the gates Sir Robert Cecil proclaimed that since God had called the high and mighty Princess Elizabeth, James the Sixth, King of Scotland, was now true and lawful King of England, France and Ireland. The proclamation was repeated in Cheapside. The people listened with great expectation, but in silence. There was neither dissent nor disturbance.

So the fear which had brooded over England for a generation was dissipated in a morning. The Queen was dead and few could remember when last a King ruled in England. The new King had come in unopposed. For a while there was a feeling of numbness at the event, and sorrow for the old Queen, though she had outlived the best of her days; but as the hours wore on, the realisation that England was at last delivered, so unexpectedly, from the vast confusions of civil war bred a sense of wild relief; and when day faded into darkness, from the turret on the Globe playhouse could be seen the line of bonfires flickering along the edge of the Thames.

COMMENTARY

ACKNOWLEDGMENTS

I WISH to express my gratitude to Dr. Helen Waddell for many valuable criticisms of the manuscript; to Dr. W. P. Barrett for reading the proofs; and to the Editor of the *Times Literary Supplement* for permission to embody portions of two articles on *Shakespeare's Topical Significances*, originally printed on 13th and 20th November, 1930.

The debt to the usual books of reference is obvious and considerable, especially to Dr. W. W. Greg's *Henslowe's Diary* and *Henslowe Papers*—from which all modern work on Elizabethan stage conditions originates; to Sir Edmund Chambers' *The Elizabethan Stage* and *William Shakespeare: a study of facts and problems;* to Professor J. Quincy Adams' *Shakespearian Playhouses;* to Professor Edwin Nungezer's *Dictionary of Actors;* to Professor J. Tucker Murray's *English Dramatic Companies*. The original authorities for the historical events are recorded in my *Elizabethan Journal*.

Page 1, line 17. *charges laid out upon his playhouse.* See Dr. W. W. Greg's *Henslowe's Diary* i, 7.

Page 2, line 27. *bending his brows.* See E. S. *The Discovery of the Knights of the Post*, Siq $C2^{v}$: "with that S. bent his browes and fetcht his stations vp and down the room with such furious Iesture as if he had been playing Tamburlane on a stage."

Page 3, line 18. *Admiral's new play.* Dr. F. S. Boas in his recent edition of *Dr. Faustus* seems to establish convincingly that Marlowe's play was not written before 1592.

Page 3, line 22. *his dissolute and licentious living.* These choice details are given in Gabriel Harvey's *Four Letters* and Nashe's *Four Letters Confuted.* See also Greene's two autobiographies *The Repentance* and *The Groatsworth of Wit*, Bodley Head Quartos, vol. VI.

Page 4, line 20. *scorning those scholars who wrote for the stage.* See the address to the Gentlemen Readers in Greene's *Perimedes.*

Page 6, line 12. *Jew of Malta drew a good house.* Henslowe's takings (i, 13) were: 19th February at *Friar Bacon* 17s. 3d.; 26th February at *The Jew of Malta* 50s.; 3rd March at *Harry the Sixth* £3 16s. 8d.

Page 6, line 26. *a young man from Stratford.* Nothing is known of Shakespeare's life between the baptism of his twins Hamnet and Judith on 2nd February, 1585, and Greene's attack in 1592. It should not therefore be assumed that he did nothing but "dully sluggardize at home." In Bagehot's words: "First of all, it may be said that Shakespeare's works could only be produced by a first-class imagination working on a first-rate experience. It is often difficult to make out whether the author of a poetic creation is drawing from fancy or drawing from experience; but for art on a certain scale, the two must concur. . . . We may assume that Shakespeare had a great experience." Bagehot's essay, *Shakespeare—The Man*, which is the best thing ever written on this problem, is too often overlooked. Several professions, notably lawyers and schoolmasters, have claimed Shakespeare. Those who have had some first-hand experience of war will recognise that he knew more of soldiers and soldiering than he was likely to have picked up listening to the unavoidable Elizabethan sea dog by the inevitable tavern fire.

Page 8, line 28. *Harry the Sixth.* The question whether Shakespeare was mainly responsible for *I Henry VI*, or simply for a few passages is still unsolved. Mr. Peter Alexander certainly destroyed the *external* evidence for revision in his *Shakespeare's "Henry VI" and "Richard III."* The unevenness of the style, however, remains. But style, especially in early work, is poor evidence; a young man's first efforts are often imitative and indistinguishable. When one remembers that the author of *The Epistle from Esopus to Maria* also wrote *Holy Willie's Prayer*, it is as well not to dogmatise on style.

Page 14, line 21. *he was . . . a recusant.* E. I. Fripp in his *Shakespeare Studies*, p. 81, showed that John Shakespeare was a recusant (but regarded him as a Protestant) and that his troubles in Stratford were due to non-conformity and not to bankruptcy. The spiritual testament, however, that was found in his house points to the fact that he was a Catholic.

Page 15, line 1. *deer stealing.* The deer stealing legend is hotly disputed. J. S. Smart in *Shakespeare—Truth and Tradition*, pp. 91-103, produced evidence to show that Lucy had no deer. It does not, however, follow that Shakespeare was innocent of deer stealing. Had he got into trouble for deer stealing, and also fallen foul of Lucy it is quite likely that the two stories would have merged into one. A good example of this mingling is Aubrey's jotting that Ben Jonson "killed Mr. . . . Marlow, the poet, on Bunhill, comeing from the Green-Curtain play-house"; here the killing of Spencer (the player) by Jonson has been merged with the killing of Marlowe by Frizer.

Page 21, line 14. *Greene slipped in a paragraph.* The offending passage occurs only in one surviving copy, now in the Huntington Library: it is reprinted in my *Shakespeare's Fellows*, p. 58.

Page 22, line 25. *upstart crow.* The word "upstart" had been prominent in Greene's mind, for *A Quip for an Upstart Courtier* was finished less than a month before. In that book "upstart" conveys the suggestion not merely of a man who has suddenly risen to wealth but who gives himself airs.

Page 23, line 9. *hurried down to Greene's lodging.* See the Second of Harvey's *Four Letters*, Bodley Head Quartos, vol. II.

Page 26, line 10. *Lord Strange's men came back.* The Company visited Oxford, Coventry, Gloucester and Leicester (19th December) in this autumn. Had Shakespeare been with them, it is unlikely that Chettle would have met him between the publication of *The Groatsworth* and *Kindhart's Dream.*

Page 36, line 5. *Christopher Marlowe.* For the survey of the documents connected with Marlowe, see Dr. F. S. Boas' *Christopher Marlowe and His*

Circle; most of them are reprinted in C. F. Tucker Brooke's edition of *Dido* in the Arden Marlowe.

Page 37, line 20. *Their discussions were even noted in print*—in a Jesuit pamphlet entitled *Responsio ad Elizabethæ Edictum*, 1592, reprinted in my edition of *Willobie His Avisa*, p. 207.

Page 39, line 6. *The poem was passed around.* This seems the likeliest explanation of the parallels noted between *Hero and Leander* and *Venus and Adonis.*

Page 41, line 17. *Richard Field.* See the article by A. E. M. Kirwood in *The Library* for June 1931 entitled *Richard Field, Printer 1589-1624.*

Page 42, line 8. *Henry Wriothesly, Earl of Southampton.* See his biography by Mrs. C. C. Stopes for details of his life and times.

Page 46, line 16. *These sonnets were indeed written from the heart.* Miss Mona Wilson in her *Life of Sir Philip Sidney* has clearly demonstrated the drama behind *Astrophel and Stella.* Many of the Sonnet sequences have their true story, and even beneath the artificiality of the Euphuistic novels there is often a stratum of fact.

Page 47, line 18. *Shakespeare followed in the movement.* I follow, generally, the view of the Sonnets put forward by J. A. Fort in *A Time Scheme for Shakespeare's Sonnets.*

Page 51, line 4. *There was the usual inquest.* The account of Marlowe's death was discovered by Dr. Leslie Hotson and printed in his book *The Death of Christopher Marlowe.*

Page 52, line 17. *Love's Labour's Lost.* See the edition in The New Shakespeare by Sir Arthur Quiller-Couch and Professor J. Dover Wilson for evidence of the date of the play and identifications of the persons; also my *Elizabethan Journal*, p. 398.

Page 56, line 7. *Holofernes.* This is a likely pseudonym for one of Ralegh's atheistic circle for "Holophernes had his head cut off by a woman, and all for blasphemy" (Lodge's *Wits Miserie*, Hunterian Club reprint, p. 66).

Page 62, line 9. *Willobie His Avisa.* For a suggested solution of the problems of this poem, see my edition in the Bodley Head Quartos, vol. XV.

Page 64, line 22. *She was a courtesan . . . in Clerkenwell.* There have been several claimants to the dubious distinction of being the "Dark Lady." The tone of Shakespeare's Sonnets to her suggests that she was not a person of any position, and there is scattered evidence that in the 1590's one of the well-known courtesans was notoriously dark. In the Gray's Inn Revels, amongst those brought in to pay mock homage to the Prince of Purpool "*Lucy Negro*, Abbess *de Clerkenwell*, holdeth the Nunnery of *Clerkenwell*, with the Lands and Priviledges thereunto belonging, of the Prince of *Purpoole* by Night-Service in *Cauda*, and to find a Choir of Nuns, with burning Lamps, to chaunt *Placebo* to the Gentlemen of the Prince's Privy-Chamber, on the Day of His Excellency's Coronation." (Malone Soc. Reprint, p. 12.) This "Lucy Negro" I would very tentatively identify as the Dark Lady. In Guilpin's *Skialetheia*, 1598, Epigrams 57, 61 and 62 are to a light lady called Nigrina. Both Southampton and Guilpin were members of Gray's Inn. In Weever's *Epigrams*, 1599, Third Week, Epig. 12, are verses *In Byrrham*:—

Is *Byrrha* browne? Who doth the question aske?
Her face is pure as Ebonie ieat blacke,
It's hard to know her face from her faire maske,
Beautie in her seemes beautie still to lacke.
Nay, she's snow-white, but for that russet skin,
Which like a vaile doth keep her whitenes in.

To which should be added the idle chat between Lorenzo and Launcelot Gobbo (*M. of V.*, III, v. 40) concerning the Moor, which is obviously topical. That there were coloured prostitutes is apparent from a letter dated 1602 from one Denis Edwards addressed to Thomas Lankford, secretary to the Earl of Hertford or Mr. Cross, Clerk of the Kitchen. He writes, "Pray enquire after and secure my negress; she is certainly at the Swan, a Dane's beershop, Turnbull Street, Clerkenwell." See *S. P. Domestic*, 270: 119.

Page 67, line 5. *able to acquire a player's share.* According to Rowe, Southampton is said to have given Shakespeare a gift of £1,000 "to enable him to go through with a purchase which he heard he had a mind to." It is not unlikely that the gift was made to enable him to buy a share in the Company.

Page 72, line 23. *Valentine forgives him.* The sudden transfer of Silvia to Proteus shocks most critics; but it is the rapidity rather than the action itself which is shocking. If Professor Dover Wilson is right in his claim that there are cuts in the text, then some elevating dialogue, after the strain of Sonnet 42, on the superiority of friendship to love may have disappeared.

Page 73, line 22. *tragedy of a few weeks past.* For details of the murder see Mrs. Stopes' *Life of the*

Earl of Southampton, pp. 70-84 and authorities therein noted.

Page 79, line 32. *Set about some revels.* A long account of this elaborate entertainment exists in *Gesta Grayorum*, reprinted by the Malone Society.

Page 82, line 2. *commanded to present a new play. A Midsummer Night's Dream* is obviously a wedding play, but that it was written for this particular wedding is a guess.

Page 100, line 27. *It was now three years.* The significance of Sonnet 104 is demonstrated, to my mind convincingly, in Mr. J. A. Fort's *A Time Scheme for Shakespeare's Sonnets.*

Page 101, line 30. *a certain William Gardiner.* Dr. Leslie Hotson's brilliant discovery of the complaint of William Wayte against William Shakespeare, Francis Langley and others, published in *Shakespeare versus Shallow*, added one more fact to the definite records of Shakespeare's life. His argument, however, that William Gardiner is the original of Shallow creates more difficulties than it solves, especially when he proposes April 1597 as the date of the first performance of *The Merry Wives.*

Page 107, line 16. *passed out of her grand climacteric.* I set forth arguments for supposing that Sonnet 107 referred to the Queen's grand climacteric in the *Times Literary Supplement* of 28th November, 1928.

Page 121, line 21. *The Isle of Dogs.* See Dr. R. B. McKerrow's edition of Nashe's *Works*, v. 29.

Page 121, line 27. *Ben Jonson.* This paragraph is founded on Section 13 of Jonson's *Conversations with Drummond.* For Jonson's life see *The*

Oxford Jonson, vols. I and II, by C. H. Herford and Percy Simpson.

Page 129, line 23. *the gross embodiment of the shadier side of the war.* It seems not generally to have occurred to editors of *I* and *II Henry IV* and *Henry V* that when these plays were written England was engaged in a considerable war, and therefore that the comic scenes had a special contemporary significance. Mr. J. Dawtrey in *The Falstaff Saga* produced an interesting and striking contemporary parallel in the person and utterances of Captain Nicholas Dawtrey, who was so bulky that it needed eight soldiers to carry him when he was wounded. There were other stout captains: see, for instance, the letter of Sir William Russell to Sir Robert Cecil (*Salisbury Papers*, ix, 339). The name Falstaff apparently is a memory of a line in *I Henry VI*, I, i, 132, "If Sir John Fastolfe had not played the coward."

Page 131, line 8. *honour pricks me on.* Whether Shakespeare invented this little jest, or whether it is one of the phrases produced in a war—like "If you knows of a better 'ole, go to it"—it appears in a letter of Toby Matthew written on 20th September, 1598:—"In Ireland the Lord Ormond is hurt and since the great overthrow four hundred more throats cut. Sir Francis Vere is coming towards the Low Countries, and Sir Alexander Ratcliffe and Sir Robert Drury with him. Honour pricks them on, and the world thinks that honour will quickly prick them off again."

Page 137, line 22. *A certain Monsieur de Maisse.* See *A journal of all that was accomplished by Mon-*

sieur de Maisse . . . translated and edited by G. B. Harrison and R. A. Jones.

Page 142, line 10. *Much Ado about Nothing.* The arguments for supposing that *Much Ado* is an old play re-written are set forth by the editors of The New Shakespeare.

Page 146, line 30. Guilpin's *Skialetheia.* See the Shakespeare Association Facsimiles, No. 2.

Page 149, line 10. *Every Man in His Humour.* The text usually read is that of the folio published in 1616, which Jonson revised thoroughly. In the original play most of the characters bore Italian names.

Page 166, line 26. *Kemp sold his shares.* See J. Q. Adams' *Shakespearian Playhouses*, p. 240.

Page 166, line 29. *In July the new theatre was finished.* The probable date of the completion of the Globe may be deduced from the contract of the Fortune, which was built by Street after the pattern of the Globe. Street began the Globe presumably in January 1599. He signed the Fortune contract on 8th January, 1600, and agreed to complete the work in July: it is likely that he reckoned that work on the Fortune would take about the same time as on the Globe.

Page 171, line 11. *its melancholic.* For the importance of the study of Elizabethan melancholy see Miss Lily B. Campbell's *Shakespeare's Tragic Heroes* and my essay on Elizabethan Melancholy in the edition of Breton's *Melancholic Humours.*

Page 186, line 3. *He made a nuisance of himself.* See the complaints made against "Horace" in Dekker's *Satiromastix.*

Page 198, line 10. *a new playhouse.* See Greg's *Henslowe Papers*, pp. 4-12.

Page 200, line 28. *he would dance a morris.* The account of this memorable feat is to be found in Kemp's *Nine Days' Wonder*, Bodley Head Quartos, vol. IV.

Page 203, line 2. "*Not without mustard.*" The coincidence of "Not without mustard" and *non sanz droict* is not likely to have been accidental.

Page 204, line 15. *slipping in a couple of jibes at Jonson.* In the earlier plays of the Stage War the personalities were confined to occasional speeches or gags. Critics have erred in trying to draw over-elaborate parallels. Thus Simpson in his *School of Shakespeare* identified Brabant Senior with Jonson; but Brabant Senior has a page and a brother; Jonson at this time was only 27 and far from employing pages. Similarly Small (in *The Stage Quarrel*) identified Jonson with Lampatho Doria, ignoring the most significant fact that Lampatho was a University man of seven years' standing. Until *Poetaster* there was no consistent or elaborate caricature.

Page 209, line 7. *It was thought prudent to prune the text.* See Professor L. L. Schücking's article in the *Times Literary Supplement for* 25th September, 1930.

Page 215, line 24. *spoke with a blunt rudeness.* See Sir Henry Wotton's comparison of the Earl of Essex and the Duke of Buckingham in *Reliquiæ Wottonianæ.*

Page 217, line 28. *Vicissitudo rerum.* See the edition in the Shakespeare Association Facsimiles, No. 4, by D. C. Collins.

Page 249, line 5. *they are blazoned there.* The granting of a coat of arms to a player seems to have roused considerable indignation. See, for instance, *II Return from Parnassus* (Ed. W. D. Macray), ll. 1960-8:—

"With mouthing words that better wits have framed,
They purchase lands, and now Esquiers are named."

Page 261, line 2. *Shakespeare hath given him a purge.* No entirely satisfactory explanation has been given of this purge, though various have been put forward. The best is that of the editors of The New Shakespeare that in Nym, Shakespeare caricatured Jonson; seeing that Pistol is in some ways a reflection of Allyn, this is not unlikely. My own conjecture is that the words should be taken literally, and that in some play, which has not survived, Shakespeare staged a Jonson who was given a purge (as Marston had been given an emetic) with disastrous and Rabelaisian effects.

Page 262, line 1. "*The tragedy . . . aroused more excitement and emotion.*" No one can understand this (or any other period) without the aid of imagination; there is little documentary evidence of the enormous emotional effect of the disturbing personality of Essex and of the continual but subconscious panic felt at the prospect of a disputed succession. In the last ten years there have been three occasions when the whole English nation was profoundly moved: the Great Strike of 1926, the illness of King George, and the formation of the National Government in 1931. Shakespeare's contemporaries were far more emotional and excitable, for they lived closely in a small city and were dependent upon rumour and gossip. One of the curses laid upon modern scholarship is that the scholar must never venture a statement that cannot be supported by a footnote. So the imagination atrophies, and the most learned studies of fact and problem are not only dull in themselves but a cause of dulness in others; for, to say the truth, Learning and Art keep little company together nowadays.

Page 272, line 17. *a girl of Tiddington.* See Mrs. C. C. Stopes' *Early Records Illustrating the Personal Life of Shakespeare* (printed in the Shakespeare Association's volume *Shakespeare and the Theatre*, p. 217) and E. I. Fripp's *Shakespeare Studies*, p. 128.

Page 274, line 20. *And then you have some again.* This part of the speech is taken from the 1st (pirated) Quarto of 1603; the lines do not reappear in the 2nd Quarto of 1604. As Kemp had died in the interval, there was no point in repeating the personal attack.

Page 280, line 14. *eagerly contended for a barren plot of sand.* The words are from Camden's *Elizabeth.*

Page 280, line 19. *added yet another passage.* The speech from which these lines are taken (IV, iv, 32-66) occurs only in the 2nd Quarto; it does not appear either in the 1st Quarto or the Folio.

Page 292, line 20. *Sir Thomas Posthumus Hoby.* See Miss Violet A. Wilson, *Society Women of Shakespeare's Time*, pp. 23-43 and 237-256.

INDEX

INDEX

INDEX

INDEX